DATE			

THE BEND FOR HOME

Dermot Healy

THE BEND FOR HOME

Harcourt Brace & Company

New York   San Diego   London

First published in Great Britain in 1996 by The Harvill Press.

Library of Congress Cataloging-in-Publication Data
Healy, Dermot, 1947–
The bend for home/Dermot Healy.—1st U.S. ed.
p. cm.
ISBN 0-15-100304-1
1. Healy, Dermot, 1947–   —Family.
2. Authors, Irish—20th century—Family relationships.
3. Authors, Irish—20th century—Biography.
4. Family—Ireland. I. Title
PR6058.E19Z463   1998
823'.914—DC21   97-40667

Text set in Minion
Printed in the United States of America
First U.S. edition
ACEFDB

Corr baile (*Irish*). The bend for home, which gives rise to many place names in Ireland, as for example Corballa, Corbellagh.

Just turn to the left at the bridge of Finea
And stop when halfway to Cootehill

PERCY FRENCH

Acknowledgements

The author would like to thank Robin Robertson, the editor of *32 Counties* by the photographer Donovan Wylie (Secker & Warburg, 1990) in which part of "The Bridge of Finea" appeared in an earlier form, and Brian Leyden, the editor of *Force 10* magazine (Spring 1996) and Johnny O'Hanlon, the editor of the 150th anniversary supplement of the *Anglo-Celt* (June 1996), in which extracts from "The Sweets of Breifne" appeared.

CONTENTS

BOOK I

The Bridge of Finea

Chapter 1

The doctor strolls into the bedroom and taps my mother's stomach.

You're not ready yet, ma'am, he says to her.

Be the holy, she trustingly replies.

That woman of yours will be some hours yet, he tells my father on the porch. He studies the low Finea sky. You'll find me in Fitz's.

The doctor throws his brown satchel into the back of the Ford that's parked at an angle to our gate and ambles up to the pub. My father sits on a chair at the bottom of the bed. My mother has a slight crossing of the eye, and because she hasn't her glasses on she looks the more vulnerable. He has had water boiling downstairs all day. He's wearing the trousers of the Garda uniform and smoking John Players. The November night goes on. Some time later she goes into labour again. My father runs up the village and gets the doctor from the pub.

He feels her stomach, counts the intervals between the heaves, then says, Move over.

My mother does. He unlaces his shoes and gets in beside her.

Call me, ma'am, when you're ready, he says and falls into a drunken sleep.

My father is waiting impatiently outside on the stairs. Time passes. The snores carry to him. Eventually he turns the handle and peers into the low-ceilinged room. He can't believe his eyes.

Jack, she whispers, get Mary Sheridan, do.

He brings Mary Sheridan back on the bar of his bike. The tillylamps flare. At three in the morning the midwife delivers the child. Where the doctor was during these proceedings I don't know. As for the child, it did not grow up to be me, although till recently I believed this was how I was born. Family stories were told so often that I always thought I was there. In fact, all this took place in a neighbour's house up the road, and it was my mother, not Mary Sheridan, arrived on her bike to lend a hand.

It's in a neighbour's house fiction begins.

We have a surprise for you at home, my father told my brother on the train from Multyfarnham College.

Tell me what it is?

Wait and see.

Go on, Daddy.

It wouldn't be a surprise if I did.

Just give me a clue.

My father shook his head.

Can you get up on it? Tony asked.

My father laughed.

Has it wheels?

Whisht! said my father. Just wait and see.

It was a long train journey for Tony. In his mind's eye he saw a black Raleigh bike parked under the stairs. On the walk from the station he pestered my father with questions, but all to no avail. They arrived to the house. My mother welcomed him at the door. He was sent ahead into the kitchen.

He approached the pram.

In disbelief and disappointment, he looked in and saw me.

Finea sits on the river Inny which runs between Lough Sheelin and Lough Kinale under a mighty bridge that divides Cavan from Westmeath. Sheelin, troubled over recent years by pollution from pig farms, was then a powerful, whitewashed, lustrous lake. But Kinale is always magical and dark.

The seven arches under the bridge are caves where rain is always seeping. Human and animal turds steam there. Tom Keogh drives cattle down the path to drink from the river. Eels slither by. A family keeps eel-boxes upriver and you can peer through the holes to see them, all moist and black and uncoiling. The fish-stench is overpowering. The eels are more dangerous than a can of worms. Their camouflage is weed and shadow. A sudden dart across the sandy bottom. A loop-flick as they kick up a cloud of gravel. Then darkness. Sonny Coyle cuts the heads off the eels on the step of his shop. Cats carry them off down the village with angry growls.

Trout skate mid river in the shallows, watch our worms approach, then skip out of the way. They are aristocrats. All facing the same way, they feint from side to side in a pool of fast sunshine. They have two seasons – before the mayfly and after the mayfly. Meanwhile, we bake perch in a stone fire under the bushes in Fitzsimon's field, and eat them, bones and all.

Oil-skinned fishermen from abroad, with long dappling rods, steady each other as they climb collapsing walls. Flies hang from the brims of their caps like tassels. They carry sandwiches and bait. They push off in a boat. One flick of an oar and they're gone.

We swim in the river, boys and girls, tall cold water to our necks. Girls were never so white as then. Neither were we. You dive under someone's legs and frighten a shoal of minnow. Stout perch eye you. One day the cows ate the girls' clothes and they had to go up the village in their knickers.

On the east side of Kinale the water is covered with unexplained layers of dry sifting yellow reeds. On the west, whispering acres of them grow, taut and green.

There was a cousin of mine who lived in Kildare. He was by the same first name as myself. Originally he'd been called Fergus, but for fear he'd be called Fergie they changed his name to Dermot after me. I was six months his senior. His father, Uncle Jim, same as Uncle Seamus, drove a sweet van.

From the time he could talk Dermot in Celbridge heard of the doings of Dermot in Finea. Seemingly I could wash dishes, carry turf, knew my alphabet, had no bother going to school, did everything I was told and had mastered Irish. If he cried they told him Dermot Healy did not cry. Not only that but Dermot Healy said his prayers morning noon and night. If he didn't eat his dinner he heard how I could finish all before me. When he couldn't sleep they told him that I slept round the clock.

By the time he was three Dermot had come to despise the sound of his own name because it called to mind his alter ego in Finea. He was tormented. It was Dermot Healy this and Dermot Healy that till he was sick of me. Time came, one summer, when Nancy and Jim Kinane and Dermot set off in the sweet van from Kildare to visit us in the County Westmeath.

I was told the night before that my cousin was coming so I was up at dawn standing by the pier of the gate looking towards Castlepollard for a sign of the blue van. They called me in for breakfast and then I was out again. Dinner, the same. I sat on the wall and counted the hours. When anyone passed I asked them the time.

When the blue van appeared at the pump in the late afternoon I was distraught from waiting.

They pulled in some distance away. My father appeared and Jim took his hand. Nancy stepped down to greet her sister. I stood watching. Dermot slipped off the running-board onto the road and stared straight at me.

Who do you think that is? said Uncle Jim.

I looked at the ground and put my hands in the pockets of my short trousers.

Who do you think, well?

Dermot came forward. He stopped and appraised me from a few feet away.

Well, say something, said Uncle Jim.

Say hallo to your cousin, Dermot! hollered Aunt Nancy.

The adults turned to watch the two of us with benign interest.

Shake hands, said Uncle Jim.

I was toeing gravel and looking sideways. Dermot stepped up to me and hit me with all the strength of his fist across the face. I went on my arse astonished. With Nancy at his heels my cousin took off up the Green Hill.

In 1912 my mother was seven. She walked into the lower spirit-grocers to get mints. Behind the shop counter was the woman of the house. Behind the bar counter was the man, without a stitch on him. He had a black umbrella over his head.

Why? I asked my mother.

To get his own back on his wife, she told me, pressing her hands into her lap, then seconds later slapping her knees. The cursed drink, she added, shaking her head at what memory will do.

It's a thunderstorm. Uncle Tom from England, who bets on horses, and his wife Bridgie, my mother's sister, are in the small rowing boat.

My father is at the oars. We've been fishing Kinale pike.

A pike turns on its belly beyond the reeds.

Uncle Tom cries: Bloody hell! Did you see that, Jack?

Another pike, in an angry splash, devours some fry.

The blighter, he says.

The unseen sun sends out a column of light from behind a dark cloud. Bad weather races towards us. Then the storm breaks.

The boat, with a rattle of boards, goes dangerously high. Vexed waves splash in. Rain pelts down. There is nothing underneath us. And in the uproar my father loses an oar.

The curse of the crows on it, he says, and, shamefaced, he grimly tries paddling after it.

What next? says Bridgie.

A dark mist falls. We see nothing. Around us, the bated water goes calm. Then it grows clear as day. My father's face lights up like a stranger's. The rumble seems to start under water. Then the awesome crack. Aunty Bridgie is wearing a green sou'wester and wellingtons. Uncle Tom is wearing a straw hat. I sit between my father's legs, which are braced firmly against the struts. We go round in circles. Bridgie starts oaring with Tom's hat.

Blessed God, says my father.

The lightning strikes above Finea. It cracks across the surface of the lake. Then the sun shines. The water grows vexed again.

We are out there for hours. Then the keel softly parts the reeds near Brian McHugh's. We grab the reeds gratefully. Hauling reeds Tom whistles a cockney air. My father stands at the prow pushing us forward with the remaining oar. Darkness falls. The air pulsates. Frightened ducks take flight. We are in the reeds for a long time. I will never forget their sound. And the sky cracking over. At last we touch land.

All in the boat, except me, are dead.

Chapter 2

Guard Healy kept an acre of cabbages and potatoes behind the house in Finea. For fertilizer he used waste from the outdoor toilet, manure from Jack Fitz's cattle and ass droppings. The crop he divided with the village.

He'd hang the jacket of his uniform on the bough of an ash tree and dig. He was an expert, my mother maintained, on the heel of a spade. With a slap of the other side of the shovel he backed up the drills that ran straight along a length of string tied to two paling posts at either end of the field. In the evenings he'd stand in the garden smoking. Seagulls thrashed in the sky.

We were out in the winter unearthing a few spuds from the pit, which was covered with old straw and turf, when suddenly a rat leaped out. He pinned him to the earth with the prong of a grape. I mind my father and me out at Derrycrave bog. When the cart was turning, one of its wheels slipped into a bog hole. The ass reared. I slid along the driver's plank. The cart lurched. The ass's eyes and my father's eyes were wild. But they got it righted.

The wet clunk of the shovels begins. I find wild bilberries. We start tossing the sods of turf. Then someone sights her coming. Mammy is coming. She's coming the straight bog road that leads to Castlepollard. Whatever she's carrying in one hand is wrapped in white linen, in the other hand she dangles a pail of buttermilk. When she reaches us at last we sit around on the dry sods.

Westmeath is relaxing all round us.

Westmeath men are lying back and looking at the sky. Sheelin is quiet and blue. Insects keep up a mischievous drone. Everyone is wonderfully sated and tired. Mother heads off. Each Monday evening she goes to Ballywillan station to get the train to Cavan for fair day of a Tuesday. The mother's side has a business there – a bakery and restaurant called the Milseanacht Breifne. She serves at table and washes up after the Northern cattle dealers.

So while she's away he comes up early from the station to put us to bed.

It's still light. He goes back out for a drink. A wind stirs the trees. The ivy shies to and fro. It's like lying in a bed of rustling leaves. I am amazed at the sounds of the village. Brian Sheridan coughing. Charlie Clavin closing his half-door. Charlie Clavin's black Ford. The bicycle repairman still at work. A swan going over. Eventually I pick his step out from the others at closing time.

He says goodbye to men on the street.

He slips the catch. Coughs. Touches a chair in the dark. Leaves his shoes aside. Comes up the stairs in his grey woollen socks. I prepare. He enters the room quietly and undresses. Throws his big Garda coat over the eiderdown and gets in beside me. The bed rustles. There's only the sound of the ivy. I pretend to be sleeping. First I breathe in the sweet gassy smell of the Guinness. Then I wait for it.

Soon the match flares up. The cigarette glows. I watch him mesmerized. His satisfaction is entire.

At the green pump outside Kit Daley's in the middle of the village there is a monument raised to Myles the Slasher. On the first of August they used to hold a parade in honour of him. He belonged to the Breifne O'Reillys, high chieftains of Cavan, and defended Westmeath against the enemy.

In the struggle, after killing hundreds, both his arms were chopped off. But despite this terrible mutilation, which I used often imagine above in my bed, he continued to fight on to the last with a sword gripped between his teeth. It was an enemy sword that had been swung with a death-stroke to decapitate him but he clamped his teeth on it and fought valiantly on.

I know the spot he fell on the bridge. It was on the Westmeath side, in a little alcove.

There's a song by Percy French called "Come Back Paddy Reilly to Ballyjamesduff", seemingly written about a cabman who used to collect Mr French, the road-engineer, from the railway station there. Then the cabman went off to America and things were never the same. Hence the title. One of the verses goes:

> Just turn to the left at the bridge of Finea
> And stop when halfway to Cootehill.

But it can't be done. No matter how you try you can't turn left at the bridge of Finea, unless you go up Bullasheer Lane which leads eventually to the banks of floating reeds on Kinale. Some make a case for the old Carrick road which passes the weeping walls of Carrick Church that stands in a quarry, but the Carrick road is to the right. It's all cod.

For the sake of a song Percy French got his geography amiss. Even road-engineers are capable of giving wrong directions in order to get a couplet true. And that's how I found out writers not only make up things, but get things wrong as well. Language, to be memorable, dispenses with accuracy.

And it was much later that I found Myles the Slasher never stood on the bridge of Finea at all. Revisionism has caught up with him. Historians now say he was off fighting with the King of Spain at the time.

To top the coincidence my mother took the turn to the left that doesn't exist and eventually found herself in Cootehill. These things happen. That's how it is. She followed the words of the song. And despite Myles the Slasher having been elsewhere, the monument to fiction still stands outside Kit Daley's door. That's how it's done.

Call it by another name and people it with souls from another world.

Sergeant Moran was sergeant of the guards in Finea for a long period. His family and ours became very close. He had a large family. The older ones were friends of my sisters, but a number of the younger children were dreadfully handicapped.

The story of their suffering made a huge impression on the Slacke ladies.

The mother often spoke with grief of Mrs Moran. After each birth, she grew more and more reclusive. Each pregnancy brought on terrible fits of depression, my mother told me. And at the thought of another pregnancy ahead her spirits would wilt. She prayed, my mother said, to pass child-bearing age as others prayed to enter heaven.

She braved the sympathy of the village with a heavy heart and eventually never went up the village to shop. Maurice, one of her older sons, grew fond of my father, and my father, in turn, began looking after the Morans. He'd arrive on duty in the morning carrying loaves and potatoes and boiling bacon and eggs and butter. Mrs Moran stayed in the married quarters.

Bless you, Guard Healy, she'd say and retire.

Maurice clung to my father while Sergeant Moran sat in full uniform by his desk going over and over lists, frantically scribbling events of note in Kilcogy, Togher, Castletown and Finea.

For long periods of silence the two men sat hunched over the fire in the dayroom. They stood in the dark opposite dance halls, and walked the village through storms in their greatcoats till they were foundered. Then they'd return and sit by the fire again, water running from their caps and coats onto the hearth.

From the private quarters the healthy children and the distraught younger ones made their way into the dayroom. And lo and behold you, said my mother, if he didn't do there what he didn't do at home! My father helped the older girls feed the infants, scalded nappies on the stove, changed underpants and warmed their milk bottles. Often the sad sergeant would stand in the doorway watching his underling rear his children. My mother would saunter up the village with my father's dinner under a cloth on a hot plate. She'd come in, she often told us, to find her husband playing with the Moran children in one of the cells while Maurice, wearing my father's Garda hat, was sitting up on duty on the Sergeant's high stool.

He spent more time with them then he did with us, she'd recall. It was a terrible cross.

In the evenings the Sergeant and the Guard would stroll the village, part at the monument and meet again at the bridge, each with a bicycle lamp cupped in his hands. Swans careered overhead on a journey from Lough Kinale to Lough Sheelin. A shotgun went off. They'd return in time to put the children to bed, then look into the fire in the dayroom and toe the ash.

There'd be a shout from the married quarters. An infant would stand on the threshold.

None of the handicapped were long for this world, my mother told me years later. Not one of them reached the age of reason.

They were carried off to the graveyard in homemade coffins on the shoulders of the policemen. Neighbours shied away. The names of the dead children were read out at Sunday Mass, and their names sounded strange to the ears of the villagers. They were people who had never been seen and yet they had lived among them for a few short years. They were phantoms when they lived, but when they died, they suddenly became real live human beings.

As for the others, said my mother, the Moran children all did well and are scattered around the world.

But Maurice, she said, never forgot your father's kindness.

He cycled to school in Granard, did his lessons by Guard Healy in the dayroom, went out with him on duty. He spent half his days in our house. I remember Maurice arriving first thing in the morning to our door. I thought of him as the older brother I never had, as Tony was then long gone abroad. He taught me how to ride a bike and walk on my hands. In the summers he forked hay, brought turf in to a shed at the back of the lonely barracks and walked his mother along the river. He dug the garden with my father.

He was a scholar, my father would say.

He told Guard Healy he wanted to be a priest, so great preparations were made. It was as if it were happening to his own son. It meant that we would not be seeing him for a long time. While he was still young he went off to a seminary down south to be a priest on the Missions. Summers, he'd appear home looking strangely adult in a worn suit. He'd prop books written in Latin and Greek on the desk in the dayroom. In the afternoon my father and he would head up the river discussing things. Sergeant Moran retired. Himself and his wife left Finea. And so we lost touch. He died. She died. The others of the family we rarely saw again. Maurice disappeared out of our lives. Your father missed him sorely, my mother said. When he fell ill in later life, it was Maurice's name he would shout out in the middle of the night.

Chapter 3

Joe and Eileen are having a row on the doorstep of their galvanized house. I used to love to sit in there and listen to the rain with the chaos all around me. Rain on a tin roof spirits you away.

But when his parents argue Tadhg Keogh gets dizzy. Once Uncle Seamus gave him cigarettes and he got sick. He stood in the village like a clocking hen because he was afraid to go home. At last he went down to Sheridan's house. Old Mrs Sheridan had taken to the bed. She used to sleep all day and read almanacs and American magazines sent home by her dead brother's wife at night. So Tadhg slipped past the two elderly Sheridan sisters, who were sitting by the kitchen range, and went on unnoticed into their mother's room.

He climbed into bed beside her and watched the ceiling going round. He fell asleep in her heat, and got up when he felt better. When he appeared in the kitchen Biddy asked: Where are you coming from?

I got in behind your mother, answered Tadhg, because I was too sick to go home.

Glory be, said Sissy.

The old lady, in her nineties, had never found him in her bed, like our neighbour hardly cared when the doctor climbed into hers. The village was always sleeping around. You'd never know who you'd find beside you when you'd waken.

Tadhg Keogh was a great traveller, my father maintained, but not as great as his father Joe, who completed one extraordinary journey. For the day he was arguing with his wife on the step of the house, Joe cracked twelve matches and when they were lit he shoved them into Eileen's face.

Matches? I asked my mother.

Matches, she nodded.

Eileen ran to get the guards. My father was on duty in the station. When he came up the village there was no sign of Joe. He'd disappeared entirely. They checked Ballywillan for fear he might be trying to get the train to Mullingar. But he was not to be found. He'd taken with him the only loaf of bread in the house and a pot of gooseberry jam.

The fecking haverel, shouted Eileen.

Aisy, said my father, but she was demented.

Joe was gone the following day, and the day after that, and the day after that again. On the fourth morning, Eileen was sitting having her breakfast, and enjoying her husband's absence, even beginning to feel glad he was gone, when a stone dropped into her bowl of porridge from a hole in the ceiling.

It was Joe dropped that stone. His bread had run out and he was above in the rafters mad with the hunger. The sight of her eating below was the last straw. Then he came down, and Tadhg made for our house. And even though I was not born at the time, still I felt I was there to greet him.

I mind to see a man hanging from a tree. Maybe I didn't see a man but heard it from my mother. Whatever she saw I saw it again through her eyes, as I do now, writing this down.

But I know it happened during Mass and I saw the rope. I can see the noose swinging this side of the repair shop where all the bicycles stood – upside down, sideways, without pedals, without wheels, with damaged spokes, saddleless. A butcher's table under the window. A foot-pump. Spiders' webs. A tin advertisement for tobacco on the wall.

A body hanging from a tree in his Sunday best.

Then one day some of the young men in the village went off to Aden. My brother went with them. Aden did for Finea what Scotland did for Donegal. Each mantelpiece had a photograph resting against the wall of young men in shorts. There were bunches of primroses in vases from the Orient on windowsills. Tea sets of bone china decorated with dragons on ancient dressers. Postcards with photos of the pyramids sitting on the radio.

My father sits down at the table to write to Tony. The lamp flares. His script is long and loose. He writes of happenings in the village. My mother, in a handwriting that slants to the right, adds her love.

My sister Una falls off a hayshifter, down between the shafts and under the horses hooves. I am sitting holding tight to the hay rope on the top of the cock. She is very pale. It gave everyone a fright. A boy ran in front of a car and was knocked out. The petrified driver ran for the guards. When my father came up the village it was me he found lying there.

The man who rose the umbrella over his naked body died naked sitting on a smothered pig. And in the galvanized house Tadhg was sick again with the flu and couldn't make it to the evening devotions that began Lent.

So when his parents came home he called from his sickbed – What are the regulations? – for fear some new and finer penance might have been introduced.

Joe stuck his head round the door and said to his son: There's no fast for lunatics.

There were as many wonders in Finea as there were in Fore up the road where dead monks strolled round at night and water flowed uphill. Westmeath had its share of fame. It was to a small business in Mullingar, capital town of the county, that Joyce dispatched Bloom's estranged daughter in a brief haunting aside in *Ulysses*. Joyce too succumbed to the scourge of the broken family, and it was to the same town that he had once come to sing second to John McCormack in a *feis*, that he sent the fictional Millie, as years later Ireland would send their unmarried mothers to Castlepollard.

He must have thought that County Westmeath had about it that sense of separation, of inwardness, of dullness even, that was necessary to portray a guilt over unfinished things. For it is the halfway house between the magic realism of the West and the bustling consciousness of the East.

When I was three I ate a pound of homemade butter. I mind to see it in a dish come from Granard. It looked delicious. I took a long time eating it, thinking of things, sitting up at the edge of the table on my own.

The window to the garden was behind me, the table in front of me and the turf-fireplace to my left. On the windowsill opposite, which looked out on the street, the radio sat forever tuned to Athlone, the centre of Ireland. It was the radio prompted me to eat the butter.

Its various voices gave you spells of faintness, unquiet dreams, and brought hunger on. You knew night had fallen by its sleepy sound. You knew dinner-time and breakfast-time by the timbre of the voice broadcasting.

Walton's brought men in from the fields.

But who was talking the day I ate the butter I'd love to know. When mother came back from the pump with a bucket brimful of water I was puking furiously. Doctor Galligan told my mother that I'd live. Then he told her I was overactive.

Give him things to do, he advised.

She put me to bring in a few sods of turf from the shed to the back door. Then she forgot all about me. When eventually she opened the door a man-high pile of turf fell in. I had brought half the winter stack across the yard, followed by the hens. And was bringing more. And would have continued to this very day if she hadn't stopped me.

It was grand relaxed work. All Westmeath people are very relaxed if they are doing something that is both useless and extraordinary.

Jim Keogh, brother of Tom, oars by Church island with three English fishermen. A wedding party stands on the driveway at Crover House Hotel. Uncle Seamus comes in the door with three ducks he took out of the back of the sweet van.

Lovely, says my mother.

He hands me a penny toffee bar. Mother begins plucking the duck. Uncle Seamus sits by the fire a while then heads up to Fitz's to meet my father when he gets off duty. Jack Healy comes to the pub in his uniform, puts his Garda cap on the counter and calls a bottle of Guinness and a Power's whiskey. They talk of snipe. It goes past closing time. The lights are dimmed. The outer door closed. Men sit with bottles at their feet before the flaming fire. When my father goes to the toilet Seamus tells Fitzgerald and the others what's afoot, then Fitzgerald quietly lets him out the front. Seamus looks up and down the village. Then he bangs loudly on the door.

Guards on duty! he shouts, imitating Sergeant Ruane, who had recently been appointed to the village.

The men in the pub pretend to run for the back. My father coming out of the toilet darts upstairs. He meets Mrs Fitzgerald.

The bloody sergeant's below, he whispers.

Come in here, she says.

They step into Fitzgerald's upstairs toilet. Downstairs Seamus enters the small bar.

Well, Mr Fitzgerald, he says loudly.

Good night, Sergeant Ruane, Fitzgerald answers.

Have you had men on the premises?

No, Sergeant.

The men snort with joy. Seamus puts a finger to his lips.

Explain these glasses to me.

I didn't get cleaning up.

And can you explain this cap, Mr Fitzgerald? Seamus shouted loudly.

Upstairs, my father raised a hand to his head in dismay.

No, Sergeant.

This would be a guard's cap, wouldn't it, Mr Fitzgerald?

It looks like one.

I'd be obliged if you stopped where you are, Seamus ordered, while I conduct a search of the premises.

Fitzgerald pointed overhead, and Seamus ascended the stairs. He went by the bathroom and knocked on a bedroom door.

Are you in there, Guard Healy?

He opened the door and closed it. Went on to the next room. Knocked on the door, opened it, banged it closed. Onto the next. The same. Then with loud footsteps he approached the toilet. He tried the handle. The door was locked. He banged twice.

Come out now, Guard, he said.

Inside my father was frozen with fear.

Excuse me, said Mrs Fitzgerald, but I'm using the toilet.

Have you a man in there?

I have not.

I know you're in there, Guard, he said. Come on out now, Guard Healy, and do the decent thing.

My father sat on the bowl and sweated.

If you don't come out I intend to stop here till you do.

This is private property, said Mrs Fitzgerald.

And I'm on duty, said Seamus. I'd be obliged if you let that man out.

My father indicated to Mrs Fitzgerald that all was lost. She turned the key and my father timidly undid the latch. He opened the door and saw Seamus there.

God blast you, he said, you nearly gave me heart failure.

Chapter 4

Uncle Seamus tells of a wake that took place up the road. The man who died had for the previous month been digging up his American relations that were buried, one as recent as the previous spring, in various graves in the cemetery. Then he set to reburying them in the one plot.

Over the years corpses had been sent home from the States to be buried near Finea, and the family abroad had wired over sizeable sums to their one remaining relation at home, Matt Reilly, so that proper tombstones could be raised. He had tipped Yankee cousins he never knew into unmarked plots, put a wooden cross into the ground and gone on drinking sprees in Granard.

He wrote back describing the fine blue gravel from Harton's quarry that he'd spread over the dead, how the best masons had worked on Connemara marble, he spoke of massive attendances at Church for the funeral Masses. In truth the priest and himself, and a couple of neighbours called in to carry the coffin, were the only ones present at the graveside.

The lies went on undetected till a certain uncle, lately retired from the fire service in New York, spoke of coming over to Ireland to view the family graves. This drove Matt Reilly into a fury of construction. He put on his overalls, and along with the idiot son of a neighbour, he walked to the graveyard with a spade over his shoulder and began digging up the dead.

He bought a new plot and the old skeletons were dropped into it. Himself and the idiot sat supping tea surrounded by ghouls. The stench of decomposing flesh reached the roadside. The horrified priest watched what was happening from his presbytery window with a handkerchief to his nose. Matt Reilly did a deal with a mason in Kilnaleck for a mighty tombstone, he ordered the gravel from Harton's, cleaned his shovel off a clump of grass when the last Yank had been buried and fell over dead himself.

In his inside pocket was £200. With this the neighbours ordered a hearse from Granard, dug up the grave again to inter Reilly himself and held a wake in his three-roomed cottage. The dead man was dressed in a bobtail coat and put into a bed in the side room, a hard hat was placed on his head, and they said he looked himself. You were always a generous soul, said Bernie Sheridan. Up Idiot Street, said Mary Ellen Flynn. Whiskey and ham and Guinness arrived and a roaring fire was set. The house was thatched with straw and sparks caught the thatch. The house went up in flames, and the mourners ran from the building. Then they remembered Matt Reilly was still within.

Two men rushed through the cottage and rescued the corpse. He was taken across and placed under a tree. Someone spread a coat over Matt to keep the morning dew off him. Then everyone went home. Next day the hearse from Granard trundled up the quiet village and pulled to a halt outside the black remains of the building. The undertaker was flummoxed. He stood on the road not knowing what to do till a neighbour woman came and led him to Matt Reilly. By the time he'd been placed in the coffin the villagers had arrived on their bicycles to accompany him to the graveyard. The funeral cortege set off.

The grave he'd dug for the Yanks Matt now found himself in. Soon after this the mason added Matti's name to the tombstone. It was erected on a quiet summer's afternoon. And not long after that the fine blue gravel from Harton's was spread.

It's night-time and I can hear voices on the path. I look down from the window to see my father and two other men. They're carrying lamps. A pike the length of the path is stretched out. I find later he was a record forty-four pounds. One man takes a saw and cuts the fish in three. What part we got, I don't know. They had been out shooting in Kinale when this big pike, like a whale, began following them. He shifted out of the reeds in the wake of the boat.

When they came in, he was still with them.

So they shot him.

Kinale is still one of the best pike lakes in Europe. The Germans know that.

It has the strangest underwater you have ever seen. The bottom one minute is sandy and only a couple of feet away. Then it's green and swirling and six feet away. And then with a race to the heart you row over nothing. That nothingness can scare people. I've known a man in the horrors oar for shore when it happened. That stretch of water was too much for him.

I've found that nothingness in my dreams. And in my love affairs. When you feel trapped in someone else's memory. When suddenly your keel glides over bottomless water. Out of its depths recently came a bible-stand, which now sits in the Dublin Museum.

The forest of reeds, the snipe, Brian McHugh's kitchen. The mouth of the river where the girls showed us their private parts if we would show ours and we did and everything was studied very closely. And it can still bring a tremor to the voice.

There were pissing competitions. And other things.

My mother stands in the kitchen singing in a voice popular when she was young – a scatter of notes on thin ice – and in a tone contriving to sound world-weary, yet very educated:

> On broken wings
> No bird can fly
> And broken promises
> Means love must fade and die.
> I trusted you
> You can't be true
> My heart no longer sings
> Its wings are broken too.

All her life she harboured a terrible fear of insanity. At fourteen she was sent to work as a maid at an asylum outside Dublin for the wealthy female mad. Maisie, her sister, was working there as well. She too would fear insanity throughout her long life. The girls were put into a room together.

On her first night there my mother heard screams, lurchings and wild disputes. The disturbances seemed to come from the inside of her head. She climbed into Maisie's bed and cried. Next morning at seven the head nurse called her name. Maisie headed off to make beds. Winnie was placed in the strange kitchen. From there she heard wild screeches from the dining room.

The cook handed her a tray of dishes filled with porridge. She stood with the tray in her hand.

Well, go on, said the cook.

I can't, said my mother.

They won't touch you.

I want to go home.

Go, commanded the cook, and she threw open the door.

Mother entered with the tray. She expected a hush to fall, that all these crazy eyes would turn in her direction. Instead the ladies in their housecoats continued with their silences and unfocused conversation. She left down a plate before Mrs Small, which Mrs Small promptly returned to the tray.

Whisper, said the lady beside Mrs Small.

Yes, said mother.

Mrs Small does not take porridge.

Oh.

She just takes tea. Isn't that right, Mrs Small?

Mrs Small did not reply. The other ladies ate with glee. Some wore heavy jewellery. Others outdoor clothes. All had handbags. Mrs Tige clutched my mother's arm and asked about the world outside. Lady Cheevers gave her sixpence and requested a trap to the fete. The women, when they gathered in the dayroom, spoke of horses, christenings and the Royal family. My mother ran a mop down a corridor between private rooms that smelled of urine, sweet perfumes and strong female odours.

She was not allowed to speak to Maisie.

Then she had to go and wash the ladies. For the first time in her life she looked on another grown woman's nakedness. Shamefaced she scrubbed their backs while they sat in the huge bath, cut their toenails and brushed out their grey hair. She was in Mrs Pherson's room when a knock came to the door. Outside stood Mrs Flood decked out in a prim suit. She was carrying a po of piss swathed in Christmas wrapping paper.

Please, will you give Mrs Pherson my esteemed regards, said Mrs Flood, and handed my mother the chamber pot.

In innocence my mother did as she was told.

Mrs Pherson undid the wrappings.

What is this? she asked.

Appalled, my mother threw the contents out the window. She gave the chamber pot back to Mrs Flood. A few days later Mrs Flood was back at Mrs Pherson's door again.

Please, will you give Mrs Pherson my esteemed regards, said Mrs Flood and she proferred the chamber pot.

I can't take it, said my mother.

Why ever not?

Oh, Mrs Pherson is not here today.

She's not in residence? asked Mrs Flood.

Yes, that's right, said my mother.

Tell her *we* will return when she is next in town. And the old lady took off with the po held before her like some prized antique.

The doctor came to Mrs Small. She was having difficulty in swallowing. He left pills but still her tongue was swollen. Each day it grew larger till the woman could not get anything down but liquids. It was my mother's job to feed her though a straw. Relations came and went. Mrs Small grew thin as a rake.

Is there anything you really want? my mother asked her.

I'd like . . . the words refused to come.

Yes.

I'd like . . . to dye . . .

No, you won't die.

I'd like to have . . .

Yes?

My hair . . . My hair . . .

Go on.

My hair dyed, she said.

So that night my mother rinsed the dying woman's hair and dyed it black. Mrs Small looked at her new self in the hand mirror. She smiled at my mother. Next morning she was dead.

My mother goes past in a cart to the dancing class in Togher. A man with the cure for worms stands in the hall, and when later he touches your head, and mumbles his prayer, and you open your eyes, you feel you have been swimming underwater in some exalted place. He gets up on his bicycle and rides off, a timid man, with a passion for owls.

Chapter 5

My father was a Roscommon man from Elphin. He joined the guards, like many others who had been active in the IRA, in 1922, some months after the Free State was declared. He was stationed at first in Cavan town, then later in Finea.

Up the village lived the Slacke girls. Their father was the old Victorian Thomas Slacke, a retired RIC sergeant. The RIC had been regarded not only as British but Protestant as well, and the girls had suffered taunts at school because of the uniform he wore. Despite his second name, Tom Slacke was a strict Catholic who had gone for the church as a young man but then chose policing. He was a voracious reader of history, gospel stories and mannered fiction.

My mother saw him as a distant figure of a retiring nature who spoke down to his daughters, yet was possessed of small sensitive asides. He was much older then his wife. He never drank or smoked. He had what she called the Slacke hump, which came with scholarship, and suffered in his latter days from Parkinson's. He got on well in the village. Prior to the burning of the barracks in 1919 Sergeant Slacke had received a warning to vacate the old station. He got his family out onto the riverbank. The barracks and the living quarters went up in flames.

The Slacke family had to move into temporary lodgings while matters in the Free State were sorted out. In the new Ireland RIC members either went North to join the recently formed RUC or accepted a pension from England. Thomas Slacke retired on a meagre pension, built a house up the village for his wife and five daughters – Maisie, Bridgie, Nancy, Gerty and Winnie – his son – Seamus – and continued on with life in Finea.

The old barracks was restored and the Civil Guards occupied it. The young unarmed guards took note of the Slacke girls. They took note of the old sergeant as well, secure in his study, reading his books, at last finished with all that, while they breezed past in their new uniforms through a countryside embroiled in Civil War.

Through my mother the police forces of two different traditions met. She might have first seen my father maybe on the bridge as he set off on duty. Or maybe at the window in the dayroom of her old home. Or standing in Fitzsimon's field looking upriver towards an eclipse of the sun the newspapers promised. Maybe even on a side street in Cavan.

I do not know. What I do know is that she flirted wildly.

While she was walking out with him in Finea she was seeing another guard in Cavan town. When my father was posted to Gowna for a year, she took up with Sonny Fitzgerald. She went out with a traveller. She was off to dances that went on till dawn. But my father persisted. He had her haunted. On the day my father came and asked for her hand she had behind his back got engaged to a Guard McLoughlin. And meanwhile she was back courting Sonny Fitzgerald, who promised her a farm of land and contentment.

Now, this day, her mother told her Guard Healy was at the door.

Guard Healy! she exclaimed.

Yes, said her mother.

He can't be.

He is.

But he's in Gowna.

He's back to Finea from today.

Tell him to go away.

He won't go away. He said he's staying out there till you see him.

What will I do?

I can't answer that.

Well, she took off the engagement ring and threw it into the armchair opposite. Jack Healy – as these things will – came in and unknowingly sat on the ring and asked her to consider him. And often I wonder how things would have gone if Sonny Fitzgerald had been my father. I'd like to be trying that out, maybe as a buttress against nostalgia that steals material from the same source as fiction, and then leaves the reality wanting.

They went on their honeymoon to Bundoran. On their first morning there a woman joined them at the breakfast table. She was dowdy and distraught, and there were spots of blue in her brown eyes. Oh something had happened her, something dreadful. Would they mind if she joined them?

I'm supposed to be Mrs Richards, she confided in a whisper, but I think I'm still really Milly Kane.

Jack, said my father, standing.

Winnie, nodded my mother.

Delighted, she said.

Join us do, said my father.

You don't mind?

No, said my mother.

She sat down.

And we can all take a walk afterwards together, said Milly Kane.

That would be lovely, agreed my mother.

In sea-bright July sunshine Milly Kane walked along the promenade with them. When they stepped down onto the sands she inserted herself between the newly married couple and linked their arms. They walked the sands with the strange woman between them. They came up the main street. The noon angelus bell rang and visitors lifted off their straw hats. Milly looked into a draper's window and broke into tears. My father gave her his handkerchief. She blew a loud clarion call into it.

You must excuse me, she said, but if you had been through what I have, you'd understand.

Then a barking dog drove her into hysterics. She grabbed my father's arm.

Summons that devil, guard Healy, she said pointing at the dog's owner.

Why?

That animal might have bitten me.

Sure he's only a pet, said my father, and he leaned down and took the mongrel's snout in his hand and wrung it to and fro. My poor fellow, he said.

They had buns and tea in the foyer of an hotel.

This is on me, said Milly Kane.

You can't do that, said my father.

Oh but I will. Now, us two women will go to the ladies.

My mother followed the woman into the toilet under the stairs. She dabbed at her cheeks and her lips.

Men, she said, and grabbed my mother's wrist.

Look into my eyes, she said.

My mother looked.

Can you see anything wrong with me?

My mother shook her head.

Milly Kane looked long and earnestly at herself in the mirror. She frowned. She smiled. She took my mother's arm. They paraded out to where my father awaited them on a white seat overlooking the sea.

You pair are my best friends, said Milly Kane.

That we are, agreed my father.

She joined them for high tea of ham and tomato in an eating house and described how her husband had walked out on her the first morning of her marriage.

We'll have a port across the road, said my father.

He left me here alone, she said. I'm lucky I had a penny left. And how am I going to face the shame back home?

She held my father's hand in the bar and wept.

Do I, she asked my father, have any recourse in law?

I'm sure you do, he said.

How lucky you are, Winnie, she said to my mother, to find a man like this.

That evening my father danced both women at a waltz night in the pavilion. My mother sat among the old maids. She fingered her trousseau and looked anxiously at the floor. Rain beat down on the roof and the sound from the band was drowned out. The blue spots in Milly's eyes swam. She came to their room and sat on the bed talking, talking, talking.

If only you'd known Dicky Richards, Winnie, then you'd know how lucky you are. Dicky Richards is a proper so-and-so. It's not right.

It's not, agreed my father.

What would I have done if you people hadn't arrived? I was thinking of doing away with myself.

You shouldn't talk like that.

Oh, but Winnie. This man drove me to despair. Dick Richards. Dick Richards – I'd known him all my life. All my life. And the worst thing was – *he was intimate with me*. And she broke down in tears.

Next morning a tap came to their door.

Good morning all, she shouted through the door, I'll see you below.

God bless us, said my father.

For a solid week they had Milly with them wherever they went. And over sixty years later she was still running round in my mother's mind.

She was a total scourge, said my mother. The only privacy we got was when we went to bed. And even that was restricted. If he'd let her she'd have got in with us. She dragged out of us from morning till night. The nerves were at her. It was *Jack this* and *Jack that*. And *oh what a wonderful man*. You'd be sorry you got out of bed at all. And your father was too soft to send her away.

And that, lo and behold, said my mother, was our honeymoon. I thought we'd never get home.

Then a few moments later my mother added: Poor Milly, I wonder what became of her.

My grandfather had walked to court in Mullingar: now my father, some years after him, went by bicycle.

The extent of a policeman's beat in the Republic was the same as that for a former policeman in the Empire. They went to the same courts, lived in the same restored barracks and trudged the same country lanes. But the rifles were put away. The police kept out of the Civil War as best they could. Guard Healy drilled men for the fascist Blueshirts in a field off Kilcogy. Then returned home to nurse my great-aunt Jane, a leading member of the Republican Fianna Fail party, when she came to spend her last days with them.

He was wary of Dev when he took over. The Economic War with England made people bitter and patriotic. TB wasted the parish. Tony was warned not to play with children from a house affected by the disease. The people said the TB stayed overhead in the cobwebs and could never be got rid of. When she'd go to Cavan my mother would take the youngest with her, drop them into a bed and head below to work. Seemingly she threw a bunch of bananas and a handful of comics to Tony when he was a child and locked him into a room. He sat reading and eating bananas all day. And my mother forgot about him.

He was constipated for over a week.

Tony fell sick with diphtheria and spent a long spell in the sanatorium. He longed to be back out with my father on the bog. He finished his Leaving and went to Aden. Then to England. He disappeared out of our lives for years and came back a stranger. Miriam was sent to Cavan to attend Loreto College and work in the Breifne. My Aunt Maisie kept the boyfriends from the door. Later Miriam married and went to live in the States.

I remember once being taken to the Milseanacht Breifne as a child. I remember the shape of the train. The white horse of the CIE cart pawing the ground outside Cavan station. The bustle below me. The long corridors in the Breifne. The board on the landing beyond the altar that went up under your foot. The huge mirror in the dining room that looked into another room.

I was in my mother's arms. Muddy, my grandmother, was seated in an armchair in the sitting room. The windows looked onto Main Street. She was dressed in black. She was the only one of my grandparents I ever saw. The rest were long dead before I was born. Outside, a procession of brass bands was going down the street. They were celebrating Myles the Slasher for something he'd never done.

Someone lifted me up so that I could see.

He's like the other side of the house, Muddy said, but he has your eyes, Winnie. Like diamonds in a pisspot.

Chapter 6

Kit Daley sits on an easy chair outside his door. The end of his shirt is blowing. He has a low dark hat on against the sun. Swans fly over the village. The swans are always flying.

Tom Keogh brings a pail of milk across to Ledwidge's. He stops on the return journey midway across and rights his hat. A bread van comes over the bridge. The pump is turning. I fall in love with Sheila Ledwidge, whose father owns the post office. My cousins from England drive the local boys mad. Aunty Bridgie's daughter, Patricia, came here during the war years and didn't want to go back to London. She knows all the people in the village from her school days here.

I go into Fitzsimon's and have a dish of culcannon with the haymakers. Real butter melts in the centre of the spuds. There are scallions and kale and milk fresh from the byre through the potatoes. Mrs Fitzsimon's says: *Take more.* Hay is being saved. To watch the men means moving through streams of seed. The bad things that happen make people memorable. A death paints the village white. Gerry Fitzgerald, son of Sonny, sits on a step drinking ice-cream soda. Noel Kiernan is kicking ball with Gerry Coyle. *Do you hear me looking at you?* says Mr Clarke. And he sent me down the village to curse his neighbours. There is another eclipse of the sun. We gather in the middle of the village and look up through blue-tinted paper.

Roosters begin crowing wildly as the dark flies over the village. Dogs run for shelter. Midges stop. Then there is a long silence. A twilight crosses the land. A shadow.

I know there is something wrong. My father's breathing grows laboured at times. He scuffs his nose with a bright handkerchief. His lean face is troubled. There's visitors at all hours. They begin putting away things in the house. Sometimes my mother is gone for days to Cavan.

Tom Keogh sits in the kitchen with my father. There are bottles of Guinness warming before the fire. The men hold their hands to the flames.

It'll be a different world, says Tom.

It will.

You'll be missed.

I fall down the stairs. My father carries me up on his shoulders. What were you doing? he asks.

He sits on the edge of the bed to reassure me. He feels my arms and my legs.

There's nothing broke, he says. What were you doing?

I was listening.

Listening, were you?

Yes.

And what did you hear?

Things.

What *things*.

This and that.

If you hadn't been listening you wouldn't have fallen.

He tucks me in and tiptoes away. Sonny Fitzgerald comes round with a bottle of whiskey. Seamus does a recitation of Dangerous Dan McGrew. My father cuts strips of boiled bacon in the scullery. I sit on the top of the stairs again. The men go down the path as dawn breaks. I walk out to Brian McHugh's and sit in his high-ceilinged kitchen. He lets me look down the barrel of his rifle. We wade through reeds. He puts a finger to his lips. We go down on our hunkers. But whatever he thought was there never rises.

You're taking the high road, he says.

I am, I say.

But I don't know what he means.

Miriam arrives from Cavan with Sheila Reilly in their Loreto uniforms. They sit in the sun on the window ledges and go up the Green Hill to pick wild flowers for the table. Una takes down a curtain from the window. Miriam that evening packs clothes upstairs and takes them away. My father stands in his garden and leans on a spade. He is puzzled. The pom called Croney walks the wall and sits on the pier of the gate. Uncle Seamus arrives in his sweet van. Into it go the things from the living room. The house is slowly emptying.

I know something is wrong.

Noel Kiernan and me walk to school. The Gurns join us. At the church we wheel right instead of left and go mitching. We go out the bog road behind a ditch. Then make our way into a hay field and run from cock to cock. We duck and weave till we're in a field opposite the school. We watch the classroom windows and eat each other's sandwiches. Noel Kiernan has ham, Noel Gurn has jam and I have eggs. We watch the other schoolchildren playing at the eleven o'clock break from behind a group of ash trees.

An ass suddenly rears. He kicks me in the head. I came to by myself in a field where primroses were growing. That is the feeling.

There is a do in Sonny Fitzgerald's. All the village are there. My father and mother go up together. She is in a brown dress and white sandals. He has on a wide-trousered navy suit. It's late summer.

I watch them go. Horses and asses drawing carts pass by. All stop at Sonny's. Men in smart rig-outs come over the bridge. The police sergeant and the two guards come up the village together. Women cross the village street with steaming trays.

There's music.

There is.

I can hear men singing that night on the street. Someone got sick on the hill and groans wildly. The kitchen fills up with voices. I sit at the top of the stairs. The men imitate beasts roaring. I can hear people urinating against the side of the house. Croney is barking on the path. My mother steers my father upstairs and leaves the gang below.

Blessed God, said my father, where are we?

You're at home in Finea, she said.

That's right, he replied.

That's right, she says. Then she quotes out of the blue:

> Good evening, John
> your shirt is gone
> and your wife
> won't be home
> in the morning.

Next morning my father does not put on his uniform. He hangs it away in a closet. I don't know why. Through ill health he was retiring early I would learn years later. He takes my hand and we go down along the river, over the stile and on out to the mouth where the perch bask, shoals of them, watching for small fry entering or leaving Kinale; duck glide out from the reeds and leave a shimmer behind them; an old boat rots; a dragonfly drones; my father sits on a spread handkerchief, pulls up his trousers and lights a cigarette.

We're going away, he says.

I know that, I said.

Aha!

Who's going?

All of us.

When?

Soon.

To where.

To Cavan.

I don't want to go.

He flicks the match to and fro, breaks it and and throws it away.

You may not want to go now, but after a while you'll be all right. He wipes back his hair. And we'll always be able to come back.

We will?

Yes.

How often?

Often as you want to. The house will still be here.

We look out at Kinale.

In later life I made Sheelin into the Atlantic. Kinale, I've never got to the bottom of. It's got secrets that shouldn't be told. A time that can't be given back, but is, continuously. I always smoke a cigarette in the dark before sleeping, and all I've ever written about has a bridge, a man in uniform, a woman who takes the reins of a business. A girl at Loreto. A girl at the Poor Clares. In behind are the silent ones, my sisters, the brother. They too have their Finea, more complete than mine, being older.

What happened is a wonder, though memory is always incomplete, like a map with places missing. But it's all right, it's entered the imagination and nothing is ever the same.

Chapter 7

I knew it was time to go one day. A dusty afternoon saw Charlie Clavin turn his old black Ford about and stop at our gate.

The mother and Una had gone ahead to join Miriam in Cavan. So there was only myself and my father. We were sitting in the cold kitchen when the horn blew. A few battered suitcases were all that remained to be transported and a half-bag of seed potatoes. My father stacked them in the boot, then he toured the house once more. All we could see on the walls were the square shapes where pictures had been. The drawers in the dresser were empty. There was a smell of mould in the small living room now that the furniture had been removed. He lifted his shaving things off the scullery window. He tried the back door. We walked through the bedrooms and he checked the windows.

That's that, he said, and closed the small green gate.

I sat in the front with Charlie, my father got in behind. Then I called the dog. Croney was perched at the front door. I whistled. Reluctantly he came up the path, leaped onto the wall and sat on the gate-pier. I lifted him down onto my lap. Noel Kiernan looked on. Brian Sheridan waved. Tom Keogh waved. We went by the monument, over the bridge and by the barracks, and on past the forty swans on Finea Lake, the engine groaned on the long ascent as we climbed out of the valley, the car shook and Charlie stamped the accelerator, but soon we were high up, ticking over nicely, with Kinale to our back and Lough Sheelin to our right, and the whole of Westmeath and Cavan opened up before us.

We drove past the galvanized dance hall in Kilcogy where my father did night-duty, the handball alley at the crossroads in Mullahoran where he often played with the uniform of his jacket hanging on a side wall, and up through Ballinagh village. On the last stretch of road to Cavan Charlie let the car drift onto the wrong side of the road. Just as one of Harton's lorries was bearing down on us, he swung the steering wheel and we came to a stop on our correct side.

Sorry about that, Guard Healy, said Charlie.

We sat a few moments in silence. Charlie got out and shot the starting handle into the front of the car. He turned her once, twice, and looked at us with beads of sweat on his brow. The car took on the third take. We bombed into into the empty streets of Cavan.

It was half-day in the town.

I remember standing outside the closed Market House after the car stopped. There was a smell of seeds, oil and cement. I looked up and down the street – not a soul moved, signs swung in a breeze, the sun shone on one side of the street, a stray dog skidded to a stop outside Provider's and smelt the bottom of the door.

Croney began to whine. My father and Charlie crossed the street with the cases and rang the doorbell. My mother came to the door. They called me across. We walked the long hall, then the dining room and into the private living room. Everyone was there – Una, Miriam and Aunt Maisie. The table was piled with food. Charlie Clavin put his cap on his knee and ate.

I sat near Charlie and when he was ready to go I accompanied him to the door.

My father paid him in the hall. Charlie tipped his cap. He turned the starting handle and was gone. So there we were standing at the front door, looking up and down the street till he led me in by the hand. I went up the back garden with Croney and found a gooseberry bush.

I saw a lad in the garden next door.

Who are you? he asked.

I'm Dermot Healy, I said.

I'm Dermot Burke, he replied.

There can't be three Dermots, I said.

Who's the other one?

Dermot Kinane.

I don't know him.

He's my cousin.

We climbed up the back garden and onto the Gallows Hill, then down into the nun's graveyard behind the Poor Clare Convent. The sight of the tall stern crucifix among the trees astonished me. We climbed a tree as dusk fell. Lights came on all over the town of Cavan.

* * *

That night I slept like a man in a boat going upriver on strange waters. I ate a bar of chocolate in the dark and drank Cidona. I had my own room and my own light. Next door I heard the Burkes screaming as their grandmother beat them. They called for her to stop but it only got worse. I could hear the slap of the strap plain as day across their backsides.

When it was over I felt enormous relief. I went out to listen on the stairs but could hear nothing. All sound carried up the entry from the dining room below. I could hear the ladies and my father talking. The radio. My sisters going to bed. No ivy stirred on the window. There were no lake birds calling out.

The village sounds which used help me sleep were gone.

The tick of bicycles in Finea was gone. The rooster was silenced. The braying ass was far afield. I missed the door of the outdoor toilet closing behind my father. The sound of my mother singing in the scullery. Odd footsteps returning from Sonny's. Instead I heard a drinker wheeling his bike down Con Reilly's entry. I hear Con rolling a barrel indoors. A car backfired on Main Street. The bells that rang out the hour were very close. Lorries cruised past. A wooden gate closed and a bolt was shot home. Maisie laughed. Mother came out of the kitchen and opened the bakery door to check the fire in the range. My father shovelled in coke.

I stood at the window and looked over the roofs. I saw old Miss Reilly stand at her little window. She had a tiny face and wild grey hair. She rested her hands on the sill and looked away into the dark. She stood there for maybe twenty minutes, as she did every night, watching something deeply buried in her subconscious.

Then just after I'd fallen asleep I heard my door open.

Are you all right, Dermot? whispered my father.

Yes, I said.

After my father left I could not sleep. So to get to sleep I walked up the village of Finea. And all the insignificant things returned. I noticed flowerpots, lamps, upholstered chairs, the colours of front doors. I went by each house and named who lived in them to myself. I called out the names with fondness. Sometimes I'd be asleep by the time

I reached Coyle's. Sometimes I'd only have to go as far as Doherty's. On good nights I'd need only cross the bridge. On the worst nights of all I'd have to travel again that whole journey we'd made with Charlie Clavin and then I'd arrive back to where I was cowering in the immaculate dark.

But the best place of all to stop at was Kit Daley's door. Here there was quiet. I stood on the cement surround of the pump. The village was sleeping.

BOOK II

The Sweets of Breifne

Chapter 8

The next day I woke at eleven in the strange house. I studied the bathroom. I ran the taps in the bath and the sink. Then coming back I opened the doors of all the bedrooms and peered in. I counted five bedrooms. I studied the photographs of old Slackes that hung on the walls of the corridor. I stopped at the altar that stood in an alcove at the top of the stairs. A Christ, with his head bound in thorns, dripped real blood, behind huge thick glass. I went into the upstairs sitting room. It had a deep reddish carpet, a long sofa, armchairs, a large radio, a tall photograph of Thomas and Elizabeth Slacke, a sideboard stacked with silver. There were two strange paintings of rivers.

I opened the final door quietly. A whiff of stale powder emerged. There was Aunty Maisie seated on a chair before the three mirrors of her dressing table.

She was brushing back her hair.

Yes? she said. Who's there?

It's Dermot.

And what do you want, pray?

I was trying to find my father.

You'll not find your father in my room. Are we to have no privacy here? she asked sternly.

I got lost.

Go downstairs. And kindly close the door.

I found my way to the shop. My mother was behind the counter. She had a new blue rinse in her hair. I stood on the street and was mesmerized by the crowds. Then, suddenly, up the middle of the street came the town crier, Tommy Keyes. A few children followed him. He rang his huge bell, then roared something incomprehensible. I watched him, amazed. I held the handle of the hall door tight.

Dermot, my mother called.

What?

Go inside and have breakfast. And tell the girls that Tommy Keyes says the water will be switched off at two.

I opened the tearoom door.

No, she said, go by the entry.

All the downstairs windows were barred. The beater was churning in the bakehouse. The potatoes were boiling in the kitchen. Mary sat me down in the private dining room before the huge mirror. I studied myself closely. I asked for Finea loaf. That was square bread all of a piece with a bronze cap and a crisp bottom. What the girl had offered was the sliced pan.

There's no such thing as Finea loaf, she said.

There is, I said.

I never heard of it, she said.

As I sat there in the dark room in front of the mirror people passed to and fro. They walked through the room I was in, and again through the other room in the mirror. I stood in the yard with Croney. The day was filled with clashing delft, the pounding of the rollers as the bakery girls beat the dough, the rattle of the industrial mixer, big as a cement mixer, as it churned and whipped sponge-cake mix and butter-cake mix. Batters spluttered. Creams were piped. The tall geyser in the kitchen sent spouts of steam onto the wet, heavily glossed ceiling. Lard hissed on the pan.

The door to the restaurant swung to and fro, trays of fries went out to the farmers; trays of meringues, eclairs, fairy cakes, apple squares, soda farls, piped horns, chocolate tops, apple tarts, sponge cakes, cherry cakes, carroway seed cakes, birthday cakes, sultana cakes, brown bread squares which were triangles, went down the entry.

The buns were stacked in the glass-fronted shelves under the counter, the cakes went into shelves on the wall, the window was stocked. My mother measured out spoonfuls of tea from a tea chest behind the counter into little white bags. It was one and a half spoons for a single, and three for a double. Then the bags of tea were sent into the kitchen, stored in a biscuit tin and emptied into the teapots as the need arose. This way the amount of tea a customer got was rigidly controlled.

Butter patties sat in a bowl of water on the kitchen window.

What's your name? asked Josie Rahily as I looked into the bakehouse. She was piping hot chocolate. Bees swarmed round her. The bees were everywhere. Miss Smith, with rags to protect her hands, lifted a tray of fairy cakes out of the oven.

Would you like a bun? she asked me.

No, I said.

Why not?

I don't like sweet things.

Well, you've come to the wrong place and that's a fact.

I wandered the house until at last I found my father. He was up the garden setting the seed potatoes.

You had a big sleep, he said.

A few days later Una led me by the hand to the convent. They had me decked out in short pants cut off at the knee from my father's navy-blue guard's trousers. The arse was huge. As we walked past High Infants, orphans were singing. Una knocked on a door and a nun came out. I ran. I ran across the convent yard, out the gate and down Main Street.

My mother was behind the counter. I ran into her.

Dermot! she said.

Mammy, I called.

Why are you not at school?

I don't want to go.

You have to go.

No.

Why?

There's wren boys there.

What!

The wren boys are there.

Una led me back again. When the nun spoke I kept my eyes on the ground. I was frightened of the wren boys. They used come up the village in straw heads and black frocks on St Stephen's day roaring about Mullahoran and Kilnaleck and Cromwell. Keys rattled in the nun's skirt. She brought her face down till it was at my level. The skin was white and clear. A little fringe of hair showed round her ears and forehead. The eyes were wide. The crucifix swung.

Do I look like a wren boy? She smiled.

She led me into a class. I kept my head down. They were reciting sums in a sing-song voice. Matt Donnelly moved over. Ha-ho, said Raymond Green. I sat down. Look at the buff from the country, someone

43

whispered. The fellow in front lifted his arse as the nun turned to the board. He cracked in my face. A thick foggy smell of fart reached me.

I went out walking with Miriam beyond Cavan. It was late afternoon, on a Thursday, when we left. The sky was darkening. We went below the terraces on the Dublin road.

Does this road go to Finea? I asked after a while.

It might, said Miriam.

What do you mean might?

It's a long walk.

Can we go there?

We can.

Now?

Yes, she said. Why not.

Evening fell. The white railings came to an end. We stepped into the country. The haze smelt of May blossom.

This way, said Miriam.

Why?

It'll be shorter.

Are you sure?

Of course I'm sure.

Do we save miles?

Oh miles and miles, she said.

That's good.

And so we took various shortcuts to reach the village. We passed a mansion house. A woman carrying two pails of water crossed the yard. A horse fled down a meadow. We went up a cobbled lane and a man spoke to us over a gate.

Lovely evening, he said.

Lovely, replied Miriam.

The nights, he said, are drawing in.

They are.

Who's he?

He's one of the Gurns.

He's not.

He is.

I turned back to look but he was gone. We went on over a rise and walked across high ground. It was an open area of gorse and stones. An ass lifted his head to look at us.

How many miles more?

Maybe four, she said.

Are you sure?

Five, she said, at the most.

Five mile is a long way.

It's not too bad.

It's longer than four mile.

That's true.

And four mile is bad enough.

We descended into a valley. The roads were small and the ditches full. Swans dipped their heads in a flooded field. Blackbirds sang, then there were crows and fidgetings.

Are we halfway?

More than that, she said.

Are you sure?

Yes.

How far is it back to Cavan?

About four mile maybe.

Four mile?

Yes.

It was a long way back, and the further we went the longer it became. My sister walked beside me and behind me.

Will the house still be there?

Of course it will.

And we can stay?

We can.

Where will we sleep?

On the floor.

What will Mammy say?

She'll not mind.

All right.

We stepped in out of the way of a car. She took a stone out of her shoe. A bullock followed us along a hedge. A stream bucketed into a drain. The moon was out.

Is there far to go?

There's not much further.

Will there be a fire lit?

Yes.

And who will light it?

Charlie Clavin.

Oh.

The shadows of trees crossed the road. There was only the sound of our shoes. I took her hand.

Finea is my real home, I said.

Don't you like Cavan?

No.

Why?

Because.

Because why?

Just because.

The moon went behind a cloud. She stopped in the dark. I listened intently. Our eyes adjusted.

Is that the lights from Finea? I asked, pointing ahead.

They could be.

Are they? I demanded.

She stopped to look.

Yes.

C'mon, I said.

I'm coming.

I strode on. I'd wait for her then go on again. We turned up a road she said we should go, but the light in the house was gone. Soon enough though another appeared, then another.

Whose light is that? I asked.

Charlie Clavin's, she said.

And that?

Coyle's shop.

They're open late, I said.

They are.

I wonder why.

It was a long tiring walk. More lights appeared in the distance. The whole village was alight. We went behind a hill and the village disappeared. When we rounded a bend there it was again.

C'mon, I said.

I'm coming.

C'mon, I said.

Don't run.

I'm not running.

You were.

Well, I'm not now.

Hold on for me, she said.

I stopped and waited for her. We went by a garage that was not in Finea. We arrived onto a road that was overlooked by rows and rows of terraced houses, with washing flapping and mongrels barking.

I don't know this place, I said.

Sure you do, she said.

No, I don't.

Can't you see?

It's not right.

What do you mean?

This is not Finea, I said.

No, she replied, this is the Half Acre.

We came round a corner and suddenly we were in Cavan again. It had not been Finea we'd seen at all. It was a great let-down to arrive back to those dark half-day streets, to hear the door open onto the gloom of the hallway, to walk through the white marble-topped tables of the restaurant. My sister turned on the light in the dark dining room. There we were, the two of us, back in the mirror.

I was trapped in Cavan for all time.

Chapter 9

My father was sitting on the edge of the bed. He must have been there some time. He asked me was I all right. I am, I said. He looked at the po on the floor.

Are you sure?

Yes.

I'll go then.

I could not wait on him to leave, and he wanted to stay. At last reluctantly he rose. The bed rose. The bile rose in my throat. He passed by the mirror, held the door open and turned.

Is there anything I can get you?

No, I said quietly, and closed my eyes, pretending sleep.

He accepted this regretfully, the door closed behind him with a quiet click. I waited till I heard his feet descending the stairs then I leaned out of the bed and vomited profusely. The door flew open. He ran in. He was short of breath and anxious. He took my forehead in his hand. I was grateful for the pressure.

Go on, son, he said.

I pressed down, I pressed real hard down on the palm of his hand as the spasms went through me. When I was finished I lay back and he wiped my cheeks and lips with a wet face cloth.

Why did you let me go, he asked, if you knew you were going to be sick?

I don't know.

Are you all right now?

Yes.

I lay back on the pillow. He sat with his back to me and his hands on his knees. We could hear across the roofs the sound of the orphan girls screaming in the Poor Clare Convent as they played during their dinner break. Frank Lee in wide wellingtons came up the entry with the milk for the café in a can. The girls in the bakery were banging dough. Someone emptied a teapot into the drain in the yard.

Would you like some lemonade?

No.

I can't understand why you didn't want me to stay.

It was because I wanted to be alone when it happened. But I didn't say that to my father. Since I'd got the jaundice I'd got used to doing it by myself. I would hear the disturbance away in the distance, see how my wrists shone and the patterns on the wallpaper wavered. Soon one of my legs would grow indistinct. The body blur. Every smell and sound would leer violently. Then your head disappeared for an instant. That was the moment and you had to concentrate to get it right. To get it over with. I didn't want anyone else there.

I'll take this away, he said, and I'll be back in a minute. He crossed the floor holding the vessel. I lay there, as the other world came rushing back, feeling like I'd just come out of confession.

Daddy, I said.

What's that?

I feel better now.

Good, he said, good.

It might have been then, or soon after this, there was some other sickness I can't name. Maybe it wasn't a sickness at all but some nightmare that visits a body during waking hours. It meant the closing walls again and the body ridding itself of its physical presence.

There would have been a radio on downstairs in the living room. There was always a radio on in the Milseanacht Breifne. The wireless itself sat in the sitting room above Main Street and a wire from it ran downstairs to the sweet shop, along the wall of the café behind, and eventually into a speaker in the small living room that separated the restaurant from the kitchen. The radio played all day non-stop from the moment Aunt Maisie switched it on at noon when she rose from her bed till the National Anthem blared out onto Main Street bringing another day to an end.

That night the voice of the announcer came out the window through the green bars, travelled up the entry and reached me in the room above, where I lay weightless and transparent.

What the voice was speaking of I can't say. It was adult, male, nostalgic; it could have been James Mason; it might have been Perry

Mason; maybe a member of a religious order speaking of acts of charity or a voice about to announce a waltz; whatever it was, it troubled me.

At first, as always, there was the benign sense of sleep falling while I listened to life going on downstairs. I heard the ladies going away to the pictures and knew my father was down there alone.

I had this fear that he might tie his bad tooth to the door handle, and push the door. He'd done this once before and when we walked into the dining room he had a bloody handkerchief to his mouth, and the long fang, yellow and topped with black, sat in a saucer. But tonight all was quiet except for the voice on the radio.

I was walking up Finea, then the wrong thing happened, and I screamed. I screamed again. I heard his hurrying steps coming up the stairs and along the landing. By the time he threw open the door and turned on the light he was breathless and pale.

Where is he, son? he shouted.

Blessed God, son, he said hoarsely, what's wrong?

I couldn't say. He held the bottom rails of the bed and looked round wildly. His gasps for breath left two pinches of blue on his upper cheeks.

What is it? he said. Where is he?

But there was no one.

I was afraid, I said.

Afraid of what?

I couldn't answer.

I thought, he said, you were being murdered.

I must have lain down then, and turned my head sideways.

There's no one, he said.

Yes, Daddy.

I'll turn the light off now, he said.

He turned it off but I could feel him standing there in the dark for a long time, watching me, ready for the next scream when it came.

And another time he caught me walking in my sleep across the landing. He'd been to a whist drive in the side rooms of the Town Hall, and then on to see Frankie Brady in the Ulster Arms for a few bottles of Guinness, and then he'd let himself into the dark hall and caught sight of me standing in my pyjamas by the altar at the top of the stairs.

What are you doing up there? he asked.

I didn't reply.

Dermot? he said.

I put a hand out and touched the walls and began to feel my way down the steps. He approached me warily.

Are you asleep? he said, and his voice reached me from another dimension.

I struggled best as I could to stop going wherever I was going. I really wanted to go on very much to that first place and there was a sense of loss in not reaching it. Now I was losing it very fast.

What's wrong? my mother said from somewhere below.

I caught him, said my father, just in time.

Dermot? she said.

Don't wake him, he advised. They say you shouldn't wake them suddenly.

I could feel the world taking shape around me, the bloody head of Christ on the altar, the pink cups of plastic flowers, the white curtains on the windows that opened onto the flat roof, and then I saw my mother in a blue housecoat, her glasses luminous, her face shining from Nivea cream, and my father standing ghost-like below me, with one hand flat on my chest.

Where were you going? she asked.

I was going nowhere, I replied.

You're at home now, she said.

That's right, agreed my father.

He led me back to bed.

You were sleepwalking, he explained, as he pulled the sheets to my chin. He sat on the bed with his hands on his knee. His shadow was comfortable and benign. He lit a cigarette and tapped the ash into the grate of the small black fireplace.

You're a great walker, he said.

A few years later it was him I would meet on the stairs, a thin gaunt figure in a pyjama top open onto his chest, and pyjama bottoms that

51

reached to just below his knees. He was, he thought, on his way to the barracks. I led him back to bed as he had once led me.

Where I was for the night he found me I can't say. But most nights we set off for Finea. That was how we always met, somewhere on the landing or on the stairs, thinking it was the bridge or the barracks, always at one remove from consciousness, in a twilight world where certain journeys had to be completed out of an obscure sense of duty and longing.

Chapter 10

My father met people through Miriam, through whist drives, poker schools, the Ulster Arms and the Farnham Hotel.

His closest friend in the long run was Frank Brady, one of the Brady Family who ran the Ulster Arms. Frank then was in his late twenties, my father in his early fifties. Frankie had a pale laughing face, a brilliantined quiff and long painterly fingers. He always had a *Daily Express* in his sports-jacket pocket. He had trained as a pastry chef in Glasgow but now spent his days working behind the bar in his family's hotel.

They played cards over the bar and drew bottles of stout. They chatted about horses and jockeys – Joe Sime, Des Cullen, Lester Piggott. Mid-conversation Frankie would fall asleep, his chin would drop onto his chest and the night would continue for a while without him, then he'd suddenly re-enter the conversation as if he'd never left it.

My father won a pair of Clark's black shoes at a whist drive in the Town Hall, and he brought them up to the Ulster Arms to show Frankie.

Well, Jack, said Frankie, they're a neat pair.

They are.

After closing time he came home with the box neatly wrapped under his arm. He entered the kitchen. My mother was ironing sheets.

Take a dekko at that, he said.

Maisie undid the wrapping.

I won these at whist, he explained.

She opened the box. Inside was a pair of brown mud-spattered shoes, without tongue or soles.

The curse of the crows on Frankie Brady, said my father.

The business premises had large canopies over the shop windows and above the gate that opened into the entry. Over the years I painted them all kinds of colours.

The shop sold the produce of the bakery. Inside the shop was a small room where all the cakeboxes were stacked. There were a few small tables where people sat having ice-cream soda with spoonfuls of ice cream in tall glasses. To the left you went out to the toilet, past the room under the stairs where Croney slept. Straight on through was a door with a glass porthole that opened into the public tearoom. Beyond that was the private dining room that was never private, for beyond it was the kitchen and the scullery and the waitresses were always on the go.

A door in the kitchen opened onto the yard. An entry ran the length of the house. Opposite the kitchen was the old bakery in which eggs in barrels of brine, boxes of margarine and bags of flour were stacked. Further up the yard was the new bakery. One corner of it contained a vast coke oven that could take four trays at a time. Above the old bakery was a long slatted attic – once a storeroom – with a galvanized roof. It was filled with antiques and books from my great-aunt Jane's time in France at the turn of the century, when she was au pair to two girls whose family suffered a grave scandal. The father murdered the mother. And later the sisters broke up over a man. Then a Hollywood film was made about the affair.

Great-Aunt Jane, who taught domestic economy in the Technical School, never married, and started the Breifne with a small loan from John Brady, draper, grandfather of Frank Brady. It was one of the few large businesses (maybe the only one) opened by a woman in the newly formed Free State. And it thrived. She in turn left it to her nieces – Maisie and Winnie – so it passed on through the female line, and perhaps in time would have continued on to my sister Una or Miriam, if circumstances had not changed. But anyway.

It was a wonderful attic. First I found an elderly silver-bearded Santa standing in a scattering of yellow straw in a tall cardboard box. Later I'd learn that he went into the shop window at Xmas to nod at passers-by, and with a quick bow, dispense innumerable favours. In London, later still, I'd meet men from Cavan who'd turn sentimental at the days they spent in front of the Breifne asking Santa for things. He stopped there for a couple of weeks saying yes to everyone, then on the dot of twelve midnight on Christmas Eve Aunty Maisie would take him in and up he went to the attic to hibernate for another year.

But now he was a complete mystery to me. It was like he was an adult's toy. He stood resolute and stiff-bearded, staring straight ahead over the lid with silent eyes. I lifted him out and stood him on the floor. He was over two feet tall, wore a red velvet coat and little prim black boots. His eyebrows were dusty. I found a key stuck in his back. I studied the key very carefully and turned it once.

Immediately, Santa nodded. I backed away. He nodded once, twice, three times, then, as if he were on the verge of a sneeze, his chin began to move very slowly, the revolutions diminished, and he stuttered to a stop. I started him again on the instant. He nodded away and I nodded back in return. We were at that a while until he came to a stop as before. So that was it. I put him back in his box of straw for again, and replaced him on the ledge where I'd found him, gazing at the hands of a clock that had suddenly stopped.

Next I found a French medical book there that contained all manner of abnormalities. A huge foot like the trunk of a tree, an ear that opened out like a fruit, six-fingered hands, abnormal swellings on the calf, diagrams of the heart. Then the book fell open at a picture of a mother suckling a child. The fine lace shawl had fallen from the woman's slender shoulder. She was fitting the nipple into the mouth of the child. The full dipping breast was exposed. It was shockingly real. The halo of the black nipple was peppered with small nodes. I could feel the soft dimensions of the flesh.

Someone came into the old bakery below. My heart pounded. I hid the book. Went for a walk and came back again. And there it was breathing with life among the musty pages. I traced its contours. I studied the dark aureole. My mouth dried. My stomach raced. Trembling I hid it again.

I went through tall green histories of Ireland with pencil drawings of the Tuatha De Dannan and Brian Boru. Then leafed through cookery books. I came across a French-English dictionary with the flyleaf signed in Great-Aunt Jane's hand – *Paris 1912. Jane McGloughlin.* There was a signed picture of the dancer Isadora Duncan. Then there was a dull photo of a huge mansion in which the murder must have occurred. News clippings from the *New York Times*: Scandal Strikes Prominent French Family. Seemingly the dead woman had been an actress from Hollywood. The man was arrested as he tried to step on a boat at Marseille.

I read on for hours till I heard my father calling my name.

Where were you? he asked.

Reading, I said.

By God.

I was solving a murder.

That's more, said he, then I ever done. Straighten your back! They've been searching for you high and low. Your dinner's within.

I went back straight to the attic when I'd finished. The windows had leaded lights, and flushes of red and blue sunlight crossed the wooden floor. I looked into old copper pots that were filled with blue mould. I found a cardboard box of maps. An old weighing scales. A marble soda fountain. There were elaborate lamps on the shelves. In some there was still a residue of paraffin. When I touched the wicks they crumbled. I found tall receipt books from the 1920s, with each item entered in copperplate writing. The symbol for the pound note was drawn in like a ballet dancer. I found old photographs of Cavan. Photographs of women I didn't know by a lake I didn't recognize.

I sat on the floor with piles of books each side of me.

Dust travelled through the sunlight. I couldn't wait any longer. I took the medical book out of its hiding place and went back to the breast and gazed at it with a dizzy fondness. From the old bakery below the smell of fresh flour rose. The smell made me delirious. Since then I cannot smell flour without thinking of sex. Freshly baked bread makes me swoon. But the bag of flour is the most sensual object of them all.

On many of our bed sheets in letters of light faded blue you could make out the name RANK'S FLOUR MILLS DONEGAL. The flour men came up the entry bent double. They had a covering over their backs and scalps to protect them. They carried the bags of flour by the ears. The girls made the Rank's men tea, and white-faced like clowns, they sat in the kitchen scattering down.

My mother took the empty bags and made sheets from them. She sewed them under the window. So, even as I fell asleep, there was this distant smell of flour. And the first time I caught sight of a real breast flour motes fell.

* * *

It was that attic that made me want to write. The first real essay I wrote was about rain. I remember reading it out in the De La Salle Brothers school. I stole the lines from a book by Charles Lamb that I found in the attic. Imagination, says Brodsky the Russian poet in his book *Less Than One*, begins with our first lie.

It is hard for me to remember my first lie, since I've told so many. And now I'm at it again. Can I lie here and sidestep some memory I'd rather not entertain, and then let fiction take care of it elsewhere, because that is sometimes what fiction does? It becomes the receptacle for those truths we would rather not allow into our tales of the self.

The made-up characters feel their way by virtue of thoughts that novelists deny having. So I'd like to describe my first stab at fame, even though it shames me. It was a combination of lies and a fondness for words that started me. I can still remember the liquid feel of those words for rain. How the beads were blown against a windowpane, and glistened there, and ran. The words for rain were better than the rain itself. I wanted to type up words.

I went to UCD for a disastrous few terms. Instead of attending university, I spent the year selling second-hand beds and wiring houses with my cousin Vincent O'Neill, who introduced me to clients as a science student. Or, with his father, Pop O'Neill, I'd sit supping bottles of stout at the kitchen table on his pension day. We'd be waiting for Vincent to come home with the dinner. Nothing good ever came out of County Clare, sniffed Pop. That was because Vincent was born there. Like my father, Pop had been a policeman, and before that was a member of the Connaught Rangers who'd mutinied in India over England's treatment of the Irish in the Troubles.

For five days he stood in the burning sun, and sometimes the memory would come back, and he'd rage and stare at me – *A student, my arse!* he'd shout. *Useless! Useless! Useless!* Other times, I'd sit with Kitty, Vincent's wife, who was heavily pregnant, both of us looking into the fire for hours on end. I was filled with guilt at spending my mother's money, and taking a place at university that Una would have relished.

Then one day I upped and left for London, did not return to university, and found a job with Securicor. In my underpants I sat on half a million pound notes in the back of a van in Ealing during a heatwave in 1968. I lodged with a family called Healy whose youngest son was called Dermot. In that house Dave Allen was all the rage. I passed a window in the High Street and saw a manual typewriter in a window. I bought it with my first week's wages.

That typewriter was a great liar. It wrote out refurbished poems by Dylan Thomas, snatches of pop poetry by the Liverpool poets that had been published in the Penguin Modern Poets series, and many disjointed lines by virtue of e. e. cummings and William Carlos Williams. It lied beautifully at times. As a night watchman I walked factories near Smithfield Market that were filled with the rank corpses of cattle. Hides hung from the walls. There was one corner that was stacked with horns and hooves. I read Camus. Beyond the fence at the end of the yard trains flew by scattering the rats.

I disappeared from Ireland and my family. I sat by the back window of Healy's and read *Portrait of the Artist as a Young Dog*. Then I moved on to Dylan's poems. The words shimmered on the paper and released themselves from the prison of the sentences they were in. They became things in themselves. A single word collected a myriad of meanings. Verbs bounced in open spaces. A noun was like a bowl of cream. It contained vast worlds. An adjective made an image infinite.

But it was the responsibility for the everyday kept me calm. The groan of an oven in the foundry. The stiff hides. The rats racing over the railway lines. Lorries, after a drive from Scotland, blowing their horn at the gate some time near dawn. Heathrow, where two of us loaded gold onto a plane at nine in the morning, and unloaded the same gold that evening at five. In between the gold had been to France and back again. It was something to do with keeping the foreign exchange rate correct. Those gold bars fascinated me. How easy it would be to rob them. Later the same gold bullion *was* stolen.

Then I became a guard in Heathrow dealing with aliens from Pakistan. I had my own office off two cells where prisoners were put. The prisoners were young Pakistanis who had been sent to England, with, in many cases, their home village putting up the fare. They arrived without proper authorization and I led them across the tarmac. They followed in my wake according to custom. I made phone calls on their behalf to various embassies, relations and immigrant services, then locked them away and lifted out Dostoevsky.

A citizen of London I returned home to a wedding in Cavan via the Holyhead boat. I hitched to Cavan. That afternoon I found myself at the reception seated by the editor of the *Anglo-Celt*, the local newspaper where I had published my first short story.

How is the writing going on? he asked.

Oh fine, I said.

He filled me out another glass of wine.

I'm glad to hear it, he said.

Thank you.

So will we be seeing a book out soon?

Not yet. (*Pause.*) But I have a play finished.

And is it going on?

Yes.

Where? In the Abbey?

Oh no. I searched round frantically. On TV.

TV, he said.

ITV actually.

Well that's wonderful.

I got a thousand pound.

You're made up. He raised his glass. What's it called?

Night-crossing, I said.

To *Night-crossing*, he said.

We touched glasses.

It starts with two lads leaving Ireland on the Holyhead boat.

Sounds good.

The dancing began and I forgot all about the play I'd never written. A week later I was sitting in Ward's Irish House when Dermot Burke, my next-door neighbour in Cavan, and now by another coincidence my next-door neighbour in Piccadilly, came in with a smile on his face and a copy of the *Anglo-Celt*. He clamped it down on the bar.

Look, says he.

And there I was on the front page with a cigarette in my mouth over a small headline that read: CAVAN AUTHOR FINDS FAME. Oh Burke brought that copy of the *Anglo-Celt* everywhere, into every company I found myself in; he produced it out of his pocket as we sat with friends, he had it photostated and posted it around.

He'd set me questions about the plot, and the more he asked the more I had to invent.

In time I invented a producer from ITV, a Mr Evans, if you don't mind, who lived in Hammersmith. Apparently I saw him from time to time. He went over the shots and camera angles with me. I even eventually set a date when it would be broadcast to the nation – November 10th, let's say. In fact I began to believe in it myself. I believed the script existed. The more of the story I invented, the more real it became.

Then I'd suddenly wake out of a dream terror-stricken by my duplicity. Slowly I tried to extricate myself from the lie. There were problems with production monies, I said. There were production difficulties. Something had gone wrong down the line. The date for the broadcast came and went. No one mentioned it.

But in fact I had set myself a duty. Everything I write now is an attempt to make up for that terrible lie. Had I not lied I might never have tried my hand at fiction. The truth is the lie you once told returning to haunt you.

Chapter 11

I came into the outpatients alone. I handed in the card from the doctor to the nurse. Names were called, we moved on a seat, one by one, all sorry folk – ladies from the county with shopping bags, sombre pallid townsfolk, startled children on the laps of their mothers, pregnant women.

What are you in for? my neighbour asked. But before I could reply my name was called.

The young intern placed me in a bed behind a screen. Outside I heard them speaking of how serious things looked. I was terrified. He returned.

Are you not undressed yet? he asked me.

Then he went off again. I took off my shirt and trousers, then my underpants. A nurse looked in. I got into the bed and pulled the sheet to my chin. An Indian doctor stood at the bottom of the bed with my card in his hand. He read it and looked at me and handed it to the intern. He in turn read it. The doctor disappeared.

The intern lifted the sheet and tapped my stomach.

Any pain? he asked.

No.

He tapped again and pressed.

Now?

No.

Then where is it?

Down there, I said, pointing.

Here?

He sank his fingers into the flesh above my groin.

Is it the bladder as well? he asked.

I don't know.

We'll have an X-ray taken, he said, as soon as possible.

He looked into my eyes and shone a light into the whites. The doctor returned with a chart.

He's a remarkable good colour, the intern said. Take a look here, Dr Rao.

The doctor entered the cubicle and smiled at me. He looked into my eyes. He read the chart. He pulled back an eyelid and shone his beam.

He has complained of his bladder, said the intern, but I can find nothing wrong with his liver.

The two of them looked at me.

You have been very sick, said Dr Rao.

My heart took a turn.

Is your mother with you?

No, I said.

Goodness. You came here alone? he asked astonished.

I did.

You are a very brave man, said the doctor. Isn't he?

Yes, said the intern.

But someone should have come with you, the doctor continued, and he looked at the intern with dismay and shook his head as if my mother and father were totally irresponsible.

Tch, he said. Tch, tch. Have you brought your pyjamas?

I have.

Tell me now where is the pain?

I pointed at my penis.

In your willy? he asked aghast.

Yes, I said.

Goodness, he said.

They consulted the chart again, then viewed me with disbelief. I don't understand, he said. It is *Brendan Heaney*?

My name is Dermot Healy, I said quickly.

They retired. I lay there wondering what would happen next. Dr Rao returned smiling.

So you're for circumcision?

I am.

We thought you were someone else, he explained. Get into your pyjamas and I'll take you upstairs.

As I crossed the room in my pyjamas I saw Brendan Heaney enter with his father and mother. They were helping him. His skin was bright yellow and he was in carpet slippers. With my clothes under my arm I took the lift to the second floor. Forty years later I was mistaken for another Heaney, when a man stopped me up in Sligo town and took my hand and said, *You're made. You can laugh at them now.* Then he congratulated me on winning the Nobel Prize.

Father A. B. McGrath walked down the ward. Then he saw me in the bed.

What has you here? he asked.

They took a bit of my mickey off, I said.

Not before time, he replied. This is a choirboy of mine, he explained to the nurse. He sat on the bed. So why did they do that to you?

It started to itch.

Did it?

My foreskin was too long.

I see.

So they cut it off.

The same, he said, happened to Jesus.

Una and two of her girlfriends came to call. They sat around the bed, whispering and joking and enthralled by what had happened to me. The thought that I might have lost such an extraordinary organ made me an object of great interest.

Are you in pain? the Keogan girl asked.

A little.

Can we see it? said Doreen Smith.

No.

Can you go to the toilet?

Yes.

How do you go to the toilet?

Carefully, I said.

This made them laugh. A few days later I was let go and ordered to return in a week to have the stitches out. Each day I painfully urinated and grew terrified of having the doctors near me again. By the time a week had gone by I did not have the courage to return to the outpatients.

On the appointed day I walked out to Swellan Lake, returned and said it was done.

63

Now that I'd told the lie I didn't know what to do. The next morning when I woke the stitches were still there, a purple hem round my flittered foreskin. The next morning they were there again. I began to fear that the stitches might be there for all time.

I stopped outside the hospital but could not bring myself to go in. The window of the operating room on the second floor was ajar. I could see Surgeon Moloney in a blue plastic hat washing his hands. A nurse with a tray of implements passed by. Steam pumped out of the down-pipe.

I ran home.

That night in the bedroom I took a scissors and patiently snipped each stitch, then gently drew them out. I could feel the pain in the soles of my feet. I thought when I had finished that the head might fall off. But it didn't. It was a delicate intimate affair, and when it was over, it brought me immense relief. But with each hint of an erection I held my breath and tried to think of other things.

Slowly it came back to itself. Dirty thoughts no longer made me flinch. When I went jiving at the record hops Una's friends would laugh, but I'd keep my head aloft, as if I didn't see them.

The first time I heard about sex I was up a STOP sign pole where Town Hall Street entered Farnham Street. Whoever was standing at the bottom of the pole carefully explained that babies came out through their mother's bellybutton. When I heard that I climbed down very slowly.

I used stand for hours in the library on Saturday mornings, looking at the nudes in tall books on classical art, then take home *The Lives of the Martyrs* to read. Lust and pain were regular bedfellows.

The courting began next a haycock in the field. It was mild enough to begin with. Then the eldest amongst us held one of the girls down in the hay.

He shouted at us to look.

A sort of sexual frenzy gripped everyone. The girls laughed and fought. I trailed my fingers across the girl's knickers. He let go her hands. She put her arms around me and kissed me. Then we got up

64

and walked shamefaced back to town. A few days later I was in the garden at the back of the Breifne with my mother.

I told her I had something to tell her. We walked through the wild rhubarb. I struggled to tell her the guilt that was nagging at me. My sin I felt was awesome.

I touched a girl, I said.

Think, said she, if that had been your sister.

So, we parted. I was forgiven somewhat. But this led to frightening invasions of my private life. She went through my diary where all sexual acts were written in code. She demanded to know the meaning of them all. And of course I didn't tell her, but I knew by the look she gave me that she knew.

That talk in the garden had its apotheosis the first time I saw my sister Una kiss a boyfriend. I wanted to run a mile. All my guilt surfaced. I could tell what that man wanted. All my insane longings were being perpetuated through him. The embarrassment I felt was like a sickness. I'm not the better of it yet, as they say.

Chapter 12

Aunty Maisie slept at the front of the house on Main Street, below a grey print of Our Lady of the Flowers. She got up at twelve each day, turned on the radio and sauntered po in hand to the bathroom with a distracted air. She'd touch the curtains in the corridor and check each room to make sure lights were switched off. Then she broke open blood-red wax seals on bills from confectionery companies and cursed in dismay. Then she took a leisurely breakfast of tea and warm buttered brown bread. She sat watching the reflection of the girls speeding past in the mirror and smoked an Afton in the dark. No daylight reached into the private room.

Is everything all right, Miss Slacke? asked Katie German.

Yes, Katie.

Would you like something else?

No, thank you.

She'd bring in her dishes to the scullery and run a scalding tap over them. She might even dry a few from the tearoom that sat on the draining board. Then, as the time got closer to the beginning of her shift in the shop, her demeanour would change. Her cheeks blazed with disdain. Her eyes hardened at the thought of all the responsibilities ahead. She'd whack the table.

Have they nothing to do, she'd say as she disparaged her customers, but feed their faces? The cursed whores!

Slinging hash, by God!

Then she'd cast aspersions on some item in the kitchen, wring out a dishcloth angrily and pass up the entry with her head down. She'd refresh her hair and face in the hall stand mirror, go up to her room to get the cash box and at one o'clock relieve my mother.

The two ladies never spoke at the changing of the guard except to point out orders that had come in.

Mrs Smith wants a cherry cake at five, my mother would say.

Does she, the faggot.

And the man from the sugar company called.

What was he calling for? He wants a kick up the hole.

They'll hear you in the tearoom.

Let them, she'd shriek.

Have it your own way, my mother would say.

Maisie would slap her fist into her hand.

I could do that to them! she'd say savagely.

I'm going in now.

Go on, she'd say, who's keeping you?

She'd turn and find a customer at her back. A vague smile would ghost across her lips.

Yes? she'd enquire. Yes, what can I get you?

My mother, who'd been up at eight to let in the girls, would flee to the kitchen to help. It was dinner hour, the busiest part of the day. Bachelor bank clerks, clerks from the County Council, the girls from the tax office, vets, apprentices from the shoe shops, young grocers, old drapers, men from the hardware department in Provider's, coal men from Fegan's, country women who left their shopping behind the counter, road men, men from the Guinness lorries, all would file past.

Good afternoon, Miss Slacke.

Good day, Mr Igo.

As each customer entered Aunt Maisie rang a bell at the end of the counter to alert the girls within. This gave a piercing sound in the small dining room, and pressing hard down with her thumb, she always rang longer than anyone.

Does she think we're fucking deaf? Mary Kate would ask.

It would ring again for good luck.

The bitch, said Mary Kate, you'd swear she heard me.

Maisie, between customers, made cakeboxes or filled bags of tea, oft times chewing a jelly baby. It was a trial for her to go on her hunkers but this she did each day. The fresh buns were moved to the front of the display. Yesterday's were moved to the back so that she could pick them first.

Then at half past one the door to the shop flew open and in came the convent schoolchildren. Despite the Breifne being up-market it kept some of the cheapest sweets in town courtesy of Uncle Seamus. But the main requirement was a penny slice of Chester cake. This was a heavy slab of cake mixed from the trimmings of Swiss rolls, Madeiras, butter sponges – anything that came to hand. Then it was topped with a coat of chocolate and a splash of hundreds and thousands.

A Chester bun, Mrs.

A flash bar.

A macaroon.

Take your turn, Maisie would snarl.

She took the penny before she handed across the item. The crowd of children would grow. Behind them patiently stood the bankers in their suits and raincoats waiting to pay for their lunch while Maisie opened jars of gobstoppers, handed out bags of broken buns, picked out pink chewing gum or cut ice cream for threepenny wafers. At last she'd reach the bankers and the clerks. With a polite nod she accepted their bill, scrutinized it carefully, then called for what was owing in a sweet voice, and paid out the change, coin by reluctant coin.

After two-thirty all went quiet. My mother sat down to her dinner, then she'd prop her feet on the ledge above the fireplace. This was to get the circulation going. My mother had trouble with her feet. A few times a month she went off to have her corns paired, her toes done. She'd dip her feet in methylated spirits and wipe them clean with cotton wool.

In the afternoon a different type of customer appeared in the shop. Country women came for buns. The genteel wives of professional men bought meringues and eclairs. Secretaries bought snacks. Drunks fell into the tearoom for fries. The dummy arrived. Orders came in for birthday cakes. Special consideration was given to wedding cakes. The mother and the bride-to-be would be taken aside to the little room off the shop.

Here the gold wedding-cake stand was shown. Maisie would be at her most persuasive.

It's always such a difficult time, she'd say.

Sizes and numbers of tiers were discussed. Out came the top ornaments – gold braids, dwarf brides and grooms in silver, bunches of plastic flowers, a couple on a swing.

Then the order book came down off the nail. The mother would look at the prices while the bride-to-be stood apart from the transaction, awed by the costs and what was in store. As customers waited outside in the shop for service, Maisie, unmoved by their impatience, went through the costs of a wedding cake again for the benefit of the mother of the bride-to-be.

A bargain was struck. The advance was handed over.

Maisie with a false smile approached the next customer.

Yes? she enquired, as she put the pile of notes carefully away, and what can I do for you?

A few weeks later my sisters and I would walk down Main Street carrying the three tiers of the wedding cake to the hotel. The wedding-cake stand, the prized piece of equipment in the Breifne, worth oh hundreds, came on its own later.

Maisie was relieved at four o'clock.

The rutting season has started again! barked Maisie. There's a Madeline Slowey for a wedding cake.

Good, said my mother.

Another one, Maisie would reply, ready to breed!

Have you seen Una?

I have seen nothing of your offspring.

And she'd stamp out through the side door and up the entry swinging her elbows with her head down. Maisie in the far past had been let down in love, got engaged and seen the engagement broken, and never kept company again. She'd sit in the dining room till six in a blue daze, contemplating her dinner, contemplating her reflection, a fork lifted in midair or tucked against her cheek as she pondered easy tasks and quiet memories, she'd drift away, but sometimes the wrong thought would strike, she'd slap down the the fork or knife, slap the table, and curse indignantly.

The girls held their breath.

Some strange guilt would propel Maisie into the kitchen to pounce on any misdemeanour. She'd rage a moment by the geyser. Lament the waste of oil. The cost of tea. The cost of coal. Were the fires stacked with slack? *And that fucker the accountant! God in heaven! What are we to do! What are we to do! Taxes! Taxes! The wages! The wages!* Her terror was of huge electricity bills. As she raced through the public dining room she'd attack the switches and plunge the place into darkness despite the single customer having a fry in the corner.

The thought of having to return to the shop would drive her mad. But the last shift from six to seven-thirty was a quiet time.

Mrs English came for cheesecakes. Mrs Burke for scones. Mrs McCarren for puff pastry. Apple tarts dusted with sugar went away for high tea out Farnham way. Like my mother before her, Maisie would sit making tea bags. *Tea bags! Tea bags!* She'd tear the top off the tea chest. A spoon and a half of tea. Open the bag. Empty the spoon. Lift a half spoon. Empty it. Fold the bag. Drop it into the biscuit tin. Fill another bag with a spoon and a half. Into the biscuit tin. When the tin was full she'd ring the bell twice, to call one of the girls to the shop.

Go careful with these, she'd say.

Yes, Miss Slacke.

We are not a charity.

Yes, Miss Slacke.

And bring me out the empty bags!

Out came the empty bags. She sat down again by the tea chest. It started all over.

She'd slide the window back and peer out onto the street. She'd make cakeboxes. They arrived flat, you bent them at the joins, undid the flaps, tucked the flaps into openings, brought down the top and there you had it. At seven-thirty she'd close the door of the shop without looking out onto the street, turn down the lights and sit a while by the till in the dark. My mother would be hanging washing out on the line. Upstairs Maisie went with the takings to her room. Another smoke. Listen to the radio. Down for tea.

Are you coming, Winnie? she'd ask graciously.

Let me get my coat.

And the two were off to the pictures.

After the pictures Maisie would laboriously count the takings out onto her bed. Cash was prepared in piles. Next day the pound notes would be carried down to the Allied Irish Bank to meet cheques drawn out for the flour men, the sweet travellers, the Tayto man, the Jacob's traveller, the Yeast Company, the Afton man, the John Player man, the ESB – *the cursed ESB!* – the sugar company. A cheque was made out to them, sent away in the post or given to the traveller, and the appropriate sum was delivered to the bank to meet the cheque. She kept no deposit or current accounts but retained all cash in a green locker under her dressing table. Her bedroom was her vault. She made up the girls' wages there. Filled bags with pennies, half-crowns, tanners, farthings, halfpenny pieces, threepenny pieces, shillings, and had them sent over the road to the Hibernian Bank in the morning in exchange for notes.

When all was accounted for she'd smoke a cigarette, part the curtains slightly and look down through a crack in the blind at Main Street. Years before, from this same window she'd seen the policeman she'd been engaged to pass down the far side of the street with his new bride and she'd broken into tears. Now she just stared a moment, then looked away. All this time the radio was playing. She'd walk down her stairs, up the three steps and across the landing to make one last visit to the throne room. Her step was off cue. She'd burp loudly. On the return journey she'd switch off the light on the landing. I'd sometimes hear her like a nocturnal animal passing through the house checking for lights. I'd hear her step on the loose board below the altar. A hand would slip in through my bedroom door and slip the switch.

Lights! Lights! Illuminations! *We want no illuminations!* The boiler! The single-bar electric fire in the shop! The water heater! She checked them all.

Only the radio was immune.

She'd sit by the mirror and wait on the National Anthem. Then by the light from her room she'd make her way across the sitting room and turn off the radio. Main Street went quiet.

Chapter 13

My father taught me handball by beating a sack ball against Provider's wall.

Go for the butt, he said. Butts are the boy.

To butt a ball meant striking at the lowest part of the wall so that your opponent could not hit the return. The fist, my father reckoned, should not be used. You have no aim with the fist. The open hand was the instrument. I stood for hours practising. Then he taught me boxing. He made a punchball of rolled newspapers and hung it from a string in the shed. Dermot Kinane was there. He had the two of us punch the ball to and fro.

I made a number of elaborate ducks and pranced.

Stop ducking, he said. Put up your guard and jab.

So the next time the ball swung at me I tried to meet it. Instead it caught me in the face. Tears burst out of my eyes. I was mortified.

Meet it with your fist, he said, not your head.

Dermot smacked it hard again. I poked out. It caught my nose.

You're looking at me, said my father. Look at the punchball. Stop looking at me.

I tried to forget he was there as I met the ball of *Anglo-Celts*. This time I drove the return perfectly. Proudly I looked over at my father. Dermot boxed it back. I turned and ducked.

Meet it, said my father, like a man, can't you.

I stood there angry and ashamed. He turned away in dismay.

Years later I went for a walk with my son Dallan and his mother Anne-Marie along the Thames. There was a bright blue sky over London. Long dark barges plied the waters. Cranes were swinging.

We bought ice creams and listened to trains crashing overhead while we stood under a bridge in Pimlico. The London folk were lying out sunning themselves on high-rise balconies and on every available piece of greenery. Dallan ran ahead of us, waited till we caught up with him, then on again, happily. We walked through the park and watched the smoke pour from the four huge chimneys of Battersea Power station.

Kites were plunging in the upper air. A brass band played on the park bandstand. We bought hamburgers off a stall. We walked by the houses of parliament. Then made our way to the new National Theatre complex. In one of the forecourts there was a giant inflatable for children to play on. I placed Dallan on board.

At first he leaped with the others in the middle. Then he moved towards us and made a number of special high leaps.

Stop looking at us, I shouted.

He jumped again, and this time he was closer to the edge.

Dal, stop looking at me! I shouted.

He jumped again, and coming down he hit the edge of the palliasse, fell three feet and struck his head off the concrete pavement. He sat up shocked and began to cry. I lifted him. After a while he quietened down. He watched over my shoulder at the other children jumping safe in the centre.

You should not have been looking at me, I said.

He didn't say anything but stared at them. And I knew then that he too, like myself, was gripped by that awful condition of wanting to please.

I made my communion. I delivered soda farls and brown bread round the town. I made my confirmation. And the top of my arm was peppered with shots against diseases that were rampant at the time. Mother, with a dust-cloth tied round her head like a scarf, cleans the ashes out of the grate.

The town crier rang his bell for the last time and Tommy Reilly of the Regal turned off the water supply at the reservoir up in Tullymongan. We lined up in Burke's garden below the glasshouse, bent over and John Burke shot a pellet at your bum from an air gun. I get all my front teeth out because one of them is bad and in goes my first plate at twelve.

They were all downstairs in the dining room. Facing us was the huge mirror which was nearly the width of an entire wall. That mirror had given my family and me a second identity.

We ate looking at ourselves in it. We were never fully ourselves, but always possessed by others. When someone entered the room we spoke to them though the mirror. The family, when they conversed, never had to look directly at each other. We all spoke through the mirror. We learned faithlessness and duplicity from an early age. Always there were two of you there: the one in whom consciousness rested and the other, the body, which somehow didn't belong and was always at a certain remove.

This mirror and our use of it threw visitors off balance. They looked at you directly but you looked at them in the mirror. Even if the person was standing in front of you you looked over their shoulder. That warped perspective stayed with me for years.

This distance between my mind and my body has always remained and is insurmountable.

Anyway, this night some of the Fineas had come on a visit. Brian McHugh was there, Mr Dolan and Mrs Reilly. My mother asked after Brian Sheridan, who had been to primary school with her. They were led through the Breifne, then brought in for high tea and drinks to the dining room. We were scattered round the two white tables and the group of people and the tables were repeated again in the mirror.

There were two of everything – two Brian McHughs, two bottles of Paddy, two fathers, two mothers.

So then what happened? asked my father.

Well then, I said, we got onto the aeroplane.

Was it a big aeroplane? asked Brian McHugh.

It was a small aeroplane, I said and looked at my father.

That's right, he agreed. And we took off from the Curragh.

We did, I said nodding at myself.

Were you not afraid? Mr Dolan the lorry-driver who'd driven Brian over, asked.

Not then, I replied.

Not till after, said my father, and he studied me in the mirror. Not till we came over the village of Finea.

Then what happened?

The young fellow had to get out onto a rope ladder.

That's right, I agreed. The ladder was dangled out of the door of the plane till it reached the ground. And it was an ojus height and then I had to climb down.

Carrying the bottles? asked Brian McHugh.

That's right, I said. Carrying the bottles of Guinness.

And he got down without breaking one, laughed my father.

I nodded at myself. Everyone laughed.

Then I climbed back up and we flew back to . . .

To the Curragh, added my father.

To the Curragh, I said, and we came back home through Westmeath in Uncle Seamus's sweet van.

Now for you, said Brian McHugh. That was some journey.

The Fineas leaned forward and laughed in the mirror. I caught the winks. More drinks were poured.

My father clapped my knee.

You're a great traveller, he said proudly. The two of him rocked gently on the chair. My mother corrected her glasses. Aunty Maisie tapped ash, ever so carefully, into a blue ashtray.

On Saturday nights the shop closed at nine and everyone relaxed. Throughout the evening, Mrs Betty Ronaghan, a seamstress and a friend of the ladies, would tour the drapers of Upper Main Street, picking up a suit here, a hat there, all on loan, for the ladies to see, and with them folded over her arm she'd set off for the Breifne. The dresses were hung from the mirror, or over a chair, then off she'd head again for more style to John Brady, drapers, or to P. A. Smith, drapers, and across to Vera Brady's Fashions to scrutinize the latest.

By the time Maisie and my mother had come in, Betty would have collected an assortment of new and old fashions. Then Una and Miriam would go into the kitchen and undress. In they came in wide polka-dot dresses, satin blouses, and jiving skirts. They walked on nyloned feet in front of the mirror.

My father and myself would give our opinion.

Do you like it, Dermot? Miriam would ask.

It's very white.

Too white for me?

It makes your eyes look big.

Dear God, said my father.

Una's dresses were strikingly floral. She kicked off various slip-ons and turned to the side.

Well?

A sight, said Maisie, for sore eyes.

Next my mother would appear in a hat decked out in feathers, or in some prim suit, with a shiny red handbag over her arm. She'd stand in her slip as Betty lowered another dress over her arms. Maisie tried on a jumper. Betty straightened the collar and pulled down the back.

Well, asked Maisie, do I look a tramp?

It suits you, Maisie, said my father.

You'd say that anyway.

My mother would bring in the bottle of port. My father pulled the top of a bottle of Guinness. Maisie threw coal on the fire. Seamus arrived with a naggin of whiskey. My father tapped a fag into the grate. My mother drank a glass of port and danced round the kitchen, then clapped her knees and pointed at Seamus as he began imitating a company sergeant in a prisoner-of-war camp in wartime England. Una beat cream. Miriam stood in the hall with her boyfriend, the showband singer, whom she would marry, and they'd head to the States together. Betty picked a darning needle out of her hat and put it between her teeth. She lifted a blouse to the light, found the seam that needed stitching and then fed a thread carefully through the eye of the needle.

Chapter 14

It was again Thursday, half-day in Cavan town. The haranguing public were barred from the door. The ladies mellowed. It felt like a home again.

Soon after noon, all activity ceased. The town gave a sigh of relief. Potato sacks were taken in, shop gates raised, grids pulled across displays; the restaurant closed; the bells on the doors of the grocers went quiet; Maisie emptied the till, and the shop went dark; Flood's flowers were brought indoors and watered; today's bread was put in behind yesterday's; the shift changed in the barracks; the last cones were served in Katie Bannon's; Hughie Smith, the county secretary of the GAA, stood on the steps of the courthouse, stroked the sparse down of grey hair on his chin, and headed in the direction of the White Star; the cobbler wet his thumb, cut a deck of cards and began a game of poker in the CYMS snooker hall; Mr Tom McKenna, in a large neat pinstripe suit, stepped carefully on stockinged feet into his window to undress a model; Maisie paused in the entry and, with one hand on her hip, sneezed; Hickey's the butchers pulled in their awnings; the man left the caravan at the weighbridge; the bank manager's wife stood estranged at her window looking down on the town; Mother hung out clothes to dry; a dog sprinted across Breifne Park; five labourers sat eating sandwiches and drinking milk in an Anglia on Main Street; a woman steered a pram down the town archway; Brother Cyril threw the *glantoir* for wiping the blackboard at someone; a traveller from Jacob's Biscuits stood behind the faded curtains of the White Swan and wiped his glasses; Mrs Battle put away her camphor balls; Fox's shoes and wellingtons and high-heels were taken indoors; Vera Brady's Fashions was shut; business came to an end in the Central Café and Mrs McManus (*née* Moloco) broke into raucous Italian; the post-office workers leaned against Whelan's and watched with envy the town close down; Dinny Brennan dropped his ladder and tins of paint in Reilly's yard and entered the Imperial; Hugh Gough served a bottle of stout to Phil Hill; Brother Cyril slowly spat a green globule into his handkerchief; jackdaws alighted on Main Street; the miller Greene went home to Saint Felim's like a snowman; the restaurant in the Breifne was swept out; rehearsals for the pantomime began in the side room of the Town Hall; the Labour Band gathered in a shed down the Market yard; Doonegan the sweep sent a brush sky-high up a chimney on River Street, while his two sons carted bags of soot to the mill wall; the cakes were taken in from the Breifne window; the drapery assistants streamed out of town towards home on their bikes; bags of seeds were carried to the back of the Market House, the huge gates closed; Miss Foster went into the darkness of the back room; the estate agent walked The Triangle; Flood's hearse was hosed down; Clarence Frogman Henry sang on a radio down Abbey Street; clothes were hung out on the terraces of the Half Acre; Jack Flood took a fare to Killinkere; Bud McNamara, in blue overalls, crossed the Gallows Hill with his bag of tools; a dog in heat flew down Bridge Street; clouds gathered; Monty Montgomery locked his shed of eggs and went back to Farnham; blinds came down; young men climbed the stairs to the boxing club; the street sweeper paused at the Pound; Mr Corr the dentist sat in his own waiting room; Mrs McCusker switched off the hair-dryers in the Beauty Saloon; Benny Hannigan drove Phil Hill home to Latt in his hackney; the first copy of the weekly newspaper was coming off the reels in the *Anglo-Celt*; the workers from McCarren's Bacon Factory walked back down River Street; lights went off in the car salerooms; Maisie carried the morning's takings to her room; Reilly the barber brushed hair into a corner; a fire blazed at the back of ESB showrooms; butterflies flitted through the cabbages in Burke's garden; hams went back into the fridge; Mr Donoghue, the scoutmaster, drank a cup of tea alone among the silent accordions in the scout den; Mother lay in bed with her feet propped up on a pillow for a few minutes, then was on the move again; Snowball Walsh got sick and was let go home; the Clones train came in; a lorry of Armagh apples passed south; Louie Blessing fed his pigs potato skins; the Cavan mineral lorry backed into the Farnham yard; Father McManus sat in his Ford reading his breviary; Johnny McDonagh, still tipsy and wild-eyed, emerged from Straw Lodge and went down the town roaring; Tommy Lauden, who sat all day watching the traffic from a well-polished knee-high stone by the postbox, headed slowly up the steep Half Acre; a Batchelors pea can crashed onto the Dublin Road; some road men appeared; Mrs English went next door; the Miss Hickeys went upstairs; Dermot Morgan headed for the links; Dr Sullivan stopped off at the Abbey Bar; Barnie Buckley shoved a barrow of glowing coals down Tullymongan; a few souls prayed in the cathedral; crows rose in the Farnham Gardens; a man with migraine rang the bell of Burke's the chemist; Johnny McDonagh reached Hourican's; Surgeon Moloney went in the back way to Louie Blessing's; Guard Gaffey came up Town Hall Street, crossed over at Jack Brady's on Main Street and looked in at the shoes; a phone rang unanswered in McGinty's; the Breifne girls got up on their bikes; Packie Clay went into the Hub Bar – *Johnny McDonagh's outside*, he said; the sound of piano music came out of the Miss Powers'; a red hen flew out of the Pound Archway; a lorry from Monery left a stinking trail of animal effluent behind it in College Street; the sacristan trimmed the Cathedral lawn; Bill Anderson stepped out of the gates of the Royal School, lit a cigarette and steadied his hands; a rifle was discharged; some parties left Nee's restaurant; the meringues cooled in the huge coke oven at the back of the Breifne; the girls from Woolworth's changed from their shop coats into their own clothes and the manageress let them onto the street; my mother shot the bolt home in the yard gate; Lord Farnham went smartly into his solicitor's; Miss Sheridan, the librarian, stamped the date of return into Walter Macken's *God Made Sunday*; Skiddely Doonegan traipsed past; my mother did her toes; the bishop's chauffeur collected his girl up Keadue Lane in the Bishop's car; Mr P. A. Smith, draper, went quickly into Cooke's; the vet took a call; a gypsy pony came down Cooke's archway from the Fair Green and whinnied; there was a mongrel asleep outside Black's, the printers; Con Reilly tapped a barrel; Mr McDonnell, the baker, called a Power's; the coal men in Fegan's washed themselves under a tap in the yard; the sky was grey, the wind ordinary; we heard the Dublin train; Bill Anderson sat down by the piano in the back room of the Railway Hotel and played the blues; Mrs Byrne told Stick Donoghue the news; the barman in the Congo ran cold water onto a cut in his finger; the deaf Smith lifted the back off a radio and looked in; Tom McCusker chalked a cue; Johnny McDonagh left town; Frank Conlon the antique dealer put

an armchair that needed upholstery into the back of his van and drove
home to Billis; Elm Bank chickens chirped in boxes at the Bus Office;
Frank Brady went into the bookies with a newspaper tucked into his
pocket, shot back a shock of hair and put his glasses on.

So, what's the story? he said.

Silence fell.

By three o'clock the streets were cleared. Only in the banks and
the dimly lit solicitors' offices or in the County Council offices did the
working day continue as usual.

My mother put her legs up over the fire and slept. My father was
in the garden. Maisie was in her room, smoking and listening to the
radio. The Milseanacht Breifne, meaning the sweets of Breifne – and
Breifne being the old tribal land of the Reillys – rested. I had the house
and the town to myself.

BOOK III

Out the Lines

Chapter 15

My brother Tony was getting married in Brighton. My father and mother done out in their fineries left for London via Holyhead where they would stop in Pimlico with Aunt Bridgie.

They were gone a long time. I had the world to myself. I ate my breakfast with Una, said goodbye to her at Con Reilly's gate then stowed my bag behind the Town Hall and headed off on a long mitching tour of various places in and around Cavan, sometimes heading out the now defunct railway line on a cabby car that we arm-wrestled through the Loreto woods and on to Butlersbridge.

The cabby car, known as the up-and-downer or back-breaker, which used bring the railway-menders up the line, now sat in a shed at the disused station in Swellan. We lifted the cabby car onto the tracks, about five of us, and sat up. This was the Swellan gang. In the old days to join them you had to lie on the sleepers and let the Dublin train race over you. Now the trains were gone and only the cabby car remained. But the line was still intact. Snowball Walsh put on a railwayman's cap belonging to his father. With the first push of the hand-bar the cabby car took. We headed down the line singing Davy Crockett.

We cut timber for an old lady that lived along the line and she in turn gave us buttermilk. Her false teeth sat steeping in a bowl on the windowsill. We brought her coal leavings from the station in the cabby car and sat around her sooty hearth. Swallows leapt out of the eaves.

You don't like the school, she said, and her whiskers silvered.

No, ma'am.

I never liked it either. She drank her mug and clasped her knees. And I don't like the town. I'm content here.

She appraised us. What's your name?

Healy.

And yours?

Hickey.

Do you see this eye? she said and she pointed at one brown iris. We inspected the pupil. I was cutting a bush, she continued, and a branch spun back on me and the thorns shot into the socket. So now I can't see on my left side. That eye, she said, has its back to the world.

She leaned forward and sighed.

But there was no pain, she added, no pain.

That's good, said Ollie Smith.

Now, any day you don't want to go to school you come out here, she said, and I'll find things for you to do.

She waved us away. We headed on to the next house, cranking the bars that turned the wheels along railway lines that had lost their sheen. Two white-haired brothers lived in a granite house with a stave of aerials shooting from the roof. Inside, Burl Ives was singing. They gave us various jobs. We watered the potatoes. We herded cattle from one field to another, filled old baths with water and stacked turf. The brothers mended radios in the kitchen and let us listen in on things from abroad. The table and floor were stacked with blue batteries.

The men ate cold pork with their hands and explained that they had been reared in the two drawers of the dresser.

Ernie was reared in that drawer, and I was reared in this, said one brother. Isn't that right, Ernie?

That's right, Walter, said Ernie, but don't be a silly-billy now.

They oiled the cabby car and gave us crab apples.

How far are you going today? Walter asked us.

We don't know, I said.

Well you could go on that thing, if you were fit for it, to Clones, he explained.

Could you?

You could. You could. As a matter of fact, on a good day you might reach the sea. Isn't that right, Ernie?

That's right, said Ernie. Then he laid a damp hand on my arm. Did I see you talking to Mrs White down the line?

Yes, I said.

How does she do it? he said to himself. How does she do it? That's what I'd like to know. Then he spun on his foot and looked towards Mrs White's. Was there any mention of us?

No, I said.

No, Ernie repeated. Nothing?

She didn't mention you.

84

I suppose she didn't. He stood on the sleepers and contemplated her house. I suppose she didn't.

The brothers gave us a push and we headed for Butlersbridge via Loreto. Each time we took the cabby car we ventured further. We sailed along to Kansas City, taking in Delaware along the way. We hit Tombstone. And Black Creek. And passed old railway houses and dilapidated farms. Your arms grew tired on the slopes. Snowball Walsh gave the orders. We pushed and pulled till we reached the crest, the last few inches were hell, then getting to the top we cheered and took off at a nice hectic rate past old crossings and hoardings, singing *Davy, Davy Crockett, king of the wild frontier.* White numbers tacked to trees flew by. We sat in a ditch eating wild strawberries and blowing cotton.

When we arrived to a bridge over which a road passed we pulled up smartly, then came to a stop under the cold damp arches. We listened for the approach of a car. We put our ears to the granite walls and heard rain steeping. Then, if there was nothing coming, we struck out into country and spread our wings.

Other times with the Cavan town crowd I'd go down to the haunted house at the nun's lake. It was called Lavell's. There was a noose still hanging in the barn, the skulls of cattle were thrown across the grounds and a small harmonium sat in a sunny room on the first storey. We sank onto the old rusty beds and unravelled fishing lines.

There were apple trees out the back and cutlery still in the kitchen drawers. There was a dresser of blue plates with an alarm clock tilted back on one leg. We washed the cutlery and old plates in the lake and set out places on the kitchen table. We lit rushes with petrol and sat them in large fruit cans. Then we ate our sandwiches.

The last man who'd lived there had killed himself. We frightened ourselves with stories about him. There were three suits hanging in the wardrobe, a case packed for going away and a hatbox filled with old bills. Someone had been in the First World War. His letters were stowed in an oilskin bag. We searched the rooms for a gun. We tapped the walls for hidden passages. Through the grounds elderly cows with large horns wandered. They fed unceasingly. The noise of their eating filled the dark house.

One day a farmer found us sitting in the barn taking turns with catapults to shoot down jam jars. In the orchard we had a fire burning rubbish.

I saw the smoke, he said.

Good day, I said.

Good day yourself, he answered. So what are you doing here?

We're on holidays, said Matti Donnelly.

You are in my hat. Do you think I'm a gom? He entered the house. Be God, he said, what's been going on here?

The linoleum floor was swept, the delft laid out and the windows cleaned.

Well I'll be damned.

He came out and sat on the collapsed wall.

Are yous thinking of stopping long? he asked and put a cigarette in his mouth.

We said nothing.

I just thought I'd ask, he added, smiling to himself.

We're boy scouts, said Ben Gaffney.

Boy scouts, be God. Are yous in the band?

We are, I said.

Very good. Very good. He shook a stone out of his wellington. I have a gammy leg, he explained. Then he studied us. Are you not afraid of auld Lavell? he asked. He pointed at the beam. That's the very place he hung himself. See that lake? He pointed over the rushes. A nun astray in the head came down the hill and walked into it. A Sister Concepta. I dragged that water for her myself. And she came up black as peat. Then there was the jockey. But that was before my time. There was a race-course here, if you can believe it, and bedad he fell in and drowned.

He stood.

And that was the end of the racing. He studied us. Would you be young Smith?

No, said Ollie Smith.

You have the head of your father, he said. Well I'll be off. Boy scouts, be God.

Goodbye, mister, said Matti.

He touched his nose with his index finger. And if anyone asks, I didn't see ye. Right? He tipped his forehead. Take care now.

He headed off on his bad leg through the orchard striking nettles with a stick as he went. We talked of the nun, the jockey and old Lavell. We dropped lines into the lake for pike and walked through the swishing reeds. On the way back from there Ollie Smith let up a kite on the Gallows Hill. It whooshed into the air with a bark and drifted over the town. That was the signal to say we were mitching. The boys saw it from the Brothers school.

Then we headed down the Cock Hill, round the Pound Archway and along River Street. At a signal we darted across Bridge Street, up Abbey Street and into the Market yard by the monastery where Owen Roe O'Neill was buried. We studied the broad brown bones under the collapsed tombs. Shoulder blades, said Matti Donnelly, that's what they are. We climbed over the gate into the back of the Town Hall. We waited there till the lads came streaming down from the Brothers. Then we took our bags and headed home, ducking pellets Paddy Ronaghan was shooting with a pellet gun from his bedroom window. Ping! Ping! The pellets flew like sparks across the Market Square.

Chapter 16

I heard my father had fallen ill in Brighton. He had suffered a blood ulcer. Una and Miriam stood for long hours on the phone outside the post office trying to get through to the hospital. Telegrams went over and back. Bridgie wrote to say he had collapsed in the hotel after the wedding.

I wrote him a letter telling all about school. By now the lads I used mitch with had all been caught, so most mornings I headed off alone. Sometimes I'd go ahead of Una and slip up Con Reilly's archway, through Burke's yard and over the fence back into our garden. Then go on my hunkers under the windows of the bakery, and shoot into the old shed and up into the attic. Once I made my way down the entry, in the lower door and went upstairs back to bed. But mostly I headed into the country. Up by Billis and out by Behy Lake. Through the rocks at Shantemon, where the Reilly clan once had their main castle in the territory of Breifne. Sitting in a ditch I listened for the angelus bell before I made my way home for dinner.

Always afraid of being caught, and yet going further.

Then one day a woman in the shop reported me. I'd been seen walking the edge of the woods along St Patrick's College. When I came in at four that afternoon with my bag Maisie shrieked. She chased me up the entry. I stayed above in the nuns' graveyard till night fell. I slipped the latch of the kitchen door and listened. Stepped into the dark dining room. There was no one there. I took ham out of the fridge and ate four slices.

There he is, said Maisie.

Don't you know that Daddy is sick? said Una.

Go straight away to your bed, shouted Maisie.

They took the radio away so I couldn't listen to Luxembourg. The room was full of reprimanding voices. Next morning Una walked me to the gate of the school.

I won't go, I said.

You'll have to.

I'll be killed, I said.

Go on.

I won't.

So she walked me to the door of the classroom and told the head brother I'd been missing because my father was sick.

Maisie would suddenly appear in my room at dawn.

Get up for school you, she'd say.

Una and myself ate in the dining room alone. Miriam was in the shop. Una watched me from Town Hall Street to make sure I'd gone through the gate. The brother I feared was waiting for me in singing class. I turned to speak to someone behind me and he busted my eardrum and bloodied my nose. Maisie was outraged. I walked round the Brothers' like a zombie. They kicked football in the yard and I sat in the Jack's reading the *Beano* and the *Classic* comics.

I kept hearing things that weren't there. This sudden screech would shoot through my skull. Sometimes there were thunderings. Other times a sort of drone. Then a sort of bewildering silence as if you were there in the world alone. The echo of the blow persisted for weeks. The brother knew he'd done wrong and tried to be nice to me. When he'd arrive to take his place behind me at choir practice in the cathedral he'd flash a confused adult smile. His lower lip would tremble. Father A. B. McGrath pushed a bright-stockinged foot down on the pedal of the organ. We sang down into the empty church.

The silence descended. The deafness from the blow came back. We were all singing but I heard nothing. Then as if someone had pressed a button back the voices returned.

After school I went up to the handball alley and played there with Eamon Smith and Dag Carroll and the bus-drivers and Irish soldiers and house painters till night fell. Una would come up to collect me and Mr Smith would say, Let him have just one more game. Just one more, Una. In the dusk we could hardly see the ball. Your hand toughened. The palm was like leather. You learned how to skim the walls. How to let the ball swerve off your cupped hand so that it made no sound.

On Saturday mornings I was in the alley on the Barrack Hill by ten, came down for my dinner at one, was back by two and stayed till eight, maybe nine.

Instead of dreaming of Finea before I slept I began to dream of games of handball. In dreams I made perfect serves that stayed flush to the left-hand wall, or ran round the corner of the back wall and fell dead. I took butts with a neat underhand that left the soldiers astonished. I picked shots out of the air and killed them. I knocked balls on the hop dead. Then one morning I woke and came across the landing and met my father on the three steps.

Blessed God, he said and he took me in his arms. I thought I'd never see you again.

He dabbed his lips with a handkerchief. My mother in a canary-yellow outfit stood by a case in the hall. Her eyes were running. She took off an ostrich hat that Lady Ashton Smith, a cousin of the queen, had bought her.

Were you good? she asked me.

I was, I said.

Una stood silently by.

Was he?

Yes, lied Una.

My mother put on her working clothes and went into the kitchen. My father and I walked up to the garden and sat under the ivy on a seat he'd made.

I was sick, he said.

He put an arm over my shoulder. His face was thin and blue.

I'll soon be playing for Cavan town in handball, I said.

Good man, he said.

That night Maisie told what had happened to me at school. She said something should be done about it.

Go up, she said to my father, and complain.

He was reluctant.

It might do more harm than good, he said.

If you don't go, said Maisie, I will. Surgeon Moloney saw his ear, she persisted, and said it was a terrible thing to do to a child.

All right, he said.

The following morning my mother put his ten packet of Players on the breakfast table as usual, he smoked his first fag and broke into a terrible fit of coughing. Then he walked me to school. He smoked another fag on the incline and broke into another fit of coughing. We entered the school yard together. Everyone stopped playing. They looked at us. My father was nervous. He scuffed his nose with the hanky and put a hand on my shoulder. Head Brother Ultan, who was strolling in prayer, turned and saw him. He gathered his wide black skirt and came towards us. Brother Augustine left down his scythe in the field, and put on his black vest and approached. He was a tall, big-shouldered man with veins like hawsers in his neck, wide ears and holy demented eyes.

And who is this? asked Head Brother Ultan.

It's my father.

Well, you go and play, Dermot, while myself and your father have a word.

I'm afraid my son must tell you what happened him.

So what happened you, Dermot?

Brother Augustine hit me, I said, and I had to go to hospital.

I see, said Brother Ultan.

It's not good enough, said my father.

Brother Augustine appeared. There was a silence.

This, said the Head Brother, is Brother Augustine. This is Mr Healy. He shook my father's hand.

I'm sure you're aware what you did to my son, said my father.

I'm sorry, he said. I lost my temper.

He worked his mouth as he often did, his forehead shone and he moved his hands off each other.

I'm sorry, he said.

Go and play now, Dermot. And you carry on, Brother Augustine.

I moved towards the makeshift goals. Someone dribbled a ball in my direction. I stood with my foot on it. Brother Ultan touched my father's shoulder and the two men strolled through the playground. Brother Augustine, head bowed, walked out to the field. He threw off his dark vest and with long strong swoops of the scythe began to mow the grass again. I could hear the tick of the sheaves as the blade cut through them. His muscled arms were unnaturally white. He stopped a moment and looked at me looking at him. His eyes pleaded with me for forgiveness. I looked away.

The first time I took acid I thought I was in heaven. I was in my twenties living in Denbigh Street, Pimlico, in London at the time. I remember walking along the sparkling Thames till we reached the Henry Moore sculpture opposite the Tate, but it was not the sculpture I was interested in but the actual plinth itself.

Acid does not like art.

I was working in an insurance office – the Westminster County Insurance building that looked down on the hippies who were stretched out below Eros in Piccadilly Circus in the late Sixties. The morning I got the job I stood with the director by the tall windows that overlooked the goings on in the Circus.

I pity them, he said, looking down on their bandanna'd heads. Within a year I was back among them.

Each morning I'd put on my pinstripe suit, say good luck to the County Cavan men I shared the flat with, and head off to work through Rochester Row, across Victoria Street, under the portals of New Scotland Yard, past the registry offices of Caxton Hall where stars got married, into Green Park and up the Mall to my offices on Piccadilly Circus. Here, my immediate boss trimmed my long business letters of poetry, censored undue familiarity and curbed weather reports.

I ate Irish dinners in Ward's Irish house, drank a pint of Guinness and watched Francis Stuart, the novelist, sitting alone at another table. Afterwards, fell asleep at my desk with the phone cradled to my ear. At Christmas I danced the daughter of the Scottish peer who was a director of the firm. Myself and Aunt Bridgie, my mother's sister, and her companion, Leo, would frequent the Irish Club in Eaton Square. When my mother came to visit we all went off to see Danny La Rue. She thought he had wonderful dresses. And on the way home we walked into Steptoe, and my mother dug her fingers into my arm. Anyway.

Sebastian, a student from Oxford, came to live on the floor below us in Denbigh Street. Around that time we had never succeeded in getting drugs. Once I'd bought some tablets outside Ward's.

The Cavan men and myself sat in the room listening to the Beatles waiting for it to happen. Nothing did. The next evening I accosted the pusher in Piccadilly.

Hi, I said, that was bad dope you sold us.

That's nothing to do with me, fellow.

You sold it to me.

Well I bought it off someone else.

They were aspro.

I thought they were acid.

Well, they weren't.

So what do you want me to do?

You shouldn't be selling bad stuff.

Hi, listen to this, he said, calling to some other pushers.

I said, It's wrong to be doing that.

Listen to this, he said, we got a religious maniac here.

Soon, with Sebastian's encouragement, I was taking LSD every Wednesday at seven, and again on Friday evening. One Friday night myself and another Irish fellow dropped two tabs. I was wary of him because he had done me some wrong in the past but he was high, laughing, and so I trusted him. We sat there, in my small room, marvelling.

I'm sorry about what happened, he said, back then.

Forget it, I replied.

I just want to apologize.

Never mind, I said.

I just wanted to get it out of the way, he continued.

All right.

I did wrong.

Leave it.

It was my fault.

OK.

Do you understand me? he persisted.

Yes, I said, wishing he would stop.

Say you do.

Look, *stop*, I said.

What's wrong?

I don't want to hear about it.

We sat a while in the trembling silence.

You don't forgive me, he said sadly.

I turned away, seeing not him, but Brother Augustine, beseeching me.

Let's go for a walk, I said.

OK, he answered and he seemed to cheer up.

We headed off, an inch at a time up Denbigh Street. We stopped at each streetlight. Stopped in awe as a police car drove past. Held each other at the traffic lights and when it came to green we raced over. Beneath Vauxhall Bridge the river thundered. We walked to the far side but could go no further. When we were halfway back across the bridge he suddenly grabbed my hand.

Look into my eyes, he said.

I looked into his eyes. I saw there a horrendous image of myself.

I'm sorry, he said, imploring me.

Immediately I heard this plea I turned and fled into the traffic. Cars braked, there was the screech of tyres, horns blew. I fell, picked myself up and ran. A taxi driver shouted at us. I ran till I reached Denbigh Street. He caught up with me at the door. And again I saw it – his face was cut in two. I looked at him and tried to put it back together again. I tried to match the eyes, to correct the corners of the mouth, to set in place the twin nostrils. But this line of severed flesh had lowered one side of his face below the level of the other.

Don't say it, I said.

I won't.

We climbed back to the room. We talked a little, played music and slowly the marvelling returned. And just when we might have been reconciled he said he was going. I didn't want him to go. But he wanted to walk home across London. When he left, this fear – unexplainable and known to many – possessed me. It would leap out of the unknown and the familiar in the years ahead.

Next morning I was back at my desk. At the memory of the night before, and at the thought of how I threw myself into the traffic, I grew bewildered and a little terrified. As the day wore on, some comfort returned. The humdrum office work restored me. The clerks, in their shirt sleeves, talked shop. The director's secretary looked impeccably sane as she shared the lift with me down into the basement.

I searched through old files with the enthusiasm and concentration of a scholar. On the other side of the basement wall was the gents in Piccadilly underground. Through the grills I heard the toilets flush, and the attendants complaining. That other world going on without me. The horrors withdrew and secreted themselves in small compartments in my frontal lobes, lay dormant in various brain cells, from which, some day soon, they would emerge enraged and virulent, like parasites that had multiplied during their short hibernation in the recesses of my subliminal self.

I could hear them battering away at my identity and ego. Away you fuckers, I'd say.

Sebastian began to set up a deal. His father had given him £200 towards his fees at Oxford. Sebastian decided to invest the money in drugs. He bought 400 tabs of White Lightning at ten shilling a tab, which could later be resold at a pound each.

Will you try them out with me? he asked.

We dropped a tab in the house and set off by underground and bus to the Clapham Common. When we reached the park nothing had happened. So we took another tab of acid each. It was a sunny day. We lay under a tree and waited for the clouds to make their patterns. Dogs chased balls. Two lads passed with hurley sticks. An Italian, in white shoes, asked us for directions to Wandsworth Road. We watched fathers and sons sail their toy boats in the ponds. We looked at the rows of flowers. But the hallucinations did not take. Instead a deep misery seemed to pervade the two of us.

I've been done, I think, he said.

So he took another two and I took one. It was a hard struggle walking along the sunlit pavements to the underground. The faces we met were cheerless and possessed of an energy that was alien and unfriendly. The minute we stood in the echoing tunnel panic set in. I was back again running through the traffic because I could not forgive. A pain shot through my stomach.

Are you all right? Sebastian asked.

No, I said.

My mouth felt strange. I steadied myself against an advertisement poster on one of the curved walls. Sebastian's brows seemed to be unravelling. I could not look into his eyes. We sat in silence in the train and surfaced like zombies from Pimlico station. Another pain left me speechless.

What's happening? he asked.

This is some trip, I said at last.

I lay down in the flat on a sofa and faced the wall. The pains were coming more often. He brought me water. It turned to vomit in my throat. He sat on the edge of the sofa.

I'm responsible for this, he said.

Don't talk, I said. It only makes it worse.

Then this fierce hallucination grabbed me. The wall flew open and closed. I saw my own image opposite me, as I often saw my own reflection in the mirror in the Breifne. But there was no mirror. Sebastian walked me to my room. I lay down but could not find a place to rest my head. The pillow was like a bag of cement. Old demons materialized by my side. Minutes went by. My guts grew taut as hawsers.

You're having a bad trip, said Sebastian.

Is that what it is?

Yes. Don't worry. It will end soon.

But why the pain? It's real pain, I said.

I don't know. Look, I'll go and I'll be back. I'll go and find something for you.

After he left night fell on the street. The room smelt of carbide. The Italian women chatted as they hung out their washing on the balconies. The red haze of a London sky lifted. Sirens blew from the Thames. I lay in the one place as long as I could, trying to batten down the overpowering maelstrom of crazy thinking that was assaulting me.

John McCaffrey, the hairdresser from Belturbet, looked in.

How did it go? he asked.

Not so good, I said.

He went next door and put on Crosby, Stills, Nash and Young. The music, after all those times it had exhilarated me, seemed false. I wrote into a notebook and turned the other way. Shay McArdle came home. The Saturday night continued. The lads dressed and went to the pub. I stayed stock still in the room wondering for whom I was waiting.

Sudden rushes of cheerfulness would reach me, and just as quickly were spirited away.

The bell rang. I looked out the window and saw Aunty Bridgie and Leo standing below on Denbigh Street. They were dressed for the club. I slunk back to bed. They rang a few more times then went away. Daco, the Spanish guy below us, put flamenco on the record player. Eerie presences collected in the darkness. Faces swam by. But the heat of bad acid would not allow me pity.

At twelve Sebastian arrived back with a friend. I opened my eyes and found them sitting in chairs by the bed.

Dermot?

Yes.

Some of it was poison.

What?

Some of the tabs had cyanide in them.

Is that what it was?

For some unknown reason I felt a little better. At least what was happening me had a concrete reason.

I had it checked, he said. I'm sorry.

That's all right.

Did you sleep?

I don't think so.

I got something for you.

He lifted out a small white box of the type you'd put a slice of wedding cake in for guests who couldn't make the breakfast. It contained four tablets.

It's Mandrax.

It will bring you down, said his friend. It's good.

I took two of the Mandrax. Slowly the darkness began to shift. The pains ceased or at least went away to another place. I was exhausted. Sebastian took out his guitar and began to play. His friend rolled a joint. The others came home, looked in and went away. Shay brought me a beer. I babbled a little. The night went on. I struggled for sleep but just as I'd make it this big wave of nothingness would crash in. So I'd start rapping again. Try for sleep and fail.

Sebastian and his friend were still there, seated at a great distance from me it seemed, in the small room, with its window open onto the London night. They made tea and gave me the other two Mandrax. My eyelids fell, yet my mind would not let go of consciousness. It seemed as if I would be forever lodged in a rigid wakefulness. This scared me. Then somewhere near dawn I woke and saw the two men asleep on the floor beside me.

I walked to the window. I put my hands on the sill. I was amazed to see the world still out there. One of the wild cats that lived in a bomb site down the road headed up the middle of the street. It was huge. It sat, looked back and wondered.

Chapter 17

In the shaky balcony of the high crossbeamed Town Hall I joined all the sinning couples at the Sunday matinees as they looked down in ecstasy on Roy Rodgers.

Every so often Packie Cullen would send a beam of torchlight over faces from which childhood was fast fading, or had already gone. Being adult meant groping in the dark. The females were restless and soft as the men on the balcony held in their gasps, and let go, afterwards, with a sigh. From the back row came the moist slap of a kiss. As Orna Galligan loosened her hair and leaned back on Kit Finnegan's arm her white knee dug into the back of my seat. Des Hickey threw his coat over Ursula Smith's lap and turned round with a stern eye.

What are you looking at? he barked.

Nothing, I said.

You better not be.

He brushed back his quiff with his fingertips. I stared resolutely over his head at the screen. He settled his ear against Ursula's ear and continued to watch me. They listened gravely to each other's thoughts. He whispered something. Now she glanced back. *Never mind him*, she said. They turned away. The projector ticked on. Big unaccompanied lads blew sparks off the lit end of their fags and sucked in heavily. The old cowboy Walter Brennan sang. The air went dry and expectant.

Then a paper bag exploded.

Hit her again, said someone, she's no relation.

A posse of big girls in white blouses tramped down the stairs to the toilet laughing. Gerry Brady stood before the screen below and clapped. The arm of a seat broke. A bra snapped in the dark. A button shot open. The milky smell of semen spread like cuckoo spit.

One Sunday we were there as usual. On came the Three Stooges. Next the ads for McCarren's, for Provider's, for Fegan's. Then began a black-and-white documentary set in Africa. When we saw it wasn't a film a derisory cheer went up. We thought it might be something to do with the missions. The documentary was narrated by a faraway BBC voice. We tramped through jungles and heard exotic birds scream.

Then onto the screen came a village filled with black people in their skin. There was a great deal of guttural sounds, laughter and shy asides. Campfires were burning. In the background, a tom-tom. The camera homed in on breasts, groins and huge swinging penises. The Town Hall went silent.

No one touched a sweet bag. Couples left each other alone.

We were shown a child being delivered. We were shown suckling. Then we watched fascinated as an erection occurred. The voice told us something we couldn't hear. A woman, richly bearded between the thighs, approached the excited male in a wild headdress. Painted arrows pointed to her nipples. She touched the young man fondly on the cheek and made soft sounds in her throat. The other villagers began an eerie chant and lobbed their mickeys and breasts to and fro. He stood with his hands flat down by his side and his dark member aloft. There wasn't a sound.

What's going on? we heard Packie Cullen shouting.

I don't know, said Mr McKiernan.

This, said the voice, is an ancient ritual of fertility.

Good God, said Packie.

We held our breath as she ran flowers down the man's chest. As she did so she never took her eyes off his. The walls of the Town Hall seemed to strain imperceptibly. She brushed his stomach with the petals. We heard Packie running upstairs towards the projection room. Bang! Bang! Bang! She slapped the young man's buttocks.

Take that off, said Packie.

What?!

I said take it off!

The film stopped, the screen went white and there was silence. No one battered the floor. The lights came up.

There's been a mistake, said the ticket seller.

No one moved.

Your entrance fee will be returned at the door, shouted Packie.

The tired, dark-eyed projection man stood in the door of the balcony scratching his scalp. We filed past him and formed a bewildered queue. As we collected our money, Packie, scandalized by what had happened, never rose his head from the wooden box. We walked up Town Hall Street like a crowd returning from an apparition.

Did you see what I saw? asked Tony Gilhooley.

I did, I said.

By Monday the story had gone round the town. Those who had been there told all that happened to those who had not. And we exaggerated all we'd seen. As I am doing here, and not for the first time.

We broke into the golf links and stole beer. Climbed over into Colm Smith's stores and stole cider.

It annoys me to remember those days. I would rather attribute them to some fictional character who would later be given some understated moral retribution. But those acts, follies, thieving, are me.

But what awfulness do we leave out as memory defends its terrain? What images are locked away that only imagination can release? Beyond those wild sexual arousals are other plainer moments, disguised as clichés, hiding from the language of elation. They are the mundane everyday that memory does not espouse.

There was something wrong with the stew in the Breifne. It was served on Tuesdays. I remember well the heartburn from the Irish stew. Nights I'd lie in bed with a thread of bile from my mouth reaching down to a basin by the bed. Wet dreams, instead of sending spasms of delight through my groin, shot pellets of pain instead. In those dreams I was trying to ward off my wrongdoings while in my waking hours I was given over totally to licentiousness. The guilt was rearing its head in my subconsciousness. I'd put a hand up a dress in my sleep and find there a male organ much like my own. I sought in vain for the womanly fold, the honeyed lips, the promised soft place.

Instead I had to take this penis into my hand. There would be revulsion and terror and excitement. I'd spring awake, wet and in pain. The woman I'd been abusing was myself.

The boys were pulling their wire guiltily on the Fair Green, and comparing sizes in the haunted house by the nun's lake. In the slatted attic we stood with our penises out while Derek Flynn showed us how it was done. Even the scholarship boys in the Brothers merrily masturbated twice daily in their desks in full view of the class while Brother Cyril went through Irish grammar.

Hormones raced through the town.

Sixth class at the Brothers smelt of chalk and sperm. Trousers were covered in come. Derek Flynn, who had a long cock, bent over and took the head of his mickey out through a hole in the back of his trousers. Bill Crosby threw a coat over Eamon McCabe's knees at the pictures. We could see the coat jigging. A loud gasp of breath sounded behind a toilet door. You wanker, someone shouted. Fuck off, came the reply. Then Brian Leddy found a copy of *Lady Chatterley's Lover* in his mother's bedroom. We went out to Loreto woods with it. In the front desk Dennis Farrely's head went down with a sigh. When you stepped into Brother Felim's class with the roll-call book he brought you in behind his desk and felt your mickey as you called out the names.

Felim Coffey, you said.

Anseo, said Felim. Here.

Bimbo Flynn, you said.

Anseo, said Bimbo.

He undid a button, then another and curled a finger round your member. The Brother slipped your damp foreskin to and fro. That is if you had one. Once the lad from the Bridge peed onto his hand. He pulled you in close to him so that you stood between his legs. He smelt of porridge and cold tea. His blue stubble powdered. You could feel through his dress the hump of his erection against your thigh.

Patsy Lee.

Anseo.

Misey Crow.

Anseo.

You looked down at the book and out at the faces while his hand hurried and his breath grew flustered.

Dickey Smith.

Anseo.

He suddenly let you go like a bad thing. Did your buttons up. He signed the roll-book then crossed over to the window and looked out at the town with his hands stuck in his skirt. Down there too sex was raging.

Is it standing? asked the local house painter.

If it's standing let's go into the side room of the Town Hall and I'll do something for you.

Charlie McGriskin banged the organ at Benediction, the sacrament was exposed, the choir sang Salutaris in the organ loft. Incense streamed skyward. We came down from the organ loft like we'd come down from the gallery in the Town Hall and glided out into the frosty night. The aura of the light behind us spilled onto the grass. The sacristan stepped out of the shadows on the avenue below the cathedral.

I'll give you sixpence if you put your hand in here, he'd say.

Us choir boys would gather round. He'd strain the erection in his trousers in our direction.

Take a hold of that, he'd say.

We'd pretend not to be interested, but still and all we were fascinated. The bulge in his trousers was huge. He undid a button. The white head of his penis popped out. He slipped back the wet foreskin.

Have any of you lads got one like that?

He flicked the slippery skin to and fro. His touch for a rough man was somehow graceful.

Put your hand on it, he said.

Some adult appeared on the steps of the church. The sacristan disappeared off into the grounds. The lights in the cathedral went off. March snow was flying across the streets.

The cathedral on confession morning smelt of urine, moist knickers and damp trousers. The air was filled with misgivings. The marble walls ran with condensation. Candles rustled like moths. You waited your turn among pungent farts and beating hearts. We moved along the pew fearfully. Then my turn came.

I told my sins and waited.

He leaned towards me so I could see his face and purple scarf and knitted waistcoat. His breath smelt of meringue and maybe cloves.

Dermot, he said.

Yes, Father.

So who was this girl you touched? he asked smiling.

What? I said, astonished.

103

Who was this girl? he repeated.

I told you, Father.

But I'd like to know her name.

I can't tell you that, Father.

Why not?

It's not right.

Come on, young Healy.

But you won't tell anyone?

No.

Mary, I said eventually.

Mary who?

Mary Smith.

Mary Smith of Farnham?

Yes.

Isn't she a bit old for you?

Yes, Father.

And did she touch you?

No.

She didn't? His eyes widened.

A little.

A little. What does that mean?

She might have brushed up against me.

I see. She *brushed* up against you.

Yes, Father.

And she didn't touch you?

No.

Not even once?

No, Father.

So you touched yourself.

Yes, Father.

Of course you did. There and then?

No, Father. Afterwards.

How many times?

Twice.

I see. Mary Smith, he said.

Yes.

And are you going to see her again?

No, Father.

No?

No, Father. I don't think so.

And is there anyone else?

No.

Not yet, you mean.

No, Father.

And that's it?

Yes, Father.

Say an Our Father and three Hail Marys. And Dermot?

Yes.

You wouldn't be telling me lies?

No, Father.

About Mary Smith?

No, Father.

So if I mention it to her she'll know what I'm talking about?

I don't think you should do that, Father, I said, frightened.

Why?

She might not like to think I told you.

That she *brushed* up against you.

Yes, Father.

All right then. Are you sorry?

Yes, Father.

Will you do it again?

No, Father.

Ha-ha, he said, disbelieving me.

He blessed me nevertheless and when I stepped outside the confessional everyone looked at me because I'd been in for so long. I buried my face in my hands, knelt once and scattered holy water on my forehead. Then with a giddy heart I stood on the steps of the cathedral ready to start all over from scratch again.

Chapter 18

The steps to Cavan Cathedral rise to a great height. My father, with his asthma turning to emphysema, found it a difficult climb. On Mass days we left home before anyone else. My job was to proffer a shoulder for him to lean on. Every few steps we stopped so that he could catch his breath.

We stopped at the Farnham Hotel. We stopped at the top of Ashe Street. We stopped outside the Protestant hall where in autumn chestnuts rain down. We stopped at the foot of the cathedral outside the old presbytery, beneath which closed-up underground tunnels converged. He'd look ahead towards the final climb. We'd take a few steps at a time, halt, take cognizance, then go on. His breath whistled overhead. When at last we stood amongst the pillars he'd lean a minute on me and survey the town.

The glands in the left side of his neck had swollen. One was the size of a billiard ball, and sometimes it burst and a trickle of blood would run down his neck onto his crisp shirt. Today it ran. He dabbed the sore throughout Mass, and stared unblinking at the altar. Wind blew up the central aisle. It announced a latecomer. The huge doors bounced closed. Mrs Reilly, who lived nearest the cathedral, was always the last to arrive. Everyone watched her head up the left aisle, slowly, oblivious to the eyes on her; a bag propped on her right arm, a huge missal with a red tag in her left hand, she advanced in a green woollen beret festooned with an array of colourful hatpins.

A line of people in the second row from the front moved over. She sat down.

Now we were all here.

The coughing began.

Before he knelt, my father pulled each of his wide trouser legs up a fraction. He wore white socks. He held the crucifix of his old brown rosary beads by the butt, spread his elbows on the back of the pew in front of him and watched Father A. B. McGrath, who used come round to the Milseanacht Breifne to play poker, ascend the altar.

The golden door clicked open. The priest reached in.

My father liked Reverend A. B.'s talks from the pulpit. Once, the priest devoted an entire sermon to Beckett's *Waiting for Godot*; he'd gone to see a performance in London. We all wait for the messenger, he said. We wait, despite the fact that no one comes. We sat back, our knees high and candles blowing. A tenor, who worked in the post office, sang Jerusalem. Money rattled into long-handled collection boxes. The altar boys studied their joined hands. My father opened a child's prayer book.

The host went up. The heads went down. We studied the open mouths of the communicants. White tongues shot out, a sliver of a tongue slipped between heavily lipsticked lips. Some offered their mouths like fledgling birds, others gulped the wafer. Charlie McGriskin, manager of the Magnet Cinema, stamped the organ. A. B., who was also musical director of the choir, looked up quizzically at the loft as a loud abrasive chord shook the church.

My mother, in an artificial black fur coat, went by.

When we stood at the end my father's breathing was back to itself. He reached into the holy water font and scattered holy water on himself and then on me.

We were in a crowd as we went through the door. I saw two young fellows pointing at the bleeding gland on my father's neck and laughing. I felt anger, shame, terror and pride, and a sort of violent loyalty.

What are you looking at? I said.

Never mind them, I think he said.

Above the steps of the cathedral we stood a moment and he lit a cigarette and we surveyed the town of Cavan again, a place that neither of us came from – the Protestant church behind its elms, the dignified Victorian houses in Farnham Street, the Cock Hill, the Gallows Hill where rebels from the prison were hanged. We stood among the huge pillars of the vast cathedral looking down till he was ready for the journey home.

He threw away the butt of the John Player's and we made our way to the Ulster Arms, stopping at the same places for him to catch his breath on the way back. Frank Brady was behind the bar. He was reading the *Sunday Express*. My father laughed at Frankie and ordered reading the *Sunday Express*. My father laughed at Frankie and ordered a bottle of Guinness and a Power's whiskey. He ducked his head, thought about it a moment, then drank the whiskey in one go.

Good luck, said Frank.

In one of my dreams I'd fly right out of bed and wing my way over Cavan town. I'd fly directly over Cavan Cathedral. It was a wonderful feeling going by the high granite top piece that held the spire aloft – swooping, arching up, gliding.

I'd fly back and forth over the silent green grounds of the cathedral while inside the worshippers were celebrating eleven-thirty Mass. When the first of them would appear after Mass was ended I'd swoop down from a turret and fly inches over their heads, turn at the Protestant church, and back again. Over and back I'd go above their heads.

Then it always happened. I'd get so happy that I'd forget and not see that the ability to fly was leaving me. Instead of staying there I should have immediately flown back across the town and into the safety of my room. Instead, I'd make one long final dive over the last of the worshippers and then find I could not pull away.

It was a terrible sensation to feel my wings were suddenly powerless. To know that I could not fly anymore. The air that held me so buoyantly a moment before now was letting me plummet to earth. Then just as the ground met me I'd find myself in bed, face-down, with my arms by my sides. With relief I'd find I was just a wretched human being, safe in wakefulness, exhausted and sorry.

Behind my closed lids I could still see the whole vista below me from my perch on the turret. I could smell the Protestant firs. I could smell the pines above the bishops' graves. I saw the congregation spilling out of the church beneath me. Next time, next time I'd remember to fly home before I fell, I thought. But I never did. I always stayed up too long.

In Lent you woke to an alien world at seven-thirty. My mother would call me and go below to make tea. The linoleum under your feet was freezing. The windows were frosted. Una sat very pale by the kitchen table in her blue Poor Clare outfit. My father stayed in bed. The streets

Lenten masses were quiet, hypnotic affairs – cars when they came to a stop dropped turds of grey ice at the main gates; no one spoke on the white slippery ascent; the snow-laden trees in the grounds of the Protestant church winked across at us; dogs leapt into the air to catch the flakes; money landed on the tables inside the front doors; vases of daffodils were placed on the side altars; people stamped the snow off their feet, shook their umbrellas and patted their hair; the holy water font grew murky and the green tiles in the freezing vestibule were covered in slush; confession doors opened and shut like cuckoo clocks; the whispers of the strange missioners, when they handed out penance, made you want to go to the toilet; as sinners prayed, their breath rose like incense; old women did the Stations with whispered supplications, then sat near the radiators; the fasting congregation ghosted up the aisles; echoes died; there was a distant disturbance, then the freshly shaven priest, with a deliberate look around him, stepped out of the sacristy in black shoes; with a swish of his stern purple vestments he kissed the cold altar and we went onto our knees; snot dripped down the noses of the sleepy altar boys; coughing racked the silence; people dreamt of what they'd given up, others grew insanely guilty over sins they'd withheld from telling, some still fretted over venal offences; you could smell the actual wine at the back of the cathedral as the priest rose the chalice to his lips; all the memories of awkward coupling were muffled by prayer; that day's gospel spoke of the necessity of purging oneself; a bird trapped in the organ loft sang a frightened trill; certain women gave off an intense erotic aura; there was a sense of dark violence suspended, of impossible promises being guaranteed; wide-eyed nurses, with white uniforms showing under their gabardines, sat in a dream; we were preparing to gather round Calvary on Good Friday for three and a half indeterminate hours of Latin *sean nos*; we could already hear the procession on Palm Sunday come singing up Church Street; we saw the tricolours on certain doors on Easter Sunday; Biblical place names, like the Garden of Gethsemane or the Mount of Olives, filled us with a sense of tragic poetry; the Loreto girls, delirious from secret cravings, corrected their berets; the pews reeked of Palmolive soap, Pond's cold cream and Johnson's baby powder; those off chocolate chewed cloves; those with vocations soared aloft; the walls wept; a girl, sick with hunger, crumpled in her seat; adolescents with crew cuts knelt with their heads cradled in their hands; make-up was eschewed; there were cracked lips, bits of newspaper on shaving cuts, hair was oiled with brilliantine; hallucinations burned bright in the eyes of sober men; pregnant women sat throughout Mass in a daze; children with painful styes knelt like small prizefighters in the front rows; when three missioners came to help the priest distribute the host they eyed him critically as he prepared communion; they were from a more austere world, their bare feet in leather sandals, their hands covered in orange hair, their eyes luminous and strangely Gaelic; they lifted the wafer aloft like a toreador his sword and plunged it deep into our miserable beings; their prayers were loud, their genuflections theatrical, and beads rattled in their skirts; shop girls received communion and guiltily avoided the eyes of the men from the *Anglo-Celt* as they came back to their seats; three rows of shy communicants formed by the altar rails; the disabled slowly returned; with a deep bow the missioners left us; the masturbators cringed; meat-eaters turned holy; a young woman stood with a man's handkerchief thrown over her hair in lieu of a hat; in the church the brisk smell of sex was astonishingly present now that the act itself had been forsworn; whole families bowed their heads; mothers rocked yelling babies; those shamed by recent controversies kept their dignity; the bearded missioners in their grey hoods stood like sentinels at the doors and distributed pamphlets on the foreign missions into the frozen hands of the worshippers; dogs waited on the steps outside for their masters, the boys from St Pat's got up on their bikes, Woolworth's opened its doors.

Meanwhile, fish appeared in the butcher's, on the streets the townsfolk, with a cross of ash on their foreheads, avoided the slides the lads had made on the frozen footpaths in Bridge Street; the Poor Clare nuns flocked across the convent yard; orphans ran along the corridors in grey skirts. Dancing finished and whist drives began. Bad Catholics attended do's in Orange halls out Farnham way. Missioners walked down side streets in flat sandals.

Our abstinences made us feel blessèd.

Chapter 19

Around the time I started at Saint Patrick's Secondary College my father became bedridden. It can't have happened all at once. One day he was up in the bakery shovelling coke into the furnace, or on Sundays sitting in the bakery with his newspapers, then his lungs gave out. He took to his bed. I'd cycle in the mile to town at twelve-thirty and have my dinner in his room, then before going back to school I'd bring his bets across to the bookies.

His bets were intricate multiple affairs, called credit bets. You put a shilling on a horse, and if it won, from the winnings was extracted a further bet that went onto another horse or group of horses, and if the second bet won, from those winnings another bet was struck and so on. For a shilling his bet could involve as many as eight horses. If the first horse went down all was lost. When I'd come home at half past four I'd write down the list of winners in the bookies, and we'd go over his wagers.

That cursed Piggott, he'd say.

He'd hold his reading glasses a fraction from his nose.

Joe Sime, he'd say.

I'd sit on his bed and do my homework. We grew so close it was painful. While I did Greek he read the *Anglo-Celt*. Sometimes I'd look up from the Spartan wars to find him eyeing me. The right arm of his glasses was fastened with a plaster. There was another plaster on his neck. He'd lower his eyes and go back to the paper.

The mother would be wringing out sheets in the bathroom. Soon she'd pass down the corridor in a blue housecoat carrying a tray of washing. She'd knock on the door and hand the tray on to me. I took it up to the line. We hung out sheets, socks, brown stiff bras, drying cloths, corsets, hankies, shirts, Maisie's blue blouses, pillow slips made of flour bags and sometimes gold cushion covers.

Then I brought his tea upstairs. Cold ham with mustard, brown bread and sliced tomatoes. On winter nights he wore a scarf round his neck and his nose glowed. On warm evenings he undid the buttons on his pyjama top. His chest was hooped. We said little. I led him to the toilet and back again. I did Latin. He'd doze and wake with a shudder.

Blessed God, he'd whisper.

He'd sit forward and slap the sheets each side of him with the palms of his hands. For a moment we were strangers. He'd hold the newspaper tight. His breath would race. He'd look at me. Then with relief he'd find where he was.

Dermot! he'd exclaim.

Daddy, I'd answer.

You're there.

I am.

He'd lie back and brush his lips with the handkerchief. His breath would subside. He'd fold his hands.

Did you answer all the questions?

Most of them.

Good lad.

Sometimes we didn't bother putting the light on but sat there in the long evenings under the growing shadow of Burke's roof. I was reluctant to leave him. When I finished my homework he played his transistor. We listened to long plays about strange happenings. We listened to Perry Mason. The jackdaws shrieked over Leo McDonald's. Miss Reilly pulled the curtain aside and looked towards the Cock Hill. The bell in the convent rang nine. On her way to the throne room with her po, Maisie would look in.

It's very peaceful here, she'd say.

She'd drop a small bag of Jelly Babies on his bedside chair, and we'd all have one. Chewing with pursed lips she'd absent-mindedly right some ornaments on the dressing table then stand a while in the doorway before slipping away.

He began having nightmares about Finea. In the middle of the night I'd hear my mother shout, Jack, Jack, you're here, here in Cavan.

Get the sergeant, he'd shout.

Jack! Jack! It's me, Winnie.

Where's Sergeant Ruane?

He's dead.

Get the sergeant, he demanded. There's a man here who is not well.

You're in the Breifne, Jack.

Get Sergeant Ruane.

Jack! Can't you hear me?

Where's Maurice Moran?

He's in the seminary.

The seminary?

Yes. He's in the seminary. He's going on to be priest.

I have to go up the village. And he leapt out of bed.

No, Jack.

Where's the door?

Stay where you are.

I have to tell the men. The men must know.

He'd step out onto the landing in his pyjamas. My mother would click on the landing light.

Where's my uniform? he'd demand. Where's my cap?

Jack, said my mother.

He'd open his eyes and breathe hoarsely. She'd lead him back to bed. I'd stand at the door watching. He'd signal me with his finger.

I was dreaming, he said.

Your father was dreaming, agreed my mother.

I started mitching again. I found a barn out at Drumalee. I'd hide my bike under a bed of straw and climb up through a hole in the ceiling into a loft where hay was stored. I read my books and looked over the countryside.

Mice scuttled across the floor. I wrote love letters to a girl in Loreto. One day I cycled home as usual at half past four. When I came into the shop Maisie looked up from the till and said, You're in trouble.

Why? I said, terrified.

Your mother wants to see you.

I looked into the private dining room but she wasn't there. I headed upstairs to my father's room. As I was going along the landing my mother suddenly appeared with a broom. She brought it down on my back.

You! she shouted.

I ducked.

What have you been doing?! she shouted.

Nothing, I said.

You scoundrel. Scoundrel! You have not been at college in two months.

Of course I have.

Don't lie to me. The priest was here. We are scourged – *scourged*! – do you hear. Do you hear me?

Yes.

Where have you been every day?

In a barn.

In a barn, in a barn, she repeated. For two solid months, she lamented. What's to become of us.

My father hearing the commotion appeared on the corridor. He leaned one hand on the handle of the door and the other on the doorframe.

Look what you've done to your father! my mother said.

I'm sorry.

Deceiving us every day.

I'm sorry.

You speak to him, Jack. He has my heart broken. I have nothing further to say.

She withdrew. He looked at me as if I were a peer of his. I tried to hide my tears.

Do you not want to go to college?

No, I said.

Well look at it this way, go as far as the Intermediate, and if you want to leave, leave then.

I got a shock to hear it put so straightforwardly.

Is that all right? he asked me.

Yes, I said.

He made his way back to the bed.

You're hurting your mother, he said. *Don't* hurt your mother.

I won't, I said. I sat on his bed. I sat at his bedside for two years with my books propped against my knees.

Chapter 20

Then, as if my father had summoned him from that recurring dream of Finea, Maurice Moran, who had gone away at fifteen to be a missionary priest, made contact.

Once we left Finea he had disappeared out of our lives, until, along with Sonny Fitz and Jim Keogh and Tom Keogh and Brian Sheridan, and many others, his name was roared out in the middle of the night by my father. Then back came the other world – the barracks, the bridge, the dayroom, the distressed children, the screeches from the cells, the cold chapel and the small coffins – but next day he was forgotten, the Fineas withdrew into the dream world and we were back in Cavan again. Then this letter came.

It's for you, I said.

Is it from Tony? asked my father.

No, I said, it's Irish.

Who could it be? my father said.

He looked closely at the postmark.

What does that say? he asked.

Corcaigh, I said.

Cork? Who do we know down there?

I don't know.

Neither do I, he said, and that's a fact.

He opened the blue envelope. He held the letter to the light, cupped the rim of his glasses, and screwed up his eyes. *Dear Jack Healy*, he said, then he stopped. He pushed himself up in the bed and took his glasses off.

He handed the letter to me.

Read that out to me, said my father.

> *June,*
> *Wednesday 7th*
>
> *Dear Jack Healy and all in Cavan,*
> *I am to be ordained next week. I heard you had fallen*
> *ill and of course I realize you can't come but I would like*

the honour of saying my first Mass after my ordination in your home. Perhaps the 15th would suit? Please write and let me know. I leave on the 17th for America so this is my last chance. I look forward to seeing you all. You were always a father to me. I think of you often. Give my regards to Mrs Healy and your family.
Yours Sincerely,
   (Fr) Maurice Moran

Father Maurice Moran, said my father and he took his glasses off and held them in his lap.

That's right, I said.

When is the fifteenth?

Next Thursday.

Blessed God! He swung his feet out of the bed and sat there looking at the wall. He quickly brushed his lips with his hanky. A rare light shot across his face.

Get Winnie, son. Get your mother, and tell her there's a priest coming to see us, he said.

The Breifne was all bustle. My father's bedroom was re-wallpapered, the sitting room was swept clean, the door and the skirting boards painted, fresh geraniums were placed in vases along the landing. My mother shaved my father. She scoured his armpits and cut his toenails. They put a table in front of the fireplace in the sitting room and a white lace sheet was drawn across it. The silver candle holders were set in place. The eerie pictures of the rivers were taken off the walls. A black rug was laid down in front of the table.

Father Maurice arrived in the early afternoon. He had dark curly hair and a bright face. The black suit seemed a size too small for him. He set his things on the makeshift altar and knelt a moment. He seemed strangely insubstantial, like a human touched by an alien light. Then, along with my mother, I led him across to my father's room. We knocked on the door.

Come in, my father said.

He was sitting in his old blue suit on the edge of the bed. When Maurice entered he went to his knees.

Jack, Jack, said Maurice.

We all withdrew as the young priest heard my father's confession. Then we led him from his sickbed across the long corridor. My father's trousers tumbled out from his body. His feet seemed too small for the carpet slippers. He wore a dressing gown that came to his shins. He put a hand on my shoulder and eased himself down on one knee beside me and rested his elbows on the seat of one of the elaborate sitting room chairs.

Father Maurice knelt and turned to begin. My sisters and mother and aunt read out the Latin responses. Traffic moved down Main Street. A candle flickered near the silent radio.

I was amazed to see the host raised in a domestic interior, to actually hear wine drunk from the chalice. We knelt by our chairs and received communion.

His first blessing as a priest Father Moran bestowed on my father who received it like a nervous countryman. He dabbed his mouth with a hand-kerchief, and, blustering, attempted some form of prayer. The priest's hand came down lightly on his head. He kissed a blue cloth that came from the Pope. Here was something beyond a mere blessing – a kindred touching, a sign between neighbours, a gesture between familiars – although in truth my father felt embarrassed and maybe a little proud.

A swish of vestments and the Mass in the long, carpeted room was over.

My father rose and shook the priest's hand and with my mother holding his elbow and his other hand on my shoulder he made his way back along the landing. He was at ease.

Father Maurice sat with him in his room till dinner was ready. It must have been a half-day – a Thursday – because the Milseanacht was closed. We had the place to ourselves. The mother had a pot roast of shoulder of lamb cooking at low heat, cabbage was ready for boiling, and would be served in gravy from the meat. Miss Smith piped cream over meringues fresh from the bakehouse. Una laid the table with silver and bright doilies. Ice cream was taken in from the shop. My mother and Maisie sipped sherries.

The two men had been up there alone together talking for about an hour, maybe two, when my mother said, Give Father Maurice a shout.

When I went into the bedroom I felt like I was interrupting something. I could smell the cigarettes which my father was denied. The priest was in a soft chair, his back to the window and his head bowed. My father was sketching something in the air with his long fingers. The two men looked a little shocked when I entered. It was hard to get a foothold there. The priest had a small glass of brandy in his hand and my father was flushed and wild-eyed.

Is that you, Dermot? he said.

Yes, I said.

Sit down there.

The dinner is ready.

Are you getting hungry?

I'm starving, I said.

Blessed God, said my father and he started to laugh. They've been fasting since yesterday.

I better go down, said Maurice.

One more, said my father.

Father Maurice lit another cigarette and handed it over. After the first draw my father broke out into a violent fit of coughing. The priest handed him the glass of brandy. He drank a sip, then another, dabbed his mouth and looked at me askance.

When I get better we'll head to Finea.

Right, I said.

He sipped. He smiled coyly like he was trying to be the man he once was.

That's good stuff, he said.

After dinner the priest went up to say goodbye to my father. He stepped onto the street in tears. He got into a black Ford belonging to his superior. It wouldn't start and when it did he was suddenly away. After Father Moran left for his first parish in Boston we never saw him again, and he died in America, a young man.

For days after this visit my father thought he was going to be all right again. He sat in an armchair by the window of his room and looked out at Burke's roof and the jackdaws on Con Reilly's roof. His eyes were black and shameful. He began making plans. When the sun shone my mother led him to the back room so he could look out at the garden.

He rested his elbow on the sill and stared. Old cabbage stalks were rotting in their beds. Did you know, he said to me, that the cabbage stalk is good against drunkenness? The drills were overgrown. The seat under the ivy was collapsing. He stood before the mirror in the bathroom and stroked his chin as if reassuring himself that he was still there intact. He wanted to visit the Ulster Arms and see Frank Brady.

Tomorrow, he said, we'll go to the Ulster Arms.

When tomorrow came he lay in bed. He ordered up a baby Power's, dressed in his suit with the help of my mother and sat in the armchair and drank the whiskey.

Order a car, he said.

The car was ordered for eight. Word was sent to Frank. My father's old overcoat was hung on the hall stand. Maisie locked up the shop and dressed to accompany him. My mother waited in front of the mirror in the dining room. The car came. When she went upstairs he had gone back to bed.

Not tonight, Winnie, he said.

If Mahomet can't go to the mountain . . ., said Frank when he rang the bell that night at ten. He had a bottle of whiskey in his side pocket. My mother led him upstairs.

I couldn't make it, Frankie, said my father.

Is there glasses in this establishment? asked Frank.

My mother left them to it. When I went out to get coal in the yard I could hear Frank's warm laughter. I brought them ham sandwiches. I brought them tea. What are they at up there? asked my mother. Drinking, I said. And smoking? Smoking as well, I said. Ah well, she said. We sat by the fire till one then the mother decided it was time to call a halt. As she came along the corridor there wasn't a sound. She knocked on the door and tiptoed in. Frank was fast asleep in the armchair and snoring.

My father put a finger to his lips.

Whisht! he said.

What do you mean *whisht*, she said. I have to get into the bed. It's past one.

The poor fellow is tired out.

Frank, called my mother. Frank!

He didn't stir. She prodded his shoulder with her index finger. Frank Brady, it's time for home.

As I was saying, Winnie, said Frank without opening his eyes, you can't beat Sinatra. Isn't that right, Jack?

Yes, said my father.

What has Sinatra got to do with it? demanded my mother, and she nipped Frank.

Frank reached out for his glass, finished it and fell back asleep again.

Poor Frankie, said my father.

What am I to do now? asked my mother.

Wake him.

Frank! Frank!

Frankie, said my father.

Frank gingerly reached out to an ashtray that was on the bedside chair and stirred the ashes round with his fingers. Then before anyone could speak he lifted out the butt of a fag and popped it into his mouth.

He'll be sick as a dog, said my mother.

Thank you, said Frankie.

The curse of God, said my father and he broke out into a fit of laughter.

Dermot, said my mother.

Yes, Mother.

Lift Frank Brady, will you.

Frank, I said.

That's right, said Frank.

I tried to lift him but he just collapsed back into the chair.

Best to leave him, said my father.

What are you talking about? said my mother. I can't be going to bed with Frank Brady sitting up by the bed.

Well, you'll have to, said my father.

I will not.

What else can you do?

Glory be to God, she said. *And him sitting there looking at me all night.* I can't.

He'll wake sometime, I said.

And climb in beside us, I'll warrant you, and she started laughing.

Winnie, said Frank and he opened his eyes. I wouldn't dream of it. He got up. I think I better go.

You bloody scoundrel, said my mother. You were awake all the time.

Good man, Frank, said my father.

Good night, Winnie.

You blackguard, she smiled.

I'll be seeing you Jack, said Frank, then humming to himself he went along the corridor.

Chapter 21

On Christmas Eve, 1962, when I was fifteen, I went to a dance in the Sports Centre in Cavan. I was wearing the new suit and shirt I'd been bought. I don't remember who was playing but I remember the sweat drying like a second skin onto my face when I stepped out to come home. The night was bitter cold. A mirthful crowd came down the alleyway past the *Anglo-Celt*. Couples streamed away in all directions. We met old drunks finding their way home along the walls of the Protestant church. I was coming up Church Street with Teddy O'Neill when Noel Brady, a neighbour of mine, drove by, turned his car and stopped alongside.

He leaned over and opened the passenger door. I got in.

Daddy is dead, he said.

We drove on down Main Street. The crowds from the Sports Centre were walking the pavements. They were cheerful and spontaneous. Lights were still on in some of the shop windows though it was after midnight. Small holy families were gathered round cribs in straw. Revellers were shouting in Bridge Street. Parties with bottles headed towards the Half Acre. And in the Breifne window Santa was still at it, giving away presents, wishes, whatever you asked for, though it was long gone midnight.

This year as usual he'd been taken down from the attic and placed among the Christmas cakes and boxes of Cadbury's chocolates, the key was turned smartly in his back and he began to nod, graciously, at perfect intervals, *Yes, you, you over there. Yes, I said.* The greatest mistake you could make was to wind him too far, then the spring broke and Santa stood unmoving. Some icing sugar was thrown on his shoulders. Maisie combed out his tight white beard, and Una, like Miriam before her, dusted down his red coat. A doily was put under his black boots and he was stood on a low glass cake-stand at the centre of the display. And all the days of Christmas children gathered at the window and asked for a wish and Santa nodded.

Now there he was nodding, nodding, nodding, though he should by then have gone back up to the attic. He'd been forgotten.

When I let myself into the hallway, Maisie was coming down the stairs. She stopped distracted when she saw me.

Dermot, she said.

Yes.

Her jaw was shaking. She pointed behind her and headed towards her room.

Santa is still in the window, I said.

What?! she asked, and stood with her hand on the bannister.

He's still going, I said.

She turned and looked at me askance. God in heaven, she said. I reached the three steps at the altar. She went down to the shop in a panic. I walked along the dimly lit landing. The door to my father's room was open. Una was in there alone crying. I don't know what he looked like, except that his gaze was fixed and he was crooked-jawed. While the men dressed the corpse I went downstairs. There were people moving through the house. As I walked through the brightly lit tearoom which was covered with branches of holly I could hear my mother.

When I opened the door and she saw me she was so upset she was nearly angry. She stood and pointed.

Now! she screamed and she began to wail.

Now! Now! Now you are the man of the house! Her voice went up into a discordant key and the women held her.

Now! she screamed.

Visitors began taking down the holly. The Christmas tree was thrown out. The coloured lights went back into their box. Santa went back up to the attic.

Una was standing outside the post office again in the public telephone booth. She rang Ballinagh to tell Uncle Seamus; Toronto, to tell Tony, who was heart-broken, nor had he the money to come home; Grand Rapids, where Miriam was, and she was pregnant, and with the shock went into labour; London, to tell Nancy and Bridgie and Gerty; and then Elphin in County Roscommon, where all the Healys lived. Trays of sandwiches appeared. I went down the corridor.

To get to my room I had to pass his. There were footsteps but no voices. I stood in the dark and listened.

Just hold him there, said Noel.

I thought of my father perched on someone's arm.

That's right, just there, said Noel.

He's as light as a feather, came the reply.

He went quick.

I tiptoed to my room. I sat down on my bed and waited. Under the heaving darkness there were shreds of light. The doctor came. I heard his bag click open. He went. I heard him go. Someone called me. The fire was roaring when I joined them again below.

Where were you?

I was in my room.

Stay here with us, said my mother. We need you now.

Did you know he was going to die? I asked.

Yes, my mother said. We decided not to tell you.

Why?

Because we didn't want to upset you, Una said.

You were too close to him, my mother said. We couldn't tell you.

Did he say anything?

He asked after you.

Did he?

He did. He said your name. Your father was ill. Your father was very ill. What will we do now?

Don't fret yourself, Winnie, said Maisie.

I loved him, my mother said.

My job was to answer the door as people rang. I sat at one of the tables in the tearoom and shook with tears – something was wrong with the fluorescent lights. They kept flickering on and off. I stood at the front door looking down Main Street. The street gleamed with frost. A car full of party-goers stopped outside Leonard's drapers. A window went up, the door opened and the echoes died away. Neighbours came and shook my hand. Father McManus hung his hat on the hall stand. Uncle Seamus arrived. He took me in his arms.

I was dancing when he died, I said.

Never mind now, he said.

Sometime near four Noel Brady, who had washed and dressed my father, came down for us. We piled into the room. My father was in his blue pinstripe suit. A candle burnt beside him. His face was straight. He wasn't smiling but he smelt fresh. He was sixty-two. The moment I'd been putting off for years had happened.

A void opened till one day in the late Eighties my old mother emerged from her bedroom in Cootehill with a small diary I'd kept when I was young. The last I'd seen of it was when she found it under my bed when I was sixteen, and demanded to know what dirty work I was up to.

Now she smiled and put the diary in my hand.

There, she said. I kept that for you.

On the blue cover it said: *Sodality of Our Lady 1963*. I flicked through it. Pages were crammed with sordid details written down in code, and the code was so good I could hardly decipher it. Each awfulness was placed incongruously below church holidays and saint's days. The first entry read:

> Dec '62
> On the 25th Daddy died. I was just coming from a dance with Teddy and Noel told me. On evening of 26th the remains at 6.15 were moved to chapel. On the 27th the funeral. Very frosty. The undertaker Meehan forgot to send on a car for the family. It was very frosty. We were lonely going through Finea. All crying when we stopped outside our old house. Tony O'Neill and Uncle Seamus lifted the coffin onto my shoulder. On Sunday the girls came round to the Breifne. I introduced them to Mammy and made tomato sandwitches.

She had kept this diary of mine secreted away among old discarded perfumes, title deeds, tax returns, photos of Miriam in the *Anglo-Celt* high-kicking in tartan shorts at pantomimes, Una up on her toes at a *feis*, book reviews from *Hibernia* that I'd written, old stories from the *Anglo-Celt*, a photo of Aunt Jane, Mass cards, Tony in Aden, letters from Father Maurice Moran, herself at the Niagara Falls.

Well, are you finding anything good in it? she asked me.

A little, I replied.

Good, she said.

Thanks a lot, I said, for keeping it.

Does it mention me?

Now and then.

And what's it about?

Tomato sandwiches, I said, and bottles of stout.

Oh, she replied, and she looked at me. Well, read out something, she said.

I can't.

Why not?

I turned a page and looked for an inoffensive entry.

Is there something dirty in it? she asked.

There is.

I thought so.

I read on. After my father died my mother was so upset that her sister Nancy talked her into going back with her to England. I remember the car heading off and the mother looking back warily at me through her blue-lensed glasses. She waved an uncertain hand. They took the night boat and arrived in South Kensington. She wrote home immediately. After a week's inactivity she took up a job as a char, cleaning out film directors' and TV personalities' rooms in Drayton Gardens.

The Breifne was suddenly empty. I'd pass the father's room at night, stop a moment, open the door and look in. There were only the squawks from the jackdaws. A pillow with no trace of a head. The bathrobe on the back of the door. The mother's black fur in the wardrobe. And strangest thing of all, in the bathroom was the razor they had shaved him with when he died, and caught in the blade were some of the bristles from his chin.

I went on to my room, lay fully dressed beneath the sheets and listened to Luxembourg. Maisie's polite step would come across the landing, she too would look into my parents' room for a moment, next she'd flush the toilet, pause with her po by my door and look in to see was I there. Una's door would close, the cats in the entry would bawl, a tin clatter, Miss Reilly would pull her curtains to, Mr Dale would leave Noel's bar and pull the door of the yard gate after him.

Then, when I thought Maisie had done her final trek through the house to check no lights were left on and everyone was in bed, I put on my shoes and dropped out the window onto the low galvanized roof of the kitchen, stood a moment there till the sound went and my eyes adjusted to the darkness, then stepped softly across the tin roof and shinned down a drain pipe to the ground, stood again a moment to see if any lights came on and when I saw there were none I headed across the frozen earth in the ghostly garden and climbed over Provider's wall, hopped through the timber, building blocks and tiles that were piled in the yard, crossed the fence into the White Star, slipped down the entry and went off into the night on Main Street.

BOOK IV

Sodality of Our Lady

A Version of a Diary 1963

Chapter 22

JANUARY

8 Tues.

Hold on to me! Sheila shouted.

　I'm holding you, I said.

　You'll let me go.

　No I won't,

　Yes you will, she shouted, I just know you will.

　I pushed off through the snow.

　Dermot! she screamed.

　We slid the length of a field the far side of the Gallows Hill on our bellies on the upturned bonnet of a car, her left hand gripping my right, cheering. Great cant! We piped a furrow, her dress rose, I saw the town coming and we stopped just in time with a swerve.

　I thought my heart would burst, she said.

　We climbed back up and came down one more time and then she had to go home. I stayed up there looking. All of Cavan is white and everywhere the lakes are frozen.

9 Wed.

Mother goes to England with Aunt Nancy. The two were wearing large red hats and fur coats.

　Be good, you, she said.

　I waved her off and spent most of the day in the Central Café with the gang.

10 Thur.

I went off t'night to a hop in the Central Café, great! and jived Mary but then Sheila came in and she stood at the jukebox glaring and soft-eyed, and I went over to her. You're looking ojus well, I said, but she was extremely jealous.

　I saw you, said Sheila.

You saw what? I said.

You know, she said. You know only too well.

I don't know what you're talking about, I said.

Oh but you're some boy, she said.

Come on and dance.

No, she said.

Why?

I'm going home.

I'll leave you home.

No, she said, stay just where you are. I don't think I want to be with you any more.

So she left just like that. Then Dermot and myself stole a cop's bike from outside the Garda barracks and planted it behind the Farnham Gardens. Birds were walking across the frozen Kinnypottle. When we skidded stones they went for miles up river echoing, Thump! Thump! Thump!

11 Fri.

Did nothing exciting.

12 Sat.

Sat with Mary at the pictures.

Cut out the continental stuff, someone shouted. The two twins, George and Phildy O'Rourke, patrolled the cinema with their long torches. Quiet, they shouted, the lot of you!

Everywhere throughout the town frozen pipes.

14 Mon.

Got a great feed and a great laugh with the lads, then t'night off to the hop in the shed at the back of the Railway Hotel. The record player was jumping as we jived, then when they were playing Del Shannon part of the stairs collapsed and Tony Coyle who was on the door went flying.

On way home I break it off with Sheila over the phone. There's laughter and tears.

You just want to go with Mary, she said.

I do not, I said.

Well, if you don't, why are you breaking it off with me?

Because you asked me to.

Well that's not what I want any longer, she said, and started giggling.

So what do you want?

I don't know.

I was about to say something else and then my penny got stuck.

15 Tues.

Stole Mary into the house. Great court! We lay out on the bed. Then Aunty Maisie went past. Mary hid on the floor under the bed.

Maisie looked in. What are you doing? she asked.

My homework, I said.

Ask me another, she said.

Afterwards I left Mary home in the rain twice. It was teeming. Then we walked into Sheila and she crossed to the far side of the street with her head in the air. Then she ran. After I'd left Mary home I went looking for Sheila and found her standing in the rain under Woolworth's.

Desperate weather, I said.

Piss off, she said.

You're very narkey.

I have every right to be.

What's wrong? I asked.

Nothing that concerns you.

Do you want to make up?

No, never, she said.

That's fine by me.

Right, she said.

We stood a while longer there.

Can't we just be friends? I said after a while.

No.

We stood there watching for maybe an hour, just looking, and then said goodbye. Tomorrow she goes back to Loreto as a boarder.

16 Wed.

I went up the town and met Johnny who had knocked off a mission box. Come on with me, he said. We ran into Ollie McNally from

Virginia who was on his way back to college and we all went down to the side room in the Railway Hotel. The Smiths keep a piano in there and children's toys and old broken chairs and one brown driving seat from a Volkswagen car.

Ollie sat into a pram and started choo-choo-chooing. Dermot Burke arrived and began playing Benediction tunes on the piano. Andy ate two hardboiled eggs with his bottle of stout and Ollie walked back to the college.

See you tomorrow, I said.

We all sang Salutaris and drank 7 bottles of Smithwicks each. Then a black doctor, who works in Lisdarn hospital, looked into the room to see who was singing.

17 Thur.

I went back to college today on the bar of Finbar Reilly's bike. We fell at Saunderson's on the ice. None of the dayboys spoke in the bicycle shed. We smoked a fag, watched the Belturbets arriving and put everything off till the last. As we came up the drive the boarders leant out the windows to shout down at us.

Go home to the Half Acre!

Go back to Mullahoran, you cunts, we roared back.

We had free classes to begin with, the walls were fusty and running. The seats were damp, there were yells, we told lies. Then one by one the doors to the classrooms closed and the corridors quietened. The snow fell on the trees, soundlessly. We said a prayer in Irish. The priests were alien like men who had been away for years. Now that they'd come back there was no one here they knew. Old fears surfaced. And Socrates called us gentlemen. Imagine, gentlemen, he said and his ginger eyebrows rose merrily. Packie the Case slapped his briefcase on the desk and opened A Tale of Two Cities at where we'd left off in a previous life. Benny wrote a line of algebra on the blackboard as if it were a death sentence. He smelt of wine from early morning Mass. Smigs smelt of sherry. Fairy sang sadly. Then at last the radiators came on and our trousers steamed, drips ran across the wooden floor. The town lads rode home for dinner; the country lads drank cold milk and ate ham sandwiches along the high windows and talked of Celtic Rovers; the boarders streamed into the refectory.

A connor had his head flushed down the lavatory. The barber, Henderson, cut hair with a soft tick onto a cement floor. A Latt man sat in the chapel. A few boarders smoked behind the alley, which was filled with snowdrifts. Others kicked a football on the frozen pitch. Lads with gloves shot basketball and dribbled across the white court.

Fellows walked the Half, kicking up frost and talking about Christmas. The radiators went off in the afternoon and everyone wanted to go to the bog. The shit smell from the clatty toilets seeped through the disinfectant and wafted high and animal down the corridor. Some classes we just sat there leafing through books and trying to keep our hands warm. In Greek we went down to Hades.

Then t'night I slipped up Keadue Lane with Mary. Over and in behind the power station. Terrible smell of old piss.

Don't, she said.

Why not?

Because.

She fell and started laughing.

What's going on in there, someone called from the road.

Oh Christ, said Mary.

We took off over the Cathedral grounds. They were white with snow. Then later I knocked off money from out of Maisie's handbag. She was in the downstairs toilet and her bag was on the shop counter. I stole in and took her purse out. I took 8 shillings and went down to the Railway Hotel. The black doctor joined us.

The best drink is gin, he told us.

We all got pissed and Dermot played tunes from Gilbert and Sullivan. This is the life. Got 3rd in Latin, 5th in Greek and 2nd in Science. Only 6% of us passed everything in Maths.

18 Fri. Octave of Prayer for Unity.

Mary went back to college. Had hand shandy twice today. Once in the trees behind the bicycle shed, then under the dinner table.

I miss Mary and I miss Sheila as well.

Were you at my bag? Maisie shouted t'night.

No, I said.

Well someone was. She smashed her hand into her fist. And whoever it was will pay dearly.

Are you reading about the good old times? asked my mother.

I am, I said, wincing.

Aren't you glad I kept it? she said.

Oh yes, I agreed.

24 Thur. Octave of Prayer for Unity.

After college Josie handed me a letter from Sheila. She's sorry we broke up and thinks we should start all over again and be together for as long as we can, but I told Josie to tell her that I did not want to go with her any more then I went home and done nothing exciting. Then I was sorry to have told Josie that so I went out and rang her.

Say nothing to Sheila, I said. Forget what I said.

All right, she said.

I only said those things to hurt her, I said.

All right, she said, I know that.

How do you know?

That's easy, she said.

25 Fri. Conversion of St Paul.

Up at Swellan Lake on a sleigh with Andy and Hickey. The lake is all frozen over to a depth they say of two foot. We came right down the hill flying and hit the ice with a bang then went about thirty feet across. The lake thundered. I cut my hand and later broke into the bus station. Eilish had a heart attack. We smoked and talked in the Dublin Bus of going to the Jersey Islands. Maybe the Isle of Man. The bus was coated in snow. In the hotel the black doctor stamped snow off his feet, put a pound into my hand and winked. I bought a round. Then Dermot fell off the piano stool onto Kate.

When I opened the door of the Breifne Aunty Maisie was in the hall.

If this continues, she said, I'll take your key.

26 Sat.

Another letter from Sheila. *I have to see you*, she wrote. *Will you be able to come out to Loreto some night? The best time is between 8 and 9 when we're at piano lessons on the ground floor. I don't want to get you into trouble.*

What do you reckon? I asked Andy.

Dead on, he said.

27 Sun. 3rd after Epiphany.

Got sick after last night. Felt very bad this morning. When I fell asleep the room was going round and when I woke it hadn't stopped. Dreamt that there was a lump of stuff was made of nothing that kept swirling round and would turn into a face and back again. There was an arm ended before it begun. And behind that, all the wrong trees. I tried to wake but couldn't and my teeth hurt. I tried to pull out my teeth, but couldn't. Woke soaked and the bells were ringing for Mass.

Then I saw Mary D. going to the toilet through the keyhole. Boy!

28 Mon.

I wrote to Sheila in double talk and said I'd be seeing her soon. X! X! X!

31 Thur. St John Bosco.

Myself and Andy went out the railway lines to Loreto. The only lights were on the second storey. It was hard to see because of the size of the flakes that were falling. I climbed a fir tree on the lawn and stood at the top looking for any sign of the girls. Snow fell every side of me. Then a nun switched on a light in a small white room and looked out directly at me. She was bald I thought. I fell off the tree through the branches and more branches, yelling, and ran. Andy came after me. As we went under the railway bridge we heard the squad car going overhead.

That's the bloody cops, said Andy.

The lights came on all over the convent and people began looking out windows.

Come on, said Andy.

We ran back to the town over sleepers packed tight with frost and I had just scaled the roof and climbed in the window when Una looked into my room to see if I was there.

1 Feb. First Friday. St Brigid.

First Useless, Smigs called.

Yes, said Sean White from Arva.

Are you awake?

Yes, Father.

Good, good, he said.

Then Smigs leant in close to my face so I could see the grains of chalk on the hairs of his nostrils.

Good morning, Second Useless, he said.

Good morning, Father, I said.

Should I see what young Healy has in his pocket? he asked the class.

Yes, said Jimmy McInerney from Redhills.

Fuck you, Jimmy, I whispered.

Smigs tapped my side pockets.

Take out what you have in your trousers, he said.

I took out a box of matches and sixpence.

Now your inside pocket, he continued.

There's nothing in there, Father.

Let me be the judge of that, he said.

He went to reach in. I caught his hand but he moved so fast he had the pages out.

What are these? he said, backing away. He scrutinized them by the window.

Are these poems by any chance? and he started to laugh.

I reached for them but he lifted them over my head.

Sit down, Second Useless, he said.

He read out the poems to the class, and then he put them in his pocket to show them to the President.

Oh Second Useless, he said, I see you in the town of Cavan talking to the Loreto girls. Isn't that right?

No, Father.

Oh yes, Second Useless, I'm afraid it is.

He took my ear between his thumb and forefinger.

Isn't that so?

No, Father.

He pulled hard. I went with his hand.

What height are you? he asked me.

Six foot, I said as he drew me standing.

Six foot *what?* he asked.

Six foot nothing, I said.

Jimmy McInerney broke into a fit of laughter.

Six foot, *Father!* Smigs said, gritting his teeth, then he reached down with his other hand and took McInerney's ear.

Isn't that right, McInerney?

Yes, Father, said Jimmy, and his mouth went up into a v.

2 Sat. Purification of B. V. M.

I got a bottle of stout and exchanged it for a beer and then went and got four. We drank them and went out the lines to Loreto. We climbed the portals of the front door of the convent, then went along the first-storey ledge to look in at the girls in the main hall – the whole gang of beauties from Cavan dancing! A tall nun was playing a record player and the girls in white blouses and wine dresses were waltzing in pairs while a nun called out the steps *and it's one two! and it's one two girls! and it's one two!* as she moved her head to and fro. I was so mesmer-ized that when a girl came walking towards the window I stepped back and nearly fell to the ground below, but Andy reached out a hand to stop me and my leather jacket snagged on the pebbledash.

Christ, Andy, I said.

That was close, he said.

My knees started to shake uncontrollably.

Steady, he said.

He took my hand and led me along the ledge. We climbed down and waited in the fir trees till the girls at last came to the lower rooms for piano practice. A window opened and Sheila looked out. I crawled across and said Hallo. She put a finger to her lips and leant out and gave me a kiss and nuzzled her nose against my nose then whispered shhh! shhh! and then slowly and quietly she pulled the window down.

Is there any word in there about the Breifne? asked my mother.

There is, I said.

It was terrible life we had back then, she said, and you, you bugger, you broke my heart.

I did, I said.

God forgive you, she said.

3 Sun. 4th after Epiphany.

I stayed in the house after dinner by the fire reading *Huckleberry Finn*. The Town Hall fire alarm rang. Bud McNamara, the fireman, came racing on a woman's bike down Main Street. Dick Mulcahy and Joe Duffy, with the brakes on their bikes screeching, came down the Barracks Hill. Tommy Reilly of the Regal left his dinner behind him. The big engine roared up Farnham Street from the fire station at the back of the library, bell going like the clappers, and waited by the Town Hall. Next the small engine came. The firemen took off their helmets and stood around in their great high waders that opened up round their thighs like champagne glasses. And they searched the sky for smoke.

Who put off the alarm? Joe Duffy asked, but no one knew.

I wouldn't mind, said Frank O'Keefe, but up of a Sunday. Of a fucking Sunday.

4 Mon.

Well on t' night.

5 Tues.

We stole Hickey's car and drove over the Cock Hill. Then I went down to the Ulster Arms with Dermot and a stray dog. I had 12 beers and he had 11. I was never in such good form and he got sick. Later I smoked in front of Maisie.

What are *you* doing? she asked.

I'm having a smoke, I said.

You'll destroy yourself yet.

Will you have one? I asked.

No thank you, she replied, glaring at me. You have a nerve.

So we sat there smoking in front of the mirror and then I went to bed and listened to the Luxembourg and woke in the dark with the radio on a foreign station and the voices going fast like they were at an auction.

6 Wed.

Woke feeling sorry and did not go to college. Josie arrived with a letter from Sheila.

9 Sat.

I brought Josie into my house to show her our photo album and then I worked in Noel's for the night. Got my wages and 20 fags, had a bath and powdered Simon, then put on my suit and new shoes and hitched to a jiving competition in Butlersbridge marquee.

Are you young Healy? the driver asked me.

I am.

We all have our problems, he said.

The ground round the marquee was swimming in muck and the van sank. The wheels screeched.

Fuck her, he said, I'll leave her there.

We drank in the field and then went into the tent. The local men were plastered.

You fucking townee, someone shouted at me. Let me at him.

Hold back there now, the driver said, he's only a lad.

He's from the Half Acre.

And tell me this, the driver said very slowly, what's wrong with the Half Acre?

Nothing, your man said.

Would she bang? someone shouted.

The competition started. Lorraine McCarren was my partner. We got through to the last round and came second. Andy Murray and Eitna Wall won. I went out the back to piss on sawdust. The driver was asleep in the back of his van so I had to walk home. I went to bed, turned off the light and put the radio to my ear. Aunt Maisie looked in and said I was abusing privilege.

Things will be different when your mother comes home, she said.

I showed her the cup I'd won.

Don't be trying to get around me, she said.

10 Sun. Septuagesima.

Went to 11 Mass and fell asleep. Stayed home after dinner then t'night walked out the lines to Loreto with Andy. The girls were down at the piano rooms. Sheila opened the window and Andy whistled and she put a finger to her lips. Then the three windows opened and the Cavan town girls began playing various sonatas while we listened from the trees. It was lovely. A nun came into the Sheila's room. We could see them talking. She was giving off. Then one by one all the windows came down.

On the way home Andy cut the arse off a bird with a stone.

11 Mon. Apparition of Our Lady of Lourdes.
Slept in. Did not go to college. Then was sorry I didn't go. Went back to sleep. The girls in the bakery were singing. I dreamt I saw my father's face at the window. He was looking in at me while I slept. So in the dream I cried but woke dry-eyed with a thumping heart. Got up at 1 o'clock and worked in Noel's then went and played Pongo.

When I got home the girls were playing the accordion in the bakehouse. I was afraid to go asleep again for fear of what I might see.

12 Tues.
Did not go to college. Lay there looking at the ceiling while Una called me from the yard. Then Maisie came into my room.

Get up!

I'm sick, I said.

Go to *school*! she snarled.

No.

She shook the bottom of the bed, slapped her hands and her eyes blazed.

You are not my responsibility, she said. You are not mine! Do you hear?

She slammed the door. She cursed me as she crossed the landing. I lay in bed till 2, waking with a desperate hunger between dreams to smell food cooking below in the kitchen. At last I could take no more. I ate my dinner in the shed with the cats. Betty Quinn took me up a dessert.

You'll be killed by your aunt, she said.

13 Wed.

You stand aside, said the Dean at roll call this morning, and wait there till I'm finished. The dayboys called out their names and headed to class till I was all that remained in the refectory.

Where were you the last few days? he asked.

I was in bed with the runs, I said.

Have you a letter from your mother?

My mother is in England, I said.

So who is in charge of you at home?

My Aunt Maisie.

Have a letter from her here tomorrow.

Yes, Father.

Go, he said.

I could never read your writing, said my mother.

It's a good job, I told her.

But I know, she said politely, what's in there.

14 Thur.

I followed the Dean to his study. He put his cane on the table. He sat and read the letter I'd handed him. He placed it carefully on his desk, smoothed out the edges and looked at me.

Is this your aunt's writing? asked the Dean.

Yes, I lied.

You're telling me the truth?

Yes, Father.

He stood, lifted his cane and walked over to the window.

Are you sure?

Yes, Father.

Right.

He stood there a while in silence looking down on the Half and the Whole, on the white football fields and the basketball court and the handball alleys. My heart raced. His white hair blazed.

Spell diarrhoea, he said.

Diarrhoea? I asked weakly.

Yes. Diarrhoea.

D . . . i . . . , I answered. D . . . i . . . a . . . r . . . r . . . i . . . a.

143

Put out your hand, he said turning.

Why, Father?

Put out your hand, he repeated.

But I've done nothing wrong, I said and held out my hand. His face went red and he brought the cane down, six times on the palm. With the top of the cane he tipped the wrist of my other arm that I had down by my side, flicked the cane under the elbow, I rose the palm, he came down six more times.

I will be reporting you to the President, he said. Go.

I stood a while in the corridor with my hands in my armpits. Then went to the jacks and had a smoke. I felt sick. I thought of heading off back into Cavan town and lying up somewhere till all this had blown over, maybe in the haybarn, or Lavell's haunted house, anywhere. I sat out that class on a toilet seat and listened with dread to classroom doors banging and the steps of priests going to and fro, the muffled sound of singing, the skivvies from the kitchen running across the tiles. Then these steps came on steadily down the corridor as far as the toilet, halted a moment, hesitated, entered. Each toilet door was pushed open. The steps came on towards me. He pushed. I saw the wide black shoes and black trousers underneath the door.

Who is in there? asked Father Benny.

Dermot Healy, I said.

Come out!

I flushed the toilet and pretended to pull my trousers up. I opened the door and he indicated that I walk in front of him. I could feel him behind me, tramping, tramping.

Why are you late for class? asked Father Benny.

I was with the Dean, I said.

I hope he gave you what you deserve, he said.

As I went ahead of him down the corridor I could hear the lads talking in the classroom. When they heard us coming they went quiet. Everyone watched me as I took my seat.

Who told you to sit, said Benny.

I stood.

And don't you look at me like that.

I'm not, Father.

Sit down, he shouted.

I didn't sit but backed away.

Sit down, I said, he shouted.

I sat down again by Jimmy McInerney.

You! Father Benny shouted. Come here!

I got up.

Not you! he said, and slapped me.

Then he began to write on the blackboard.

What did the Dean do you for? whispered Jimmy.

I couldn't spell shite, I said.

First he tried to smother the laugh, and his eyes watered, then he gagged in the throat. I cycled in from college and went to Noel's to work and do my exercise. Then Josie waved from the street. When I came out to her she walked over to Woolworth's so I followed her in.

We can't be seen together, she whispered. There's trouble.

What kind of trouble?

Sheila is going to be expelled.

Why?

Because of you, she said. They know it's you has Loreto haunted.

I didn't know what to say.

You'll be killed, said Josie, and so will Sheila.

I walked her to the door. Other girls from Loreto going by on their bikes stared at me. I was in very bad form. I had a bad conscience. Dermot and me had a long talk. Then I called up to Andy. We make preparations to go to England. All the money we have will go into a fund and we'll hit Dublin in Sean McManus's car and get the night ferry. That night I packed a suitcase and put it under the bed.

Upon my song, said my mother, but you were the right blackguard.

What is she saying? asked Maisie, as she felt her way into the sitting room.

She says I was a blackguard, I told her.

Are you only learning that now? said Maisie, flopping down on the sofa. I say, Winnie!

What's she saying? asked my mother.

She always pretended to be innocent, snorted Maisie. But she managed to have you despite everything. Her beloved offspring, she chuckles.

The two women look at each other a moment.

What's on the box? asks Maisie, turning away. My mother goes back to her beads.

15 Fri.
Get up, said Una.

I have a headache, I said.

I lay in the bed dreaming of a new life in London while the huge mixer in the bakehouse spun dough. The story went round and round. The flour men came up the entry. Miss Reilly shook a pillow slip out of her bedroom window. A car backfired. The jackdaws screamed as they landed on the draper's roof tiles. Dark feathers flew. I slept and woke and found that nothing had changed. I went back to the beginning and ended up where I was. I tried to convince myself that none of this was true.

I turned in the bed, this way and that, and tried to empty my head of everything. But it was always there. The girls in the kitchen called me down to breakfast but I didn't answer. They called me to dinner but I didn't go. Soon the light in the room started to fade. I felt small. Miss Reilly stood looking towards the Gallows Hill. The lights came on in the dining room below, and the whitewash on Burke's side wall slowly grew grey, with long bands of yellow thrown onto it from the lit-up kitchen where the trays went back and forth, and the girls called to each other cheerfully.

Maisie spoke from the landing.

What's wrong with you?

I'm sick, I said.

I lay on. It turned black. Music came over the house. Delft clashed. I woke in the early evening from a terrible dream I couldn't remember, and all that I couldn't remember tormented me, driving great eerie distances between things that didn't exist. The geyser stopped hissing. The chairs went up backwards on the tables and the dining room was swept. The baking house slammed shut.

Noel shouted up from the entry in a faraway voice. Are you coming to work, Dermot?

I sat up in the bed ashamed and didn't answer. Then a while later Una looked into the dark bedroom and said did I want the light on but I said no, I was all right. Then I felt happy in a light-headed way because I would be left alone. I would be left alone. I knew Maisie had reached her room because suddenly the volume on Radion Eireann was raised. The hunger and the darkness and the fear gave rise to great swathes of self-pity. I dressed in the dark and dropped down into the garden. The streets were empty. I headed for the Ulster Arms and met the lads. Dermot who'd taken the half-day was there. Andy says there is trouble. Bad trouble.

That's right, agrees Dermot.

We're in the shit, said Andy. Let's hit London.

We're emigrating, he said. Myself and Healy are off across the water.

Is that so? said Mr McCusker, the barber. Give those lads a jar.

By the time we reached the Central at 11 we were footless and Andy was sure we would never see home again. Josie was there sitting at a table on her own.

You can say goodbye to us now, I said, we're leaving Sunday.

I've been waiting for you, she said. I've been up and down the town all day.

What for, I asked her.

To give you the news.

What's happened?

Everything is all right, she said. It's blown over.

I couldn't believe it. So we all went off to the amusements and jumped into the bumping cars.

16 Sat.
Turned up for role call, answered to my name and hid in the jacks till class started, then I slipped down the back avenue to the bicycle shed and hid there reading *Kidnapped* till 1 o'clock when the half-day at school was over.

17 Sun. Sexagesima
Met Josie in the Central. From a Jack to a King was playing.

19 Tues.
Did not go to school but went out after dinner because Maisie threatened me with writing to the mother. There was an enquiry.

Fairy sent me to the Dean. The Dean sent me to the President. Father Bob said I was letting my family down.

I know, he said, that you've lost you're father, but you've got to come to terms with it.

Square gave me five on each hand. Benny said I'd soon be sent through the gates. And then I read out an essay for Packie the Case entitled Going Abroad and into it I put all the things I imagined I'd have seen in London. Then I went home. I went up to my room and did my exercise and listened to Luxembourg. For a while I thought there was someone standing behind me but there was no one, and yet someone was there all the same. I began to get frightened. Then when it was dark I slipped out onto the roof, over Provider's wall and went out the Dublin Road. No car was stopping. So I walked the 7 mile through the cold pitch darkness to Josie's house. Her parents were away. We lay on the living-room floor and listened to records. Boy! Had to walk home in the sleet. I was skint. I got in through the window and went to the toilet. When I came out Aunty Maisie and Una appeared from my father's room where they'd been waiting. They kicked the hell out of me. Una fell.

20th Wed.
Andy caught hens, Dermot fell under the table, they shouted upstairs, I went up and they were downstairs.

Where are we? said my mother, suddenly darting awake.

We're in Cootehill, I said.

And you're still here?

I am.

Good, she said, and she closed her eyes again.

Chapter 23

24 Sun. Quinquagesima. (St Mathias, Apostle)

I played records in the Central Café and finished the last of 10 Players.
After 11 Mass Sheila came in for the day. She was looking lovely. Her
face was flushed and fresh and happy. She was wearing a long blue
jumper over her red pleated pinafore. A gold chain and cross hung
down across the small collars of her blouse. The striped tie was
knotted firmly. She smiled slyly and came straight across to my table,
passing her brother and his friends, and sat down opposite me.

Thank you for coming to see me all those nights, she said, and she
moved the milk and the salt cellar aside and took my hand.

Old emotions stir within me. She trailed her fingers over mine,
and we sat looking at each other, saying nothing. There were dark tints
like sleeplessness under her eyes, something warm and foreign that
made me glad. I played Be Bop a Lula. She squeezed my hand.

We're awful fools, she said. We could have been in big trouble.

I know, I said.

We're not to do it again, she said cheerfully and added, I don't think.

She took my hand across the table and pressed the palm to her
cheek.

It'll not be long till Easter, she said.

Then Josie arrived with her flash camera. We stood by the bus
station and she took photos of us, arm in arm, Sheila's hair quiffed back,
one foot askew and myself humped over to come down to her size.

Smile, can't you? said Josie.

27 Wed. Ash Wednesday.

In the bicycle shed we all dismounted with crosses of ash on our
foreheads. We had a competition swinging along the overhead beams
hanging by your bare hands. It was tough going. The boarders
had bigger crosses than us, made not with a thumb but a paintbrush.
They had black toast they said for breakfast. Everyone's gone holy,
even McInerney.

What are you off for Lent? I asked him.

Talking to you, he said. You're always getting me into trouble.

Slipped out of bed that night and went for a walk down Main Street. Met the hard lads. Go long, you clatty fucker, said Johnny.

We drank down River Street sitting on the door step of Johnny's house. His father, a tall tipsy man with an old gash across his cheek, came along from the CYMS carrying a billiard cue.

I like to see our Johnny in good company, he said, taking the piss.

Don't start, Daddy, said Johnny.

Start what? he shouted.

You're always cribbing.

Healy, he said to me, go back where you came from.

Then Mrs Galligan, her hair tied back with pins, came down the stairs in a man's pyjamas. James Galligan, she said, come in from the street.

Yes, Mammy, her husband said.

There's nothing but class distinction in this town, he said and went in.

I lit a fag. Johnny puked into the Kinnypottle. Andy was pissed. We are all bad cases. I ended up shouting on Main Street.

Did you come across Shamey Slacke in your travels in that yoke? she asks.

He was mentioned, I say.

And any word of Nancy?

A little.

I should never have left you after your father died, she says and her chin steadies. Nancy got it into her head that I needed a break and I ended up a char off the King's Road. And you—she looked at me—you went asunder.

MARCH

2 Sat.

Did not go to school. Bad headache. I'll never do it again.

3 Sun. 1st Sunday in Lent.

Left Josie out part of the way home on my bike and then headed off alone to the Railway Hotel to see if any of the gang were there but the only man at the bar was the black doctor in a smart grey gabardine coat that detectives wear.

Where have you been? he said. Give this fellow a gin.

I had my first gin and tonic.

It tasted great. We had another. He spoke about Calcutta and lit a cigar and drew it away quick and wide from his face. He clapped me on the shoulder and ordered again. His eyes were cream-white and his knuckles were pinched and blue. He laughed a lot to himself and talked of being lonely, so we hired a taxi and went off to the first opera I'd known of to come to the Town Hall. People there were astonished to see us together.

Have you booked? asked Miss Connolly.

No, I said.

Well, all we have are the dear seats, I'm afraid, and she righted her glasses.

That will do, thank you, said the Doc.

Reluctantly she peeled off the tickets and so we found ourselves up the front among all the folks in evening dress. The women wore white gloves and the men dicky bows. In front of us the orchestra were tuning up. Violin, violin, violin. Cello. The drum. A scatter of notes from the flute. A head through the curtain to see was the house full. And all the time the Doc kept laughing. When the lights went down he fell asleep, and woke when I poked him. The worst thing was – it was a sad part, and he jumped to his feet and clapped. All eyes turned to us. I was mortified. Afterwards I took him home to the hospital on the bar of my bike. On the avenue we fell off into a bush and lay on the lawn laughing. Every time we tried to get up he started another burst of laughter.

We must do that again, he said, some time.

4 Mon. (Novena of Grace begins)
The college lost the McRory cup so we got no free day. Everyone was badly disappointed. That night all the school boarders from Saint Pat's and Loreto were let out for the opera, so off I went to the opera again. The girls were in the front and just before the start Sheila stood and waved at me.

6 Wed. Ember Day. (Fast and Abstinence)

Josie took off her roll-on. Would not but was nearly going to. We had some of her father's gin then.

10 Sun. 2nd in Lent.

Did not go to the alley but stayed in and studied. Asked Maisie for money for the pictures.

You are abusing privilege, she said.

Please, I said.

No, she said, a thousand times no.

I just want to go to the pictures.

No, she said. You'll see no more money from me.

So Dermot paid for me in and Josie bought me 10 fags and a 99. Josie and I broke the seat at the pictures while courting. She hit the floor and said Fuck. Everyone in the Magnet laughed. Afterwards we hitched through the cold to her place towards Killeshandra and I met her mother and played her some records. She poured me a gin.

What age are you? she asked me.

Nineteen, I said.

Have you any interest in politics? asked her father, the doctor.

Not really, I said.

Well you should, he said, certainly, certainly. We talked about Ireland. The mother stoked up the fire. It turned 2. He said he'd leave me back to town. I got into the car and he poured a kettle of hot water over the frozen windscreen. He started to reverse. Josie was standing at the gate to wave goodbye but the car skidded on the black frost and hit her.

I ran to her.

Dermot, she said, I feel sick.

She's suffering from shock. He hit her on the leg. The father was upset.

It's all my fault, Daddy, she said.

I led Josie back to the fire. She held my hand. Her father wrapped her leg in a bandage and the mother gave her a hot whiskey. Josie didn't want me to go but I had to. I said I'd walk home because he was too drunk to drive. I got lost coming down the lane from their house in the snow and felt my way by the branches. Cows were bellowing in sheds. It was pure cold. I slid along the ditch. Stars were everywhere. I must have been walking a long time when the squad car stopped me on the Farnham Road and the guard rolled down the window. I could feel the hot air from inside. He asked me my name.

What are you doing out at this hour of the night?

I said I was walking home.

I can see that, but where are you coming from?

A Fine Gael meeting, I said.

Is that so.

And then my wheel went flat.

Ah *h-ard* luck, he said.

It was 3 when I reached the Breifne and Maisie was waiting for me on the stairs. I said I had an accident. The only accident you had, she said, was the day you were born.

12 Tues. St Gregory the Great.

Got six slaps from Square, the Dean, because Fairy reported me for throwing orange peels in singing class. Then Barney chucked me out of science for causing a disturbance. Then Mutt hits me. Josie gets into the car.

I have a sore arse, she says, and she gave me a letter from Sheila.

It's a fair day in Cavan. The town is full of ponies and cows and carts of pigs. The Market House is running with seeds. The Market yard is filled with carrots and heads of cabbages and onions. Everyone is on the move up and down from the Gallows Hill where the cattle pens are. The pubs are overflowing. The Northern farmers, in squat wellingtons that suck as they walk, piss down the entry and stalk the streets with hefty sticks. They're having fries and high teas of ham and tomato and sliced pan and butter pats in the Breifne, and Katie German is on her feet all day by the range with a plate over the frying pan. Maisie is flying in the shop. Una is serving in her Poor Clare's uniform.

Get in there, says Katie.

I wash up in the Breifne till the restaurant closes. The girls collapse in the dining room and light fags. Then I work next door in Noel's bar. The skin on my hands is white from the soap and hot water. In the yard a man broke a stick over his son's back then drove him before him screeching up Main Street. The door in Woolworth's slammed shut on a woman's arm. I served a snail in a bottle of Guinness. The farmer spat it out into the palm of his hand, studied it and asked Noel when had the shop turned into an eating house.

That's a good one, said Noel and gave him a Power's before compensation set in.

A small man ordered a drink and came up on his good leg to get change from his pocket. He was 6 feet tall. The pub was full till 10 and Noel paid me 9 shillings and 20 fags. I go for a stroll. The town is littered with dung and walking sticks.

Howareya.

Howareya.

Oh how is it going?

The same. The same.

13 Wed.

Don't go to school, still have the *cruiscin*. Dermot left me in a few books to read.

14 Thur.

Do not go to school. Spent the day in bed. Then in the middle of the night there was a tap on the window and Andy in a long green FCA coat climbed in off the kitchen roof. Next thing Dermot brought a ladder up the entry and two girls climbed up into my room. We thought you'd like the company, said Dermot.

16 Sat.

Working all day washing delft, then went off to see *Ben Hur* at the pics. There was no seat beside Josie but one beside Andy, so at the break Andy took Josie's seat and she took his and we ate apples I'd stolen from Blessings. Quiet, shouted George O'Rourke and he shone his torch at me.

Where are we? says Mother, wakening.

Here, I said, in the bungalow.

She closes her eyes and sighs.

17 Sun. St Patrick, Patron of Ireland. (Holiday of Obligation)
The Saint Patrick's Parade came charging down Church Street. There was a pipe band from Downpatrick and another from Kingscourt. Then the floats came. Provider's, Fegan's, the ESB, Jackson's garage, Smith's garage. The scouts. The Brothers' band with Gerry Brady marching in front of them with Brother Cyril. Irish dancers. Roadstone.

I'm not going back to St Fucking Pat's, said Ollie.

All right, I said.

I've had enough of that place, he said. I'm for Manchester. Will you come?

I might.

Good.

I don't feel right, said Dermot and he went home.

I've just cut my finger, said Ollie. How did that happen?

I haven't a notion, I said.

Myself and Ollie walked round the town. I slept that night with him in our single bed. He got up at dawn fearing trouble. I've done it this time, he said. He put the dicky bow in his trousers pocket and headed off for college at half past 6 looking miserable.

19 Tues. St Joseph, Spouse of B. V. M.
Ollie got 10 slaps from Square and a warning that his parents would be told. He said he felt ill and had slept in the Farnham Arms. He denied he was with me. In Packie the Case's class Bob the President called me up to his room.

Have you been out near Loreto? he asked.

No, I said.

Are you sure?

Yes, Father.

Well, the nuns say it's you. They've heard the girls talking.

It's not me, Father. Not at all.

I suppose I must believe you.

Thank you, Father.

Should I tell the Mother Superior it's not you?

Yes, Father.

All this, Dermot, is very sad, he said.

That night I walk out to Josie's house on my own. Nearly dead tired when I get there. We listen to music for hours. I ride back to town on Josie's bike and leave it in the Regal yard. It's 12 o'clock. Aunt Maisie is at the door. She takes my key.

21 Thur. St Benedict.
Josie thinks I went with someone else last night. And also thinks something happened on Sunday night. I say no. We go on talking over the phone. Then the operator breaks in. *Stop that dirty talk*, she says. We go on talking. The manageress of the Ulster Arms arrived. *Get out of that phone box*, she says, *I've had a complaint*. She dumped me onto the street, I went up to the phone box at the post office and rang back. We talked on, and on. But it was no deal. She doesn't believe me.

You only want Sheila, she says. Only Sheila.

23 Sat.
Did not go to school. McInerney called out my name during role call so Square didn't know I wasn't there. Watched boxing match in Burke's, went to the matinee (*The Canadians*) with Josie who expects me to break it off.

When Sheila gets back you won't want me, she said.

Yes I will, I said.

All I'm good for is bringing you her letters.

That's not true.

Wait till Easter comes, then we'll see.

You're wrong.

And the strange thing is, said Josie, I don't mind.

I watch *Thank Your Lucky Stars* in Andy's bar and at 8 Mammy comes home.

Were you good? she asked me.

I looked at Una.

Was he?

Yes, she said.

Can I go to a dance in Oldcastle? I asked.

Yes, you can.

She opened her purse, lifted out a pound note and threw it on the ground.

There, she said, there you are. Go where you like.

Dressed in the new shirt she'd bought me I went to see the Clipper Carlton showband in Joe Hill's car and danced the Sheridan sisters. Joe found a woman from Kells. When we stepped outside it was snowing. At 10 mile an hour we drove to Kells. Sometimes he'd drive into a ditch. We spun round on corners. At last we reached Kells. The girl made us a cup of tea and I waited in the car while they had a court then we turned towards Cavan. We could see nothing because of the snow blowing against the windscreen. We slithered all over the place. This side of Lavey we tipped into a drain.

That's that, said Joe, and I haven't even a coat.

So we walked home.

I arrived into the Breifne covered in white at dawn. My shoes went slapslap across the landing. Mammy woke when she heard me closing the door. She came into my room without her glasses on.

Look at you, she said. Just look at you.

The car broke down.

I've heard, she said bitterly, I've heard all about you. Dear God of almighty. What's to become of us! Your father is looking down on you, she said. Remember that.

Chapter 24

25 Mon. The Annunciation.
Studied. Did not go out.

26 Tues.
Did not go out. All night we talked of my father and of London. The mother looks at me for long periods as if I was someone else.

27 Wed.
If Mammy had given me money I would have won on Kalminos in the Lincoln. Did not go out.

30 Sat.
Put 6 shillings on races. Out and About led till the third last. Afterwards went to *The Lost Continent* with Josie. Silly picture. Silly court. Studied, took a spin in the car and went to bed.

APRIL

2 Tues.
Asked the blonde from McDonnell's but moved the Farnham model instead. The thaw began and the ice broke with a roar on Swellan. Then the town was full of burst pipes.

Have you the money ready for the milkman? asks my mother.
    I have.
    And you'll take me to Mass?
    I will.
    She studies Padre Pio's face. She reads her prayer, puts it aside in the silver vessel, and grips the arms of the chair.
    Get me out of here, she shouts.
    No, I say.

3 Wed.

Put on our finery and myself and Dermot went out to Loreto to the annual concert. Sheila introduced me to the Mother Joseph Cupertino. All the young things nearly fainted.

I hear a lot about you, said the nun.

She lifted my hand in the air, squinted and sighed and nodded, not too severely. Then she gave me my hand back – daintily. It was like being forgiven. Sheila was very proud. We sat among the parents like saints in the hall I used to climb up to. Burke turned adult. The girls played the tunes on the pianos that myself and Andy used to hear from the trees, they sang and recited poetry, dressed as men in blue tights and pointed shoes they delivered speeches from Shakespeare, and the night finished with beetroot sandwiches, Jacob's marsh-mallows and tea. We had great cant. Went on afterwards to a bazaar on the Railway Road where I hit the bull and won a reed bowl for the mother from a dwarf.

A dwarf no less, said Maisie. When I was young I thought of running away with an acrobat.

You should have, I said.

I'd have been killed.

We sat by the fire talking and toasted bread. Mammy did her toes and soaked her feet in methylated spirits. We were all in great form.

4 Thur.

Loreto get holidays but though I searched the town I could not find Sheila.

6 Sat.

Did not go to school. Ma ripping. Cut lip while shaving. Searched the town again but could not find Sheila. Go to links. Sat in the café but she never came. Jumped out window in the middle of the night and stood outside Sheila's house till 1 in the morning. No one. Nothing. Nobody.

7 Sun. 2nd Sunday of Passiontide. (Palm Sunday)

Today records great events. Went to High Palm Mass with Dermot then to the Central Café. All the dames are there but no sign of Sheila.

Went home and sat by the fire. Done composition called Contentment and went to Devotions. The cathedral was rustling. The priests looked like altar boys that have just climbed out of bed – all white-faced and tired. Got money off Una for pictures. Sat by myself. At last I heard the door open after half-time and saw her at the back waiting for her eyes to adjust to the dark then Sheila came straight across to me.

My parents kept me in so I couldn't see you, she whispered.

I was wondering where you were.

They won't let me out. Especially my brother.

Why?

They say we are too serious.

Do you think we are too serious?

No, she said. The trouble is we are not serious enough. Do you love me?

I do.

She looked into my face.

I keep dreaming about you.

I kissed the back of her hand. She brought my hand to her lips. I have to go, she said. If my brother sees us together, I'll be killed. We put our arms around each other and then she left.

Had a brandy by myself and listened to the *Top Twenty*. Then had tea. I feel awfully happy.

8 Mon. Holy Week.
Fr Terry told me he is about to make investigations into my grasp of Greek and my general intelligence. I took a half-day and met Sheila outside Katy Bannon's. She was crying. I brought her into the baker's room. She kept on crying. I couldn't stop her. The parents want her never to see me again.

9 Tues. Holy Week.
Dermot Burke gave me a run-through of what to expect in Greek. Terry gives me an examination by myself in the back seat. I get 98 out of a 100.

There's something strange going on, he said.

Then there's Geography, then Maths. The hours drag. Then at last comes 4 o'clock. Come the Holidays! But the boarders have to stay in till tomorrow morning. Ollie leapt out of a window and raced away through the trees to where I was waiting for him on the road. Away we went like fuck round the back of the triangle with Ollie on the bar of the bike. He has the dicky bow on.

Give her stick, he shouted.

We hit the Railway Hotel round 6 and he took a taxi out at 9. I did not get in till half past 2. Mammy gives out shit.

10 Wed. Holy Week.

Ollie calls to the Breifne. He has his case with him.

There's trouble, he said.

Square saw him leap out of the window. The Dean came into his dorm, and said, McNally! Get up! He smelt his breath. Square asked him did he go to see Healy. He said no. Was it a girl? He said no.

When you pack your case in the morning, Mr McNally, said Square, it will be for the last time. You won't be coming back here.

Now Ollie doesn't know what to do. So we smoked 20 fags and went to Balihaise to pick up Harton's lorry to take him home. I went to the pictures and sat down by Sheila. She got up and moved away.

I followed her. What's going on? I asked.

You've been double-crossing me all this time with Josie, she said.

Not at all, I said.

Yes you have.

No I haven't.

You needn't lie any more, Dermot. You needn't lie. Josie told me.

Let me explain.

No, she said, I'm not talking to you anymore.

Quiet! shouted George O'Rourke.

After that I couldn't follow the picture. I went to bed in bad form.

11 Thur. Holy Thursday.

Met Sheila outside Woolworth's. Her parents are taking her away for a few days.

To keep me away from you, she said.

Josie doesn't mean anything to me, I said.

That, said Sheila, only makes it worse.

We said goodbye. I slipped in the backway to Stick Donoghue's.

Courted Mary. Saw Pat. Skipped Mass. And banged my head running up yard to climb in window.

12 Fri. Holy Friday.
Sheila gone to Wicklow. Not a soul stirring on the streets. Played records. Josie bought a loaf. Had some toast and went home early.

14 Sun. Easter Sunday.
Are you going out with Sheila? asked Mary.
    Sometimes, I said.
    Sometimes, said Gerty. What does that mean?
    We broke it off.
    Did you, now. Well we don't want anyone else's leavings, she laughed sarcastically. We all know about you, you glick fucker. Look at Dermot Burke – he wouldn't ask to put his hand up.
    Is that right? I said.
    That's right, said Burke proudly.
    Would you like to go to the pictures? I asked Mary.
    I would, she said.
    You should not let him have his way so easily, said Gerty.
    Can you not mind your own business, I said.
    Mary arrives at 9 o'clock.
    I thought you weren't coming, I said.
    Oh, I didn't want to let you down.
    So I put a hand on her tits and she pulled it away.
    No, she said.
    Why? I ask.
    Just.
    So I stared at the screen with my hands in my pockets.
    Are you crabbed? she asked.
    Oh I'm in terrific humour, I said.
    I'm glad to hear it, she said. You see we differ too much to be together.
    I hope I'm free, I said.
    What does that mean? she asked.
    I don't know, I said importantly. The twins marched up the aisles waving their long torches.

15 Mon.

Dermot lost four balls on the links and we danced to the wireless on the road. We bought ice creams and played a game of doubles in table tennis. Dermot and Gerty against Mary and me. Then I went off to the amusements. Garret's teeth fell out when he was up in the swingboats. We gambled at roulette and throwpenny, then sat into the bumping cars. Save the Last Dance for Me was playing and you could hear it at the far end of Main Street.

On way home saw that Sheila's father's car was back. I was in great humour.

Can I have a party? I asked the mother.

If you paint the house, you can have a party, she said.

16 Tues.

As I write this I'm swivel-eyed. Painted the hallway then brought Sheila out to the golf links. Ah I love Sheila. She said she'd forgive me for going out with Josie because Josie said it wasn't serious. She brought me a present of 20 Pall Mall from Wicklow. I love Sheila. I'll make Gerty eat her words. Afterwards Dermot and myself went out to Lisdarn and collected the black doctor. I have 2 gins and tonics and 9 beers. I love Sheila.

17 Wed.

Ollie arrived to give me a hand and we painted the corridor, and the landing, and the wall above the three steps. Then made arrangements for the hop in our house. The gang arrived with records and the cant started. At last Sheila came. She was by herself.

I can't go in, she said at the door. That crowd don't like me.

You only think that, I said, come on.

No. She looked down the street. Who's in there?

So I told her.

That does it, she said, I'm not going.

Who's at the door? asked Mammy.

Sheila, I said.

Hallo, Mrs Healy.

You're welcome, Sheila, said Mammy. Well, what's holding you? Come on in, we're about to eat.

When we went in Gerty made lousy remarks. We helped my mother serve. We ate in sixes and spun the bottle and danced. Kevin ran into the pillar and knocked himself out. Croney started barking like mad. Una came out for a jive with me. Maisie went down the entry and looked in the window and sneezed with the knuckle of her index finger to her nose.

Stay with me, won't you, said Sheila.

I will.

Don't dance with anyone else.

I won't.

She put my arm around her waist.

I love you, she said.

I danced Sheila all night and we courted under the stairs.

18 Thur.
Ollie and myself painted the rest of the landing and the door of Mammy's room. He asked Pat to go with him but she wouldn't because she wanted to go with Andy so Ollie hitched off to Virginia. I went to the pics with Sheila. The seat collapsed from under me in the middle of a murder scene and Sheila went to bits.

21 Sun. Low Sunday.
Went to see Sheila at half past 3, supposed to be there at 2 but the fire in the bakehouse went out twice and so we had only time to talk before she had to go. Ollie calls on way back to college. He says he'll go out and see what happens in the morning.

22 Mon.
It's our last time together before going back to college. Myself and Sheila tear up Reilly's archway into the loft. She has no buttons on her shirt. There are no prying eyes. She begins to cry. We say goodbye.

24 Wed.
After school played tripe golf and go to the pictures. *Marx Brothers Go West.* Terrific picture. I miss Sheila. I could've enjoyed it better if she was there.

25 Thur. St Mark, Evangelist. (Rogation Day)

Ollie can't come back next year. They are blaming my bad influence. Father Terry put a map of Greece on the wall so that we could follow the wars of Sparta. He sneezed, the map fell and Parrot farted. Ollie went off round the Half on his own. Met Josie, and told her to tell Sheila to start the ball rolling by writing first then I stood in the handball alley till night fell.

26 Fri. Our Lady of Good Counsel.

I went up to Bob and pleaded on Ollie's behalf but he says there is nothing he can do. He'll see but at the moment it's out of his hands. It's gone too far. Myself and Ollie walk the half. The 5th years stood and watched us.

It'll not be long now, lads, said one.

They walked behind us, taunting us so we headed across the lower pitch.

The minute the term ends, said Ollie, I'm taking the boat across the water. Are you coming?

I will, I say.

We'll go into antiques, he said. I have an uncle doing well at that.

Right, I said.

And fuck these crowd.

Right.

Fuck them.

28 Sun. 2nd after Easter.

Lit the fire in the bakery and walked Maisie and the Mother round the triangle. Told Maisie to keep her voice down as we passed Sheila's house and she roared laughing.

29 Mon.

Got word that there's 25 women up the pole in town. Got a lovely letter from Sheila but Josie does not stop to talk.

30 Tues.

Skipped the last two classes and met Sheila who was having a tooth out. Her mouth was bloody. I walked up town with my arm around her and didn't care who saw us.

I didn't know you had any bad teeth, I said.

I hadn't, she said.

What?

I only pretended so that I could get into town and see you.

Then she went back to the convent.

MAY

1 Wed. St Joseph the Worker.
Have bad old stye. Square gave me six for skipping the two classes after dinner.

4 Sat.
Gave Josie a tiepin for Sheila.

5 Sun. 3rd after Easter.
I hear that Sheila is up the pole, said Andy as we came down the steps after 10 mass.

Is that right, I said.

So they say.

Who?

People. People talk about it.

Do they now.

Yeh.

Well fuck them.

You'll be in trouble yet.

No I won't.

There's people in this town don't like you, you know.

Why?

There'll be trouble, he said. I heard, he added.

I went up to the alley and played all day with the soldiers.

8 Wed.
Vomited this morning. Bad form. The mother looked in.

Time to get up, she said.

I'm sick, I said.

I'm sorry for you, she said but didn't give me a spiff. The inside of my head was racing. The wallpaper was upside down. After dinner in good form so headed to Noel's loft. Fixed it terrific. Looks smashing, all boarded and nailed up. Laid out a carpet that Frank Conlon was going to throw away and carried up a chest of drawers from Burke's. Tacked Eddie Cochran and The Searchers to the wall, then lit a candle and looked round for ages at my new home.

Maisie looked over at Winnie and said, Poor Winnie.

What's she saying? asked my mother.

9 Thur.

Brought a mattress from our loft round by the garden into Noel's. Then came back with a few roles of wallpaper. We pasted them up.

12 Sun. 4th after Easter. World Sodality Day.

I had the fire lit in the bakehouse when the bell rang and Father Bob was at the door.

I'd like, he said, to see yourself and your mother.

What has he done now? she asked.

Nothing, he said.

I'm glad to hear that, she said.

But I think it would be proper, he continued gravely, if Dermot was booked in as a boarder next year.

Whatever you think, Father Robert, she said glaring at me.

And I think he should go to a *Gaeltacht* during the summer. It will help his Irish.

Do you hear Father Robert? she asked me.

I do, I said.

So you'll go?

I will.

That's that then, said Father Robert.

13 Mon.

Put up more wallpaper in Noel's. Done a bit of painting. Left half a flagon of cider up there.

Noel's head appeared in the opening.

How are things in the Castle? he asked.

14 Tues.

The girls are coming into town tomorrow. We put in divisions between Kevin's mattress and mine and shoot air-freshener through the loft. Then we invited Dermot up to see the Castle. Very nice, he said.

15 Wed. St John Baptist de la Salle.

I watched the Loreto girls arriving at the Town Hall. They trooped out of two buses in their red uniforms and brown nylons and the town girls gave us the nod. The rest looked on knowingly. Sheila never let on to see me. We kept our eyes aloft and when they'd gone in myself and the lads go onto the balcony.

The two films showing are *Lord Save my Soul* and *Daniel and Lions*. Sister Gabriel gave a religious talk to the girls, we clapped, the light went off and Sheila slipped up onto the balcony.

Dermot, she whispered, where are you?

Here, I said.

Where's here? I lit a match and she sat down. I could hardly get my breath. She touched my cheek with her hand and kissed the side of my neck.

Come on to the Castle, I said.

Are you mad? she said.

I've missed you something terrible, I said.

And I've missed you.

We kissed.

And you haven't been going out with anyone else?

No, I said.

You swear.

I do.

Then she went below and her brother suddenly appeared in a seat behind me. Watch yourself! he said.

18 Sat

Gave a book called *Golf for Ladies* to Josie to give to Sheila.

19 Sun. 5th After Easter.
Take half a flagon of cider in the morning. Feel fine.

20 Mon.
Since Easter have pulled wire nearly every day.

Chapter 25

23 Thur. Ascension. (Holiday of Obligation)

Knocked on the back door of Slowey's shop to get some milk in the afternoon. The red-haired girl working there said it was a Holiday of Obligation. I know that, I said, but we haven't a drop in the house. She said she'd have to get the key.

I see you on the town a lot, she said.

That's right, I agreed.

And you're always at the pictures.

I am.

We went into the shop. When she bent down to get the milk her blouse fell open wide.

What are you looking at, she asked.

Your freckles, I said.

You're some man, she laughed. She gave me my change. Is there anything else?

No.

Well then. She opened the door and laughed again. You're a funny wee cunt, she said. Would you care to go to the pictures with *me*? she asked.

I'd love to, I said.

Now what have I done? she said to herself.

So I had a bath and washed the hair and shaved and powdered Simon. I stood outside the Magnet thinking she wouldn't come. But she appeared in a blue frock and high heels.

I thought you wouldn't be here, she said.

I thought the same of you.

We passed by the lads and she bought us tickets for the balcony. She had the exact money in her coat pocket. She looked a little lonely. We were the only couple up there. When the pictures started she reached over and her hand came down on my knee.

You don't mind me doing this, do you? she said.

No, I whispered.

She ran her hand along my leg, stopped a while and looked into my eyes.

Are you sure you don't mind?

Yes, I said.

She walked her fingers along my thigh.

Do you like that?

Yes.

That's good.

She walked them to and fro, then gently rested her fingertips near the lad.

Now, what have we got here?

Oh.

Who is this fellow atall, atall? she said. She gently traced the outline through the trousers. Has it a name?

No.

And now it's moving by itself.

That happens.

So I see. It has a life of its own.

That's right, I said.

Am I hurting you?

No.

I've never done this before, she whispered.

Don't worry, I said.

I feel funny, she said.

So do I.

I thought the likes of you would be very experienced.

No, I'm not.

Is there something wrong?

What?

You've stopped breathing.

No I haven't.

And your voice sounds strange.

Does it?

You're deadly, she laughed.

A whiff of Palmolive and cherries and sweat flew by. Slowly she undid the buttons.

What age are you?

Fifteen.

I'll be arrested, she said.

She reached into my trousers.

God, she said, you're boiling.

Yes.

God, she said.

Ah.

Oh. Is this the right way?

Yes.

You won't think bad of me afterwards?

No, I said.

I'm very fond of you, she said.

And I'm fond of you.

Is that nice?

Yes.

Very nice?

Yes.

Oh, she said. Oh.

Oh, I said.

Oh dear, she said.

24 Fri. Our Lady of the Wayside.

Jesus, cannot walk today. Felt ojus bad. Could not hit a ball in the alley. Ellen tried to fix a date for tonight but I didn't go.

What happened you, said Maisie, you're in early? Did they all go off and leave you?

Then at 11 the doorbell rang.

I'll get that, I said.

No you'll not, said my mother.

She came back in and said there was no one there. When I was going to bed I found a letter under the front door.

What happened you? it said. *Are you sorry about last night? Love. Ellen.*

25 Sat.

Asked Ellen to come up to the loft. She stood a moment in the dark entry.

Come on, I whispered.

What's up there?

A mattress.

A mattress?

A mattress, I said, and a bottle of cider.

She took a few steps up the yard and stopped.

It's very dark, she said.

There's candles up there.

It's not right.

You'll like it.

I don't know.

C'mon, I said.

No, she said, backing away.

Why?

Because I'm scared.

But you weren't scared the other night.

I knew you'd say that, she said. That was different.

How was it different?

That was then. This is now.

All right, I said.

Now you're thick.

No, I'm not, I said.

You think I'm not good enough for you.

That's not true.

Well, I couldn't go up there, she said.

That's all right, I said, because I don't want to go up there either.

You don't? she said.

No.

We stepped onto the street.

Will I see you again? she asked.

Sure you will.

You don't mean it.

Yes, I do.

No, she said, you don't. I can tell.

I left her to the door of the shop.

Goodbye, I said.

Goodbye, she said, you yoke you.

26 Sun. Sunday after the Ascension.
Went with Noel to Castleblaney to see match between Cavan and Down. Very good.

27 Mon.
Day of revision.
    On the way to bed at 12 looked out window of the sitting room and could have sworn I saw Ellen standing under a streetlight at Con Smith's. But when I went to the front door there was no one.

28 Tues.
The exams have started. Done arithmetic and Irish. Got caught with a note in Arith by Father Hurley. Passed both exams. Came home and revised.

29 Wed.
Done English. Had date with Ellen but didn't go. A note arrived from Ellen under the door. *See you at King of Kings*, it said.

30 Thur.
I gathered timber and lit a fire in the Pleasure House, a small lodge on the edge of Killykeen Lake, and threw my arms around her.
    No, Ellen said.
    Ah please.
    No.
    Why?
    I want you to respect me.
    Oh but I do.
    You do in your gob.
    Honestly I do.
    I've heard that before.
    But I mean it.
    Stop that.
    I can't.
    You wouldn't do it to the Loreto girls.
    What does that mean?
    You know.

Ah, Ellen.

I know all about you, she said. Now stop or I'm going.

All right.

Just lie there, can't you.

I'm trying.

Try harder.

One minute you're mad for it, the next you're not.

That's the way it is, she said, with us ladies. Next thing I knew the mother was calling me for school.

31 Fri. The Queenship of the Blessed Virgin Mary.
Done Algebra, History and Latin. Honours in Latin, pass in History. Don't know about Algebra. Up to the Alley!

Afterwards met Andy.

You're looking for trouble, he said.

What do you mean?

Sheila's brother is after you.

For what?

There's rumours going round, he said.

JUNE

1 Sat. Vigil of Pentecost. (Fast without Abstinence)
Got the holidays. I blew a round in the Ulster Arms and slipped away on the qt to meet Ellen, who had her father's car again.

Where will we go?

Once it's some place out of town, she said.

I have a friend in Lisdarn, I say. So we drove out to the hospital and I knocked on the black doctor's door. He was delighted to see me.

I have a woman in the car, I say.

But bring her in, he says.

He took Ellen's hand and bowed.

We sat on his small bed and he sat in an armchair. He opened a bottle of gin and poured it into mugs. We drank it with water and it didn't taste like it did with tonic, but Ellen got awful giddy all the same and threw her arm round the doctor.

Isn't Dermot a funny wee cunt, she said.

He lit a large cigar and showed us a photograph of his parents and the house he grew up in. She took the album from him and studied it. She wanted to know everything. Who this was. Who that was. His sisters, his brothers, his aunts. Then she wanted to hear all about operations. He wanted to bring us for a drink in town but I said that might mean trouble. So we drove to the Park Hotel in Virginia. There was a wedding on and the guests made us join them. The black doctor was all the rage. They were all over him. The drinks flew. He danced sedately with Ellen and I danced the bride, who was from Crosserlough.

Her new husband was from up Denn, she said. She stuck her groin tight against mine and said she was for Majorca in the morning on her honeymoon.

This is an excuse me dance, said Ellen, and she stepped between us. So I danced her and the doctor danced the bride.

She drove me home at 4 in the morning and taught me to French-kiss in Main Street.

I could see the shape of my mother through the glass in the front door. I let myself in.

Do you know what time it is? she shouted.

I was at a wedding.

You were seen, she says, with tramps. Tramps! she repeated.

3 Mon. Whit Monday.
Painted all day in shop. Go up to Swellan Lake. Lovely day. Rose was there. Great fun.

4 Tues.
Painted gate.

5 Wed. Ember Day. (Fast and abstinence)
Painted outside of house. Got terrible rubs from the house painters like Tom Dale and Dinny Brennan. Look at the gimp of him, said Dinny. Then walked Sheila down by the riverside.

7 Fri. (First Friday) Ember Day.
Fixed the seat in the garden that Daddy made and gave it a coat of blue.

8 Sat. Ember Day. (Fast without abstinence)
Tramps, said Mammy when I came home. Nothing but tramps and your father hardly in his grave! One day you'll be sorry and by then it'll be too late.

9 Sun.
Brought Sheila and her friends from Balihaise out in the boat. I was rowing. We landed at Death's Point.

I don't like it here, said Sheila. I think something bad is going to happen.

10 Mon.
I asked my mother for 4/- to go to see Ollie in Virginia. She opened the till and scattered the money on the floor of the shop.

Go where you like, she said.

I thumbed to Virginia. Walked round the lake and had a lovely tea in Heary's who long ago knew my Aunt Jane. Then I walked out to Ollie's house. He lives on the side of a small mountain in a farm. There's two women there and his father. His people are nice. Myself and Ollie headed to the American Bar for a coupl'a bottles of stout and walked home the 4 mile at 1 o'clock. His mother was by the fire. She fried us up a feed. She asked me all about college, told me how Ollie was the first of hers to get the chance of an education. I felt bad knowing that soon she'd find out that Ollie would not be going back to St Pat's. The rafters groaned during the night and I heard this voice talking, maybe in my sleep, maybe in the real world, talking of some place foreign, whether Joe White was still there, was he now? I haven't heard from him in ages, thanks awfully but no, no thank you, no thank you all the same, then came names and ailments, scourges sent from heaven, rats and asses and carts and the blight, where was the bucket, where was the cursed bucket, God in his heaven where is the bucket gone? what's to be done? tap water and spring water that's what, the gutters, the eaves, the calf in the back field, the eel, the cat has a bird in his mouth, the scutter, when I hit him both eyes flew out of his head – it was dreadful out, I've told you all you need to know, who's that at the door? there was never anyone like Michael, never again Sadie, no more Sadie, no more Joe White, only the same crowd day in day out, then someone called out and the voice went silent.

11 Tues. St Barnabas, Apostle.
Started thumbing to Oldcastle but couldn't get a lift. Sat in a ditch and smoked my last fag. I was thinking of Kells, anywhere, even Navan, when Sonny Walsh came along and took me home to Cavan.

Are you finished with your wandering? asked my mother.

I went to see the Hearys, I said.

You did not.

I did.

Well there's some good left in you yet, she said. And how are all their people?

They're very good.

I'm glad to hear it.

Then myself and herself and Maisie went off to the pictures to see *Some Like It Hot*. Aunt Maisie laughed herself sick and my mother thought Tony Curtis made a lovely girl.

The thought of it, said Maisie. They'd want their marbles seen to.

We sat by the fire and had tea. I told them all about Ollie's house and Virginia.

You see, said my mother, how happy we can be when you stop at home.

12 Wed.
I rang the bell. Una's boyfriend answered it. When he saw me he nearly fainted. I was covered in blood from a fight in Bridge Street when Sheila's brother tackled me.

Stay away from my sister, he said and he head-butted me. Then his friends, including Andy, lashed in.

Sacred heart of Jesus, said my mother. What's to become of us?

What happened? asked Maisie.

I got hit.

Get the guards, Winnie, said Maisie.

No, I said.

I'd have them strung up, said Maisie and she struck her fist into her palm.

What has you on the streets, the cursed streets, lamented Mammy.

I sat in the kitchen and Una dressed my face. The new shirt was ripped. In bed I could only lie on one side.

Are the bins out? asked my mother.
  Yes, I said.
  You'll stay with me?
  I will.
  Good.

13 Thur. Corpus Christi. Holiday of Obligation.
I felt bad in the morning. I put on a pair of Una's dark glasses and stood in front of the mirror in the dining room.
  You look a sight, said my mother. Where do you think you're going?
  I'm going out.
  You're not going out looking like that.
  I have to, I said.
  Stay where you are.
  No, I said.
  I went down to Hickey's the dentist and even though it was a Holiday of Obligation he took a fitting for a new plate. Then he sent me across the road to the hospital for an X-ray. I was waiting for ages because everyone was at Mass.
  You took a bad hiding. What did you do to deserve this? asked the doctor.
  It was over a girl.
  That was a mistake, he said. Have you a headache?
  No.
  Anything else?
  My ear is ringing.
  I'm not surprised.
  Myself and Dermot stepped down Main Street. The Corpus Christi procession went by. Andy was at the corner of Bridge Street talking to Rose McNamara and Josephine Bravander.
  You were asking for it, he said, looking at me.
  When we turned into the Central Café there was a lot of sniggers from the crowd that was gathered there after Mass.
  Mama Mia, said Sean McManus.

We sat at a table by the jukebox. Sheila's brother and his friends kept pointing at me and laughing.

What happened you? asked Lila Little.

I was in a fight.

You look a dread, she said.

Then the door of the café opened and Sheila came in. The place went quiet. She looked round, saw me and, passing by her brother, came over and sat down.

I heard what happened, she said, and I'm terribly sorry.

Never mind, I said.

It's all my fault.

No, it's not.

And they said if I ever spoke to you it would all happen again. Then she left the café in tears.

15 Sat.

Ellen said she was sorry about my face, and we broke it off. Had a vodka and a Carlsberg Special in the Ulster Arms. Jack Healy was a good man, said Frank Brady, I miss him. Andy broke the handle on the door of the toilet. I was looking for a fight. Andy said they'd made him hit me. They told him I'd been saying bad things about him. So we made up. We stole bottles of McArdle's and planked them in the Castle. Then we hid a bottle of sherry in the Cock Hill. I am drunk. We went across town and out the railway lines with a bottle of whiskey. I take none. There was some argument out there. And Andy said Castro was the man, he was sorely wanted here, they killed Connolly, but we'll take the fucking six counties back tomorrow, won't we, he said, the Black North has had its day, and he started to cry on my shoulder over the United Ireland.

16 Sun. 2nd after Pentecost.

Up to the alley first thing and served 10 aces on the trot. Drank the sherry before the pictures, passed by Sheila without a word and moved Emer.

18 Tues.

I sleep in till 12 because every night I listen to *Music in the Night* till 3 o'clock. I went to Hickey's to get a fitting for my new teeth and

Sheila met me and said she wasn't afraid if I wasn't afraid. So with Eamon Smith we cycled out to Lough Oughter. We brought biscuits and lemonade. He got one perch. The midges were going mad and the water was sleepy. Then we took a boat and oared out to O'Neill's Island. We fished off the rocks, and cooked up in the castle. Ate big out there, and cycled back in and parted just outside town. She went on ahead and I followed her.

21 Fri.

I was on the road at ½ past 6 with £25 in my pocket. Got a lift with a vet who was going for a test in a Dublin hospital for suspected brucellosis. He dropped me off in O'Connell Street. Wish me luck, he said. I went looking for a suit. I had to keep from smiling in the shop so that they wouldn't know I'd lost my teeth. I bought a grey suit in Kingston's, a Burton outfit with tight trousers and wide lapels. I took the coat, they will send on the pants later. Had dinner in the Castle Hotel in Gardiner Street, and was on the road by 3. Off to Kells in the back of a Rank's flour lorry, then a Yank who'd been a pilot in Korea took me as far as Cavan. I arrived in time for the pictures. Later I headed up to the loft, and sat there a while by myself, then I paraded before the mirror for my mother in the new coat.

He has good taste, said Maisie. A surprising thing in a man.

22 Sat.

Slept late with huge dreams.

I buy a new pair of shoes, real pointy, with high heels.

I take that back about taste, said Maisie.

I wore the shoes and the new coat up Main Street. Met Sheila on the quiet outside town and we cycled out to Lough Oughter again but on the way there we took another road to the private lake which is owned by Lord Farnham. It was strange territory. There was a sign saying PRIVATE – KEEP OUT. A lane led across a small wooden bridge and on into miles of cobwebs. To the right a flooded place where there wasn't a leaf but everything rotting and some sort of lice stripping the bark. At last we came out into an opening packed on all sides with rhododendrons. The lake was flat calm. The sky filled with oceans of birds. In a wooden boathouse was a lovely blue vessel ready for launching. It had long perfect oars and oarlocks. Behind the boathouse we found a circle of huge exotic trees, the likes I'd never seen before. The leaves were blue and red.

With my first cast I took out a pike. Sheila had a fire going at the edge of the woods. I found two tin plates in the boathouse. We roasted the pike and lay down. I hung my coat on a branch and Sheila took off her bra.

23 Sun. 3rd after Pentecost.
We sat in their living room and listened to *Pick of the Pops*. Then, later, we went off to see *Inn of the Sixth Happiness*. Sheila surprises me in the dark, and I tell her I love her.

26 Wed.
Sheila is going to Dublin to see President Kennedy so I go off to Castleblaney, Ballybay and Clones with the Jewman, Harry Ross, who collects scrap and wool. He pays me 5/- a day. A few days a week Harry appears in the private dining room for his dinner of a boiled egg and brown bread. He has powerful glasses that look like the bottoms of stout bottles. His eyebrows are huge, dark and bushy.

He has been coming to the Briefne for years and so he has gained access to the inner sanctum. He runs a rambling shed down the Market yard, where he collects lead, iron and sheep's wool. That scrap, Maisie says, has put his three children through university in Dublin, where Harry returns to his home every weekend. Harry says little. He never discusses his family. We call on tinkers and farmers and garages throughout Monaghan and fill the small lorry with batteries, sheets of tin and some wool.

Are you not shamed to be at this work? he asked me.

No, I said, I like it.

27 Thur. Our Lady of Constant Help.
The shed was heaving with wool. Harry hurled huge bales overhead with a wheeze and I moved batteries and lay lengths of iron one on top of the other. He began breaking down an engine with a mallet and I set baths into each other. We broke up iron beds, hammered lead into balls and stopped to smoke.

Monty Montgomery, the man who has the next shed along, looked in.

I see, he said, that you've an apprentice.

That's right, said Harry.

After dinner we sat into the wagon and took off for Meath County where Harry says the best wool is. We pulled into a farmhouse where shearing was still going on, and sat in the kitchen drinking tea till the men were finished. Harry was called out to inspect the wool.

Eventually the deal was struck and we loaded up the pick-up. The whole family helped us. Harry hurled the bales to me and I packed them up. It was good work.

28 Fri.

We drove off to see the gypsies that were parked outside Oldcastle. The McDonaghs sat on the steps of the caravan and watched Harry as he picked through the gas cookers and lead from roofs and engine parts and agricultural machinery and old ranges, all the time mumbling to himself.

Look, Mr Ross.

I see it.

It's worth five shillings be itself.

It's worth three.

Ha-ha.

Take it or leave it.

I'll take four and six.

No.

Four.

No.

Ah Jasus, sir.

Three and six it is.

I have the wife here, and the childer to feed.

You heard me, James.

You and me, Mr Ross, we go back.

I know that.

We've been dealing together for years, sir.

Dermot, said Harry, get in the van, we're going.

We climbed into the van. The gypsy man came over to my window.

Can you not speak to him, son, for the love of God?

No, I can't, I said.

He went round to the driver's window. Harry started up the engine.

There are other dealers I can sell to.

Well, do that.

Three and ninepence, Mr Ross, God bless you, said James McDonagh. We loaded up and headed to Kells and into the back kitchen of a small restaurant in the town. Out came his egg and brown bread, with boiling bacon and cabbage for me. We had a cigarette. We unloaded in Cavan. Stiff and tired we parted ways on Main Street. He shuffled off to the Farnham Hotel. I went back and told mother of all the places we'd been.

29 Sat. SS Peter and Paul, Apostles.

The dentist fits in my new teeth. They seem too big for my mouth, but still and all I put my new suit on because the trousers arrived yesterday. So I head up Main Street in the shoes.

You look lovely, said Sheila, as she passed me.

When I was walking home that night some of the older fuckers shouted, *There's a smell of Healy the pavee. Jew lover! Are you with the pavees now, Healy? Healy for scrap!* I just walked on pretending I didn't hear them. It was all because of Harry Ross. Dreamt tonight that my teeth were full of meat and I couldn't spit it out.

30 Sun.

Sheila came up to the alley to watch me play. Doc Galligan was there with Seamus Ennis the famous piper, long in the leg, famished looking, thin-shouldered and nervous, peering over the wall and making comments. I grazed my knuckles on the side wall by showing off and trying to get a ball I couldn't reach. The piper lifted a baby Power's to his head and said he was calling it a day. The Doc and he drove off in a blue Volks.

The soldiers were fierce quiet. And all the stray dogs that followed the soldiers were quiet.

Sheila and myself then went out to Killykeen Lake on our bikes and it began to rain. It rained and rained. We got drenched on the way

184

home. It was warm rain. Again we parted on the outskirts of town. When I was passing the Ulster Arms I heard the pipes coming from the bar onto Main Street. When I looked in there was Seamus Ennis playing the uileann pipes and Garret Brown, the Guinness heir, was in a corner with Seamus White, the dancing teacher. Frank was behind the bar in his element and the Doc was dancing with a lady singer from Gowna. She danced prim with her arms by her side while he was using tiny little steps and twisting his shoes and slapping his thighs.

When the tune stopped, the Doc bought me a beer and told a conundrum.

Where, he asked me, did Irish music come from?

I said I didn't know.

Well, this man was above in the bed dying. He was on his last breath, and he said to the son, Son, he said, bring me up a glass of rum. So the son did. He filled out a tot of dark into a glass and fed him slowly with a spoon till the glass was gone. *Da*, said the son. *Da*, said the son again. *Did-the-rum-do-Da, did-the-rum-do-day!* And that's how music started.

Do you mind, said Seamus Ennis to me, as he scrutinized my face, if I ask you something?

No, I said.

Did I see you somewhere before?

JULY

1 Mon. The Most Precious Blood.

Coming on down the Navan road a Mercedes suddenly shot out of a by-way and Harry had to jam on the brakes. We spun across to the verge. He parked and climbed down angrily.

Did you not see us? he shouted to the driver of the car.

We are sorry of course, said the German.

What do you mean sorry – you could have killed us all.

I was not seeing you.

Suddenly, Harry banged the roof of the car. The driver covered his head and Harry began raving aloud in another language. He circled the front of the Mercedes. He kicked its front wheel and banged on the bonnet.

Stop please, said the driver and he began to raise his window.

Get out of this country, roared Harry. Get out!

The driver reversed, pulled round the back of the lorry and took off with Harry racing behind him. He stood shouting in the middle of the road in his long white coat till the Mercedes had gone from sight.

At last he got back in beside me and cradled the driving wheel.

Did you see that? he said.

Yes, I said.

I could feel his heart pounding. His sallow face was very pale. It was the last words he said that day. We drove home in silence. He gave me 5 shillings and I got washed and shaved and powdered Simon and went to a party in Doli's. Great feed. I was asked in a quiz who my favourite male singers were, so I said Joe Brown, Ray Charles, Elvis Presley, Del Shannon, Gene Pitney and Mario Lanza. My favourite female singers were Helen Shapiro, Shirley Bassey, Connie Francis and Brenda Lee. In instrumental groups I picked The Shadows, Kenny Ball and his Jazzmen, Mr Acker Bilk, The Tornadoes and Joey Dee and the Starlights. Then went off to meet Sheila on Keadue Lane. In the morning I leave for Rannafast *Gaeltacht.*

Write to me, she said.

I will.

I know, she said, that you're not to be trusted.

We said goodbye.

Ich liebe dich, Sheila wrote into my diary and signed her name with five X's. I went home and packed my bag for tomorrow. Felt lonely. Mammy ironed three shirts and gave me £6. I listened to Luxembourg till it closed down.

Chapter 26

2 Tues. The Visitation of B. V. M.

The bus stops in Donegal town and we have a few bottles of Harp. Then when we go on through the mountains we're dying for a piss. Tried to pee into a bottle but couldn't and it got very painful. Eventually I told the bus driver there was a man sick in the back. He pulled in and six of us jumped out. We went behind a sandbank for a piss. It was some relief. But then the bus moved on a fraction and we all came into view with the lads out dribbling away. The women cheered at the sight and the driver blew the horn. And then when we arrived in Rannafast there was no house for us.

Na labhair Bearla, a man said.

We were sitting starving on the side of the road till ½ past 9. Then a woman arrived and said *Rachamid go Teach Eamon. Na Labhair Bearla*, she said. We got a boiled egg apiece and two pan slices, and that was that. Myself and Peter and Paul share a room with two Holy Boys. No one slept with the hunger.

3 Wed.

Reading of the Rules today. *Na labhair Bearla*. Do not speak English. *Labahir as Gaelige*. Speak in Irish.

Then we were brought to the hall where we inspected the women, and were given a free afternoon. The food is terrible in the house. There's blue mould in the bin. The plastic potatoes are piped onto the plate. And the gravy would turn your stomach. Then tonight we went to a *ceili*. A local band played and a man barked out the jigs *as Gaelige*. No remarkable women. I'd say, said Pete, that they're all mad to go. The Holy Boys stood by the wall and danced with their heads down and their eyes on their feet. Pete and me had another bad night in the bed with the hunger. Then the *fear-an-ti* (the man of the house) started to snore through the thin wall so we lay there and looked at the ceiling and whispered.

4 Thur.

An bhful einne anseo as Cabhan? the storyteller asked. Is there anyone here from Cavan?

Myself and Pete put up our hands.

He studied us and winked and laughed.

Dia dhuit, he said. It won't be long now.

Won't be long till what? asked Pete.

The storyteller tapped his nose and told us a tale in Irish.

There was this man, a man from Gweedore who wore women's clothes till he was ten. When he was five the father said to the mother that lad should be in trousers, it's not right to see him going about the country in a dress.

Wait till he earns it, she said, and she put the frock back on her son.

When the son was seven the father said, Now Bridie, he said, now Bridie, he said, let him into his trousers.

Not yet, she said, not till he's earned it, and she put him back in his dress.

When he was nine and had his muscles the father said, Now Bridie, now he's ripe for the trousers.

Not yet, said the mother, and she combed out her son's long curls that fell like snow to his waist.

So the father feeling low went to the priest. But the priest wasn't at home. Oh no. He went to the schoolmaster but he was on holidays. Oh yes. At last he went to the doctor. Good day, Doctor Timothy Brown, he said, a thousand blessings. Good day to you, Michael Joe, said the doctor. My wife, he told Doctor Tim, thinks her son is a girl. Is that so, said Doctor Tim. It is, the father said. It has me *máinte*. Feeble-minded.

And he went on. When the rest are kicking football he's by the fire mending socks and a puss on him.

Ho-ho, said Doctor Tim.

She has him, said Michael Joe, in a dress each hour of the living day.

Since when?

Since the cratur I'm sad to say was a bairn.

He has his equipment, I take it? asked Doctor Tim.

He has indeed, said the father. And the father looked astray. So what's to be done?

What you'll do is this – and here the storyteller suddenly stopped. We'll hear the rest of it tomorrow, he said, and he put his cap on his head.

5 Fri. First Friday.
Where was I? the storyteller asked in Irish.

What you'll do is this, said Pete.

That's right, he said. It's good you remembered or I could have gone off on another tack. He took off his cap and beat his knee a blow and began.

What you'll do is this, said Doctor Tim. Take the nail varnish of the toes of a woman who is over sixty, crack it up in your fist and tip the scales and the leavings into the bellybutton of your good wife while she's sleeping.

Can I do that? asked Michael.

Of course you can, said Doctor Tim.

I can, I suppose, said Michael Joe.

Next get a glass brimful of spring water from Tobar Brid and have her wash her fangs in it when she wakes. You have that?

I have.

Next admonish her to prayer. Let the prayer be of your own choosing. Then put the lad in wellingtons and walk north.

North, your honour? asked the puzzled father.

North, said Doctor Tim.

Right, said the father.

Do this, said Doctor Tim, then come back to me.

So the father set off round the parish of Gweedore looking for a woman over sixty with varnish on her toes. He inspected the feet of the women at Sunday Mass. He went on his hunkers in the shop. He stood like a thrush in the post office. But no woman over sixty with varnish on her toes could he find. A year went by. He was giving up. Then the visitors came. And one day a strange white-haired woman pulled up in a smart car at the hotel and as she went up the steps in her sandals Michael Joe caught the hint of red varnish. Well the woman sat down in the lounge for a cup of tea and a chicken sandwich and the father came over on his tippytoes.

Grand day, said Michael Joe.

The woman nodded and he went down on his knees.

What are you doing? said the scandalized woman – and the storyteller stopped and put on his cap and went out through the door. Then he looked back.

How are the Cavan men today? he asked.

Taimid go mait, I said. We are fine.

Not for long, he said and he winked. Wait till Sunday week, he said.

Then I wrote a letter home to Mammy. There's a storyteller here, I wrote, that's off his head.

6 Sat.

I dropped the letter in at Sharkey's post office and walked to school with a girl called Phyllis. She said one of the girls in her house had been proposed to by a fellow from ours. The master kept looking out the window and glancing at his watch. Speak among yourselves, he said, *as Gaelige.* We saw the storyteller come up the path looking very sorrowful. The master indicated with his finger that Peadar Rua should come on in, but Peadar put a hand on the gate, stopped to spit, looked pale then turned away.

We'll soon see about that, said the master.

He went outside.

Peadar, he shouted, Peadar Rua, come back here! But the story-teller said, I have the gawks and continued down the road and never looked back, and the master stood around a while not knowing what to do and that's how we went swimming in Poll an tSnamh. Phyllis from Ardee, who was an inch taller than me, put her towel down beside us. She had a big sweeping navy dress on, a buckle on her waist and black hair kicked out on her shoulders. I had on a pair of jeans, a check shirt and a sweater knotted at the waist. She had thin flat pointed shoes and I had a pair of gutees laced to the shin.

We went together to the *ceili* that night. The local men home from Scotland ambled by in a group and stood in blue suits with whiskey in their glasses at the lemonade bar. They'd shout *as Gaelige* when one of them would set off to dance the older girls. They pelted the floor. You were not let sit down. You had to dance. I left Phyllis home. They were tall kisses. I made up names for the stars. She took off her shoes on the strand. We passed a pub and the storyteller came out the door and started shouting back in English – Anytime, anyday, whenever you like – and someone came out and put an arm round his shoulder.

It's all right Peadar, never mind them, he said, and they went off down the road.

The Holy Boys were listening to a wireless in the room. We shared a chicken, Cidona and biscuits and listened to the *Top Twenty*. The *bean-an-ti* (woman of the house) bangs on the wall and shouts *Ciunas! Ciunas!* (Quiet!)

The *fear-an-ti* wakes from his snoring.

What's wrong now? he shouts.

We opened the window and had a smoke and listened to the seabirds.

7 Sun. 5th after Pentecost.

Stood under a rock on Tra Mor with Phyllis as a storm blew over. Then we stepped into the sea and walked out at low tide to the island. Collected a few crabs. Got fierce wet. That night threw the crabs among the women at the *ceili*. Great laugh. Well fixed with Phyllis.

11 Thur. B. Oliver Plunkett.

Where was I? asked the storyteller.

What are you doing? said the scandalized woman, Pete told him.

That's right, What are you doing, said the scandalized woman, get up out of that this very instant, and have manners.

I'd be grateful, said Michael Joe, if you'd part with some of your varnish.

Oh, said the astounded woman, and she looked at her toes. Why didn't you say so in the first place?

I don't know.

Well, I don't mind, she said.

So Michael Joe peeled a few chippings of varnish off her toes with a small penknife, tossed them carefully into a handkerchief and thanked her most profusely.

Anytime, said the woman.

He went the road for home a happy man at last. The gorse was burning and the mother was putting the lad to bed in his petticoat.

That's a terrible night, Michael Joe said.

Do you think so?

I do. We should go to bed.

Not yet, said the mother.

She put her feet up by the fire. He turned on the radio, then turned it off. He ate a slice of bread and marge.

Will we go now? he asked.

Hold your horses, she said, not yet. It's too early.

He went out to check the ass. He kicked a sod across the street. He emptied his pockets onto the draining board.

How about now? he asked.

What's wrong with you, she said, it's only gone ten.

I'm tired, he said after a bit.

Well you go on ahead, Bridie declared, and I'll follow you up after a while.

And that's what he did. He landed in the bed anyway, put his handkerchief under his pillow and lay waiting. The next thing it was the following day. He looked over and there she was sleeping. So very gently he drew back the bed clothes and lifted her slip over her bare stomach, reached in under his pillow and got the handkerchief. Then very quietly he tipped the shavings of the varnish into her bellybutton.

He lay back and thought, That's it. I've done well there. Then he suddenly remembered the glass brimful of spring water. He jumped up to run to Tobar Brid when the woman woke and – *Sin e*, said the storyteller, that's it. And he put on his cap and left. There was an argument on the doorstep between him and the Master.

Fuck off yourself, said Peadar Rua and that was the last we ever saw of him at the school.

6 Sat.

Went swimming. Lost my togs, found a local girl called Catherine O'Donnell and Skinny took her shoe. We played cards. Started with Old Maid, moved on to 25, then into a game of poker. I bluffed and lost 5/- to Catherine. She can box the cards like a pro. And renege like hell. I walked up Rannafast to her house. We went by the sea. It smelt like jelly that had just been boiled. Oh Catherine is a lovely bit. Very sexy. I have it bad. You can smoke fags here whenever you like.

7 Sun. 5th after Pentecost.
Met Catherine under the rock. A woman threw her arm round Peter.
He kept looking at me. We all got very sexy there, then we went off to
play cards.

12 Fri.
Went down to the Poll an tSnamh. The boys and girls from Annagry
were swimming. We made our way behind the top of the hill to watch
the girls dressing. We crawled over the dune and looked. They didn't
see us. Two of them had nothing on under their towels and they were
trying to pull the towels off each other. I began shaking and Pete
started sneezing.

Then a priest saw us. He broke into a run and started roaring.

Is Cuma, is cuma, he shouted to Pete. Come here you! What do you
think you're doing?

We said we were playing cowboys.

And you weren't looking at the girls? he asked.

What girls? asked Pete.

He asked for the name of the house we were in then marched us off the
dunes. Everyone saw us. We were shamed. We went back up the strand.

And home. When we got there the priest was waiting. The *bean-
an-ti* turned blue.

Nothing like that has ever happened here before, she screeched.
These ones have disgraced us, she said to the *fear-an-ti*.

You've let down this house, she said, slamming the door behind us.

Looking at the girls in their skin, sniggered Catherine at the *ceili*
that night. Have you nothing better to do?

14 Sun. 6th after Pentecost.
Went to Siopa Cassai to listen to the match on the wireless between
Cavan and Donegal. At half-time the storyteller looked in and said,
You couldn't kick shite.

Cavan lost.

15 Mon.
Did not go dancing. Stayed home, but the *bean-an-ti* caught us. She
marched us to the *ceili*.

19 Fri. St Vincent de Paul.

Fixed a date for the middle of the night with Catherine. Slipped down the drain pipe and away. It was lashing. I stood by the rock and then heard a dog barking. I crawled back up over the dunes and hid. Someone came by in a rainproof coat and stood at the water's edge. Whoever it was cut a fearful figure. They looked round them a couple of times. I didn't know whether to call out her name. Then a dog came out of the darkness. I slid away, and went home by the road, avoiding cars. I climbed back up but the window was closed.

I tapped on the pane.

Nothing. Then the ladder broke. The Holy Boys opened the window.

Are you all right? they said.

I got in anyway and we had apple tart and biscuits the Holy Boys had raided from the pantry.

24 Wed.

Went off to the *Ceili Mor*. The boys made a big circle round the women during singing and we all made our way up the hall. The *Runai* gives off and the *Uachtarain*. The Donegals from Scotland got out together to do a rowdy set.

We danced till 10 and photographs were taken. After the *Ceili Mor* we sat looking out to sea and talking. About where we were from and what we'd do. And giving over addresses. People were arranging to meet there again the following summer. And then we went home. We threw our wet clothes onto the Holy Boys and woke them up. Great laugh. Stole out onto the landing and tied Charlie's bedroom door to the handle of the bathroom.

26 Fri. St Anne, Mother of Our Lady.

Woke first thing to hear Charlie banging on his door. Fierce cant. Left Rannafast at 2 o'clock on the buses. Said goodbye to all the crew in Cavan town, and met Dermot.

And he said: Sheila is going out with someone else these days.

Is that so? I said.

I just thought you'd like to know.

I stepped up on the weigh scale at Burke's and saw I'd lost a half a stone. Rang the bell and my mother, in her blue housecoat, answered the door.

You're welcome, she said. Say something in Irish for me.

Nil aon tintain mar do thintain fein, I said.

Is it something nice? she asked.

It is.

Good, so tell me what does it mean.

There's no fireside like your own fireside, I said.

Oh if only it was true for you, she said.

So I told them all that had happened in Rannafast. When I came to the storyteller my mother looked aghast.

Nail varnish, she said, where in heaven's name did the cur get that?

I don't know.

That's your Irish for you now, Winnie, said Maisie and she chuckled. We don't know the half of it.

But nail varnish, repeated my mother, nail varnish of all things. And tell me this, why did he not finish the story?

Maybe, said I, there's no ending.

She gave me a sharp look. You cur, she said, you made it up.

I did, I said, laughing.

Chapter 27

27 Sat.

When I come in to the Central my hands start to shake. Sheila is at a table with some girls. She looks straight at me. I walk by her in the same way she'd walk by me and play a record, a record I don't know though I spent time over it as if I did, then sit at a table with my back to her. Of all things – Frank Sinatra. This goes on a long time. I feel a gom. I can hear them between tunes laughing and talking.

I don't know what to do and I don't know how long I can keep this up then suddenly I feel her behind me.

I turn. She stands there at my side with her arms behind her back.

So who did you go with in *Ran-na-Feirste*? she asks.

No one, I say.

That's not what I heard.

Well, you heard wrong.

Oh yeh?

Yeh, I say, and you – you went out with Jim.

She measures me. Who told you that?

Never mind.

Well I wouldn't have done that if you'd been faithful.

But I was faithful.

Blah!

Suddenly she leans in over the table, lifts a pepper pot and shakes it into my face.

What the fuck, I say.

Don't you sit all high and mighty with your back to me, she says. I start sneezing. She marches out the door followed by the girls. Adel Murphy who works behind the counter goes by laughing. My eyes water. A few minutes later Sheila is back, alone.

I'm sorry for going out with Jim, she says, sitting down.

OK, I said.

And you, did you go with anyone in Donegal?

Not at all, I said.

Are you sure?

I am.

I heard you did.

Don't believe it, I said.

I don't know what to believe. I get tired thinking about it. All I know is that I'm stuck with you, for my sins.

It could be worse, I say laughing and hoping she'd laugh too.

She smiles at least.

Are you still going to marry me? she asks.

Yes, I say.

Sun 28.

Crossed over the fence from the Royal School into Breifne Park and got in for nothing to the pitch to see the match between Donegal and Down. Lift money and head to the Congo for a few stout, then on to the pictures where I've a date with Sheila. But she doesn't come.

At half-time I get Mary to ring Sheila's house. Mary hands the phone on to me.

What's wrong? I demand.

There's no use in being cross with me, Sheila says.

I waited on you.

They won't let me out.

Oh.

You see, she says, this is how things are with me because of going out with you.

Will you be at the dance?

I don't know. Look I have to go now. Someone is coming.

OK.

So I sat with Mary at the pictures, then went off to the dance in the Sports Centre. But Sheila doesn't appear. So I moved Rose Reilly and slept with Dermot, who tells me again that Jim and Sheila are still going out together.

30 Tues.

Today couldn't get rid of the feeling that something was wrong. I paced the town. The street did not know me. The Breifne did not feel like home. I tried to stop the feeling but it got worse – so I went up to the bed and lay in it, falling in and out of sleep and each time waking with a worse sin on my mind, not sins I could place but some sort of dark insanity that makes people fail to know you – they think, who's that fucker coming? – thoughts raced past then revisited but made no sense, none at all, twitchings, not that I could remember anyway. So I went to the pictures alone. Rose sat down beside me.

Do you mind? she asks.

Not at all, I say.

Sheila was sitting two rows in front of me with her father, the bank manager. I watched her head tilt against the screen. One of the twins shouted for silence. When the lights came on at the end she turned in the aisle and looked at me. Her father prodded her forward. They go by like eternity.

Isn't that your girlfriend? asked Rose.

She used to be, I said.

The look she gave me! said Rose.

31 Wed. St Ignatius Loyola.
Today told Sheila that Rose only happened to be sitting next to me last night at the pictures.

And you didn't go with her?

No.

You swear?

I do.

We went up to the Castle in the shed with Noel's wireless, fags and cider. We said we'd start all over from the beginning again. Fuck the brother, I said. Listened to Radio Luxembourg and sang. Then the galvanize began thundering. It was Andy and the boys throwing spuds and stones onto the loft. After a while they stopped.

She told me her family wanted her to have nothing to do with me.

Will you run away with me? I asked.

When? she asked.

Tomorrow night, I said.

Tomorrow night?

Yeh.

Are you sure?

Yes.

Where are we going?

I don't know.

AUGUST

1 Thur.

I packed a bag and dropped onto the kitchen roof round 3, then went by Provider's onto Main Street. Stood in Fox's shoe shop opposite the bank and looked up at her room. It was in darkness. Half 3 came and went. Then maybe round 4 the light went on in the second storey for a second. I stood well in. I thought I saw her head, as I'd seen it before, tilted. The light went off. I waited, but the front door didn't open. So I started to bark like a dog. Mrs Reilly from next door looked out her window astounded.

I gave up and went home, put everything back in the drawers and lay in the bed seeing behind my closed eyelids the bank in the light of the streetlamp. It seemed to be forty storeys high.

2 Fri. St Alphonsus Ligouri. (First Friday)

What happened you last night? I asked Sheila.

You mean you came?

Yes, I did, I said bitterly.

I didn't think you would.

Why?

You're always saying these things.

Well, I meant it.

And where would we go?

Anywhere, I said. She tucked her arm in mine. Did you not hear me barking? I asked.

Barking? she said, and she started to laugh.

Yes, barking, I said serious-like. Did you?

No, Dermot, I didn't hear you barking.

All right, I said, that's enough.

6 Tues. The Transfiguration.

Her family are at a do in Dublin so myself and Sheila go to see *Gone with the Wind*. We had ice-cream cones and a great long court during the Civil War, then we strolled over the Gallows Hill. The sky was night-blue. The gypsies sitting around a camp fire on the Fair Green called out to us through the smoke, wondering who we were.

We talked about running away again.

I don't know, she said. Have you any money?

Not a hate. A few bob maybe. But there'd be no problem getting a job.

Don't you want to finish college?

No.

How can you be so sure? She went on ahead of me, stopped and seemed to be by herself. I feel lonely thinking about it, she said. You'll have to give me time to think.

The best thing to do, I said, is not to think at all.

It's easy for you to talk like that.

What do you mean?

You don't seem to care.

I care about you.

Do you know what I think – I think you're out of your head.

We could be in England this time tomorrow night.

Oh God, she said, don't rush me.

We climbed down into the nun's meadow. A snipe skirted the lake. A mist travelled over from the green lake.

I'll race you to that fence, she said.

You want to race?

Yes, I do, she said and she took off.

7 Wed. St Cajetan.

I threw myself on the floor of my mother's bedroom and said I didn't want to go back to college.

And what do you want to do?

I want to be a writer.

Will you get up out of that, she said, and don't be making a show of yourself.

She went back to *Woman's Own*. I went back to Luxembourg.

8 Thur. St John M. Vianney.

After getting home from Trim with Harry, I hitched out to Annagh Lake for a swim to clear the wool oil off my skin. I swam out beyond the reeds, turned around, did a few strokes and went for bottom but there was nothing there. Next thing I was underwater trying to yell. I went straight down thrashing. And still there was no bottom. The light crashed overhead and turned black. Then I touched something with my hand. It was Pat Gaffey swimming past underwater. I grabbed his togs. He pulled away, taking me with him. When we surfaced he took off his goggles and shook his head.

That's not funny, he said.

I was drowning, I said.

He undid my arms from round his waist and swam away. He thought I'd just been playing. The rest were there swimming as usual. No one had seen what had happened. I tiptoed in, searching ahead for ground before I put my foot down. This shaking went through me so I sat in the shallows in my togs till I got back to myself. I tried to undress but couldn't get my togs down, so I pulled my trousers over them and hitched home. The house felt stone cold. There was no one in the Breifne, the women had gone walking round the Triangle, the girls had gone to the country for the half-day, I was back to high D, it was all made up again, it was making up time again, the radio was playing by itself, and in the kitchen all I heard was this constant whispering, and loud noises in my eardrums that I'd heard some-where before but couldn't place, buffetings and asides, even in the garden where I sat on the blue seat my father made under the ivy there was the same dangerous overlapping, the same uncertainty, too many I persons, the hatred-voice, and I ran back through the house and out to the front door as if I was being chased, and stood under the Breifne canopies looking up Main Street, then it passed, and I went in.

10 Sat. St Laurence.

I hung around the town waiting for Sheila to appear, but there was no sign of her so eventually myself and Dermot and Mac head off for a drink in Stick Donoghue's. I have 13/-. We're drinking Smithwick's Number 1. We meet men from Kilnaleck and women from Killeshandra. I get very drunk. Then meet one of Sheila's brother's crowd on the street.

Why the fuck did yous gang up on me? I say.

Fuck off, Healy, he says.

I'll break your face, I said, you cunt.

We made a run at each other. I bled his mouth and he kicked me between the legs, then he spat blood into my face. He tore the shirt off me. The others pulled us apart and then the lads took me to the Ulster Arms and washed me down in the toilet, and Dermot brought me a shirt from his house. I paid for a feed in McGinty's but couldn't eat it. Started shouting in the street. Up the Half Acre, I roared, and all that ever sailed in her. The mother met me at the door.

You're drunk, she said.

I'm not.

Tomorrow, she says, you get a Pioneer pin. Do you hear me?

I hear you.

God in heaven, she said, what's to become of me? And she started to cry.

I'm sorry Mother, I said. I'm sorry.

We knelt in the dining room and said the rosary. Opened the window and vomited into the yard. When I went to bed I saw the toe of his boot had missed my balls by a fraction.

11 Sun. 10th after Pentecost.

Listened to *Pick of the Pops* with Sheila, she lay with her head in my lap.

You know what I could do?

What.

I could go ahead of us and get a job. Then you could come and join me. How about that?

OK, she said. If that's what you want.

I love Sheila. Let them do what they like whoever they are.

12 Mon.

Up at break of dawn and on the road with Harry Ross to Athlone, where we dropped off over 50 bales. Ate a dinner of leg-a-lamb looking down on the river Shannon.

16 Fri. St Joachim, Father of Our Lady.
In the Central Café I tell Sheila how much she hurt me when she went off with someone else. Got a load off my chest and feel in Great Humour. Went to the pictures and did not expect her to come, but she does. Love her.

What's going on over there? said George O'Rourke, and he shone his torch on us.

18 Sun. 11th after Pentecost.
Was in the Central with Uncle Seamus's kids. Talking to Sheila and lift letter out of her cardigan pocket without her seeing me. Find out from it when I read it at home that she went with a fellow from Ardee when I was in Rannafast. Ar – *fucking* – dee, no less. Oh he wants to meet her again somewhere down the line. I get mad. Very mad. Ar – *fucking* – dee. I read the letter over and over till it sickened me.

Then the bell rang and Sheila's at the door.

Are you coming to the hop in the Sports Centre? she says.

So I gave her the letter. She touched her cardigan pocket, glanced at the sheet of paper and looked at me.

Dermot, she said.

I said nothing. We start off up Main Street. She cries her head off.

Dermot, she said again, say something. Give off to me but don't stay quiet.

We keep going.

But you're no better than me, she says, can't you see that? You're no better than me.

At the door of the Centre we parted. She stands underneath the stage, her eyes running. The lads have *poitín* in the jacks. Mal Elliot is half shot and Dermot is half cut. The drink goes to my head and so I only dance Sheila a couple of times. She holds me closer than ever before.

Are you still mad?

No.

We dance to Buddy Holly.

I'm going on, I said, in the next few days.

You're running away?

Yes.

203

For ever?

Yes.

Oh.

You can come after me if you want to.

Do you mean it? she asks.

I do, I say.

On the way home I rang Ollie and he told me to come on ahead to his brother's pub in Parnell Street and we'd take it from there.

20 Tues. St Bernard.

I have a job in Dublin starting tomorrow, I told Mammy.

Have you?

In Ollie's pub, I said.

If you want to go I can't stop you.

It'll only be for a few days.

Yes, she said. I suppose you want some money.

No, I said, I've saved what Harry gave me.

There's a stain on those trousers of yours. Give them to me.

So I gave her my trousers and she soaked the stain.

They'll be ready for you in the morning, she said. We went from the bath to the line and hung out the washing.

That night she tapped on my bedroom door.

So you're for the big city?

Yes.

Well, I've set the clock.

Thank you.

Come back to us in one piece, she said. And don't make a spectacle of yourself.

I won't, I said.

She put the clock on the floor, one of those round clocks whose hands shine in the dark.

22 Thur. The Immaculate Heart of Mary.

Was on the road at 7. In the Parnell bar at 11.30. Ollie was working as a waiter in a white jacket, bow tie and white socks.

Will I start now? I asked Ollie.

Go off and enjoy yourself, said his brother.

So I headed off up O'Connell Street and went to see *55 Days at Peking*, then back to Ollie, who got the afternoon off. We went for a few pints of Dublin Guinness after the happy hour in a pub down Capel Street, then he went back to work and I go to see Elvis in *It Happened at the World Fair*. I forgot I was in Dublin till I walked down the warm carpeted corridor and saw the usherettes with their spry caps and dark nylons, and heard the newspapers boys yelling *Herald! Herald!* on the crowded street. Twilight fell from some unreal place. Pigeons flew through the dark air.

There was a dwarf photographer asking to take your picture outside the Metropole, the flash from his box camera lit up a girl with her hand to her cheek, he peeled her off a ticket and swinging round asked to take mine. I said I hadn't a hate. Well what are you doing here? he said, and he went straight by me. Walked round by Moore Street to see the market women putting away their vegetables and fruit for the night. They were in great humour. An ambulance raced round Parnell Square. I thought I could go on for ever. The pub was full and Danny Doyle was singing ballads. I helped clean up. We sat by the bar till 1 with the four waitresses, who smoked and studied the ceiling.

So you're the fellow goes to college with Ollie, said Mick, his brother.

I am, I said.

And I hear you're looking for work.

If there's anything going.

Are you expensive to hire? he asked and started laughing. The waitresses went home and all the waiters and barmen slept in the one room in three beds talking of Cavan.

23 Fri.

When do I start? I asked Mick.

We'll see, he said. Don't be in such a hurry. Does your mother know where you are?

Yes, she does.

Are you sure?

Yes.

Take a daunder, then we'll see.

So I went off round the city in the morning – Capel Street, Parnell Street, Moore Street, down Abbey Street, then along the Liffey and back.

Do you want me now? I asked Mick.

Not yet, he said.

So I made a friend of Johnny, a barman with a white face who'd slept in the bed beside me the night before, and I asked him for his jumper. We made dinner in the small kitchen – pork chops and beans, then I went down to the bar in Johnny's jumper.

Well? I said to Mick.

Don't worry, he said.

So I headed off again and at last after taking many wrong turnings I found Gerry Moore, another Cavanman, who was working in a bar down at the Four Courts. He put up a round. I told him I had a job starting but I didn't know when, then I had a Wimpy hamburger. It tasted great.

What's the story? I asked Mick.

Ah, he said, take the night off – here's an advance.

He gave me 10 shillings. This time I went further than I had before. I got dressed in my suit and found myself in Stephen's Green. Rang Sheila from a phone box outside the Shelbourne Hotel.

Is that you? she asked.

It is, I said.

And where are you now?

Dublin, I said. Are you coming?

There was a long silence. I don't know, she eventually replied.

Why don't you know?

Because.

So what do I do?

Come back, she said. Just come back.

I went round the Green twice but couldn't find the way home till a man pointed me down Grafton Street. At last I found myself outside the National Ballroom in Parnell Square. I told the man at the door I was nineteen.

Go on, he said.

Honestly, I said.

Go on, he said, opening the door.

No one would dance with me. The Dixie Showband, dressed as women, were playing a bunch of melodies. I met a young thing in the mineral bar. She was a nurse in Stevens and took me back to her flat in Phibsborough. There was a lot of other women there, with eyebrows pencilled painfully on, eating tuna fish and discussing menfolk in the kitchen.

So you scored, said one to Mairlish. They looked at me. You've been baby-snatching.

We sat outside on the stairs talking. She asked me what did I do and I told her I was going on to be an architect.

Where? she asked me.

I couldn't think.

I haven't started yet, I said.

Do you always tell lies?

Yes, I said, it was what my father taught me – always tell lies.

I got lost on the way home and ended up in a fruit and vegetable market. It was the middle of the night and all the lights were on. Lorries of apples and spuds were being unloaded. A pub was open. I asked my way home. I rang the bell of Parnell House and after a long time Mick answered it.

I thought you were the cops, he said.

27 Sat. St Bartholomew, Apostle.

Are you right?

Right, Mick, I said.

It was 8 in the morning. Down we went to clean up after the night before. I hoovered out the lounge, washed glasses and emptied ashtrays. Then, just before the doors opened at 10.30, Johnny tried me out in his waiter's jacket and it fitted. It was his day off. He handed me a tray.

Do you know how to use one of those?

A' course I do.

Let's have you then.

He put three pint glasses and an empty Babycham bottle on the tray and I lifted it up.

No, he said, don't hold it by the edges, balance it on your fingertips. Like this, he said.

The first man through the door was a policeman. After him, a man with a wild head of hair shuffled by in a long tweed coat. He untied his shoe and knocked it off a table. The two men sat at opposite ends of the long bar. I stood by the door, the tray in my hand, the hair flattened back with Brylcreem and a shake in the knee.

The silence went on. I took the three glasses and bottle from the bar onto the tray, and moved quietly down the long lounge, one foot at a time, turned, and trying to keep the tray steady served an empty table at the rear, waited a second then lifted the glasses and bottle and returned with a firm step up the lounge, and left the order back to the counter and stood by the door.

I have the dry gawks, said the policeman to no one in particular.

I served the empty table again, returned, took up my former position, and the red-haired man glanced over at me, then looked away. I aligned the same order on the tray and, taking great care, set off down the lounge and served the four imaginary people at the empty table. I moved round each person that wasn't there as if they were, reached in and served the pints with a smile, and for good measure, *a bottle of Babycham for the lady.*

I took their new order, lifted the glasses, and gaining confidence, swung round with a neat flourish to find both drinkers looking at me aghast. I smiled weakly. The glasses slid. Oops, I said, I took off and their eyes followed me as I came back up the lounge. I deposited the glasses and stood by the door. The policeman stared steadfastly at me waiting to see what I'd do next. The red-haired man looked from me to the empty table and back again.

I stood my ground, looking off into the middle distance.

He's just started, said Mick, without raising his head from the paper.

25 Sun. 12th after Pentecost.
I went to bed only to find that Smith was in it. What are you saying? he shouted out of his sleep. What are you saying! I said, You're in my bed. And he said *Leave it at the door,* so I pushed him over and got in. Next thing I woke in the early morning to find him jigging against me.

Oh Marian, he mumbled.

Stop it, you fucker you, I shouted.

He woke and looked at me softly, then shot up in dismay.

What the fuck is going on? he asked.

You were trying to ride me, I said.

Oh Jasus, he said and he leapt out of the bed.

All the barmen got up to go to Mass so I did too. We shaved in front of the one broken mirror, dashed our armpits with *cauld* water, shook talcum down our vests. Shoes were polished in the kitchen. Suits came down off the hangers and we ate white bread and jam. We filed through the dark lounge. Johnny opened the pub door and the five of us marched up O'Connell Street through the pigeons and into the future.

Later I rang Cavan.

Sheila?

Yes?

Dermot.

What are you doing?

I'm a waiter.

I mean what are you going to do?

I don't know.

I miss you.

Then this other conversation between two people broke in and I put the phone down. Later that night after we'd finished we headed off to hear Dickie Rock Showband at Palm Beach.

Stop pawing me, shouts the blonde American in the back of the car. Stop it!

Ah come on, says Smith.

Stop! she screamed.

We swung through the dark wet streets.

The car brakes to a stop outside Palm Beach with the sound of a ripped skirt. Something dark has happened. Across the carpark Dickie Rock is singing a slow melody. We walk past the men in tuxedos. The American got onto the floor to dance, then excused herself to go to the toilet and she wasn't seen again.

26 Mon.

My good shirt nearly went off to the laundry and I only got it back just in time. I rang Sheila, packed my stuff and Mick gave me £1.10s. od. I swopped one of my jumpers for Johnny's and said goodbye.

Ollie walked me towards Phibsborough. We shook hands at the church, and I headed on, glad to be going home in bright sunshine. I started to hitch on the North Circular. A man seated on a park seat was watching me.

Where are you headed? he asked.

Cavan.

Can you not take the bus?

No, I can't afford it.

Well here's a fiver, he said.

Even if I had the fiver, I said, I wouldn't take the bus.

That doesn't matter, he said, take the fiver anyway.

Can I have your address, I asked, and I'll send it on?

No need for that, he said, just give it to someone else down the line.

I got a direct lift to Cavan with Phil Cullivan the architect, and headed straight down to the Central in my new jumper and met Sheila. Then I went up the town and bought Una nail varnish, got my mother a brooch, Maisie lipstick and for Sheila a lovely neck-chain belonging to Miriam that she left behind when she went to America. Along with that I bought her a ring.

So what happened you while you were away? asked my mother.

I told her all as best I could.

Remember, said Maisie, that fiver.

I will, I said.

Chapter 28

28 Wed. St Augustine.
Only six days to go. Went for a walk up Shantemon Mountain with Sheila to see Finn MacCumhaill's Five Finger stones.

Are you glad you didn't go away? she asked.

I am, I said. Are you glad I came back?

Oh I don't know, she smiled.

That's a good one, I said.

Would you quit! she snorted.

We could see for miles but couldn't find where the O'Reillys minted their coins, or where their castle stood, only saw acres of rocky fields, a couple of old ruins with ash trees growing through where the roofs once were, then turf smoke shooting west from one galvanized cabin, nothing else but the spire of the cathedral in the distance, some wild mushrooms and the giddy feeling heights give you. Then we spotted an elderly man muffled up against the wind walking a dry sheugh for shelter with his dog. He had a pile of hay tied to his back to feed a lock of calves in a far whinny field. We wished him good day.

How are you? I asked.

I'm good enough, he said. I didn't eat much but at least I did the washing up.

Sheila started laughing.

Good luck, I said.

Take your time, he said. Are yous lost?

No.

He studied us with a merry eye. Are yous courting?

Yes, I said.

Fair deuce. I mind the time I do. He looked back the way he'd come. The evenings are quare and drawn in, he said.

They are.

Well, I'll leave you to it.

Snot flew from his nose as he waved. She takes my hand. Her hair is fresh.

Will you write to me when we go back to college?

I will. Every day.

You promise.

I do.

We courted there in the grass among the stones and talked of spending our lives together.

29 Thur.

Five days to go. Cycled out to the Deredis river and threw a few casts in at the rapids. Nothing doing. Sheila cooked up sausages on a small fire. The night came down. These things happen. Time is running out. Rode home in moonshine.

30 Fri.

Four days to go. Tonight the mother ironing in the kitchen, shirts and sheets and pillowslips and everything I'll need in college, and she looking into the dining room to see if I was still there and I was, sitting up by the fire by Maisie, cause Sheila was housebound.

31 Sat.

Three days to go. We found ourselves looking down on the herons who feed off the Kinnypottle river from offal and blood swept away from McCarren's bacon factory. The birds stand nodding mid-water, or perch on long branches that reach out over the river, very white and long-legged and still in the gloom. Not a sound. As if it were a grave-yard. A manky place. She took my hand. Then a hammer hitting glavanize in the townland of Swellan. A bus backing into the station. A bicycle. Nothing else for a while, till a doll's pram sailed by, and a rat swam fast through a stretch of petrol-coloured water further on down towards the town.

We walked back to Cavan. The street lights came on.

It's eerie, she said. It's like as if someone had died.

We didn't want to say goodbye, so she went in for a while to the bank while I stood in the doorway of the Hub Bar, Teddy Maguire shouted good night and Rinty Monaghan went by on a messenger bike, she told her parents she was going to a farewell dance with the girls and then appeared in a pleated dress, white blouse, blue raincoat and another perfume, we went on walking, up Cooke's Archway, past the gypsies on the Gallows Hill who were drinking again by the fire, a piebald pony looked over the railings into the blue reservoir, a bird rose in the meadow, rain spattered on the lake, We're not going there again, she said, are we, we walked though the orchard of dripping apple trees and stepped in cowshit, then shed some of our wet clothes in Lavell's haunted house by the light of a match and scared ourselves, the sleep under her eyes darkened, Take it easy now, she said, you know we have the rest of our lives, I lit another match and we lay down, stayed like that, everything quiet but for mice or birds in the rafters, scurrying, the rain on the window splat! splat! splat!, her head on Johnny's jumper on the floor of the kitchen and her face to mine, I undid her blouse till her breast was bare, she looked down a moment and went on, her flattened palm swept over my stomach, the wind jumped through the rafters, Is that your leg? she said, Whose leg do you think it is? I said, It's hard to know whether it's yours or mine, she said, they feel the same, Da de da de dee, da dada da da dee, she hummed, Dee dada dada dum, as she undid my belt, sneaked a hand in and rummaged around and said, What's the words of that song, What song, I said, Never mind, she said, it'll come to me.

SEPTEMBER

1 Sun. 13th after Pentecost.
Two days to go. One last time to the matinee in the Town Hall. The balcony was packed. Great court. And great cant afterwards.

2 Mon.
I tiptoed past the mother's room around 2, waited on the three steps below the altar and listened, then quietly went down the stairs, and onto Main Street. It was quiet as the grave. Stood in Fox's shoe shop. The door of the bank clicked open, and Sheila stepped out, and pulled it quietly behind her. Each sound echoed down the street. She stood a moment uncertain of what to do, then ran to the Ulster Arms. I barked. Then barked again and hopped across the road.

You put the heart crossways in me, she said.

We linked arms and headed towards Provider's, then a car came on, it slowed up, and began to cruise along behind us, Don't look back, I said, don't look back, and we had to go by the entrance to Provider's, and then I thought if I don't look back it will mean we have done something wrong so we stopped at the door of the Breifne, and the squad car pulled in, and I thought this is it.

What are you doing there? asked the guard.

I'm going home, I said.

You live here?

Yes, I said.

I think, he said, I'll just have to ring that bell and check with the owners.

There's no need, I said, I have the key.

You have?

Yes, I said.

Well go on, he said, watching me.

So now I had to turn the key, open the door and go in with Sheila. For a minute I thought he was going to follow us so I said Good Night and closed the door, turned on the light a moment, then turned it off. We stood in the dark, our backs against the wall, barely breathing. Through the glass we could see him standing outside. I listened for any sound from upstairs, my mother's footsteps on the landing, Maisie coming out of the sitting room. It seemed he was on the point of ringing the bell, he peered through the blurred glass, then turned and eventually the squad car pulled away. We slipped onto Main Street, up Provider's and round the gardens to Noel's loft.

That was gas, said Sheila.

It was close, I said.

Everything was ready in the Castle. A small gas ring, chops, beans, Madeira cakes. We cooked up a feed by the light of a candle.

Talk to me, said Sheila, can't you.

I said, I don't know what to say.

It's strange, she whispered, being here like this. It's like playing housey-housey.

I had the bed decked out with clean sheets and an eiderdown that had been got ready for college. We lay down in our clothes without touching. I set the clock with the hands that shone in the dark and tried the radio but everything was finished.

That chat is no good, I said.

You're very nervous, she said. As a matter of fact you're shaking.

I know that.

What has you so nervous?

To tell you the truth I'm afraid.

Afraid of what?

Of telling you the truth.

About what?

About myself.

She sat up.

Fire away, she said.

You see, I don't think we can go on if I don't tell you the truth about me.

Well do, then.

And so like a fool I told her about all the women I'd been with, knowing in my heart I shouldn't have been doing it – starting with Mary.

Oh Mary, she said, well I know about her.

Then there was Josie.

Yes, she said sternly, but I was led to believe it wasn't serious.

Well, maybe it wasn't.

Go on, please, she said flatly.

Then there was Ellen from Slowey's.

And was *that* serious?

Not really.

And what about Rannafast.

Well, there was two girls there.

Two?

Yes.

You lied to me, she snapped.

But it was only kissing.

Spare me the details if you don't mind.

I just wanted to get everything off my chest.

Well, don't let me stop you.

And last of all, I said rushing towards the end, there was Rose.

Rose?

Yes.

You went with Rose?

Yes.

Rose Reilly?

Yes.

You bollacks, she said. You ojus fucker.

I reached out a hand to her neck and she beat it away.

But you said that you were just as bad as me.

She looked at me.

No one could be as bad as you. No one!

You are, I said.

No, she said. And to think you asked me to run away with you.

She sat on the edge of the mattress.

Sheila, I said softly.

What had you to go and tell me all that for?

I thought I had to. Because we're going away tomorrow.

Well there are some things a body is better off not knowing.

A long silence.

It's our last night together, I said.

You might swear, she said.

More silence. She sat on the edge of the mattress with her back to me, and I stretched behind. The candle went out. The clock went round. The darkness was long.

I want to go now, she said.

I lit a match and we climbed down the rickety ladder, went back round by the misty gardens, onto Main Street and she ran to her door. I stood looking after her. She turned and came back. We walked down Bridge Street, then on up College Street and back round by Mill Street. In the dark the Kinnypottle flew by. Then we climbed the ghostly Half Acre, only a dog barking behind a closed door, a pram of coal, a bicycle tyre round an electricity pole; onto Tullymongan, timber for burning piled against a gable, a Sacred Heart lamp, washing hung up on a spreading bush; and from there to the Gallows Hill. We sat against the rails of the reservoir on the Fair Green and looked down on the town. The damp smell of the old camp fire reached us. The piebald pony came out of the night and stared at us a long time.

Well, said she, since you've started I suppose I should tell the truth as well.

Only if you want to, said I nervously.

Well there was Jim, but you know that.

I know that, I agreed.

Then Kevin.

Yes.

Then that lad from Ardee.

Oh, yon fellow.

Then there was a fellow in Dublin.

She went quiet.

Is that it? I asked.

I'm trying to think.

Can you not remember?

No.

Jesus, Sheila!

No, I think that's it, she said at last.

Thanks be to God for that. I couldn't take any more.

Hold on, she said.

What! I asked, startled.

Wait till I see now.

Ah, fuck me.

Go on, she says, I was only joking.

That's a good one, I said.

She laughed and burrowed her head into my shoulder. The dawn started. An ass trotted by. Hand-in-hand we went down by Cooke's, stopping to kiss every few yards. Jackdaws sailed onto the middle of the road. We kissed outside P. A. Smith's the drapers, outside McCusker's the barbers, in the Regal Archway, then she let herself into the bank with a finger to her lips. There wasn't a soul stirring. I stood by the door of the Breifne and then I heard these steps coming from a long way away, coming up Bridge Street, then this figure came round by where the Swan Hotel used be, he crossed over to our side of the street never losing a beat, it was Mr Allen the baker on his way to McDonald's bakery to put the first batch of bread into the ovens. The top of the morning, he said.

3 Tues. St Pius X.

You're under starter's orders, said the mother.

It was 10 o'clock. I was dog tired. We were packing all morning. Then I had to nip across and get my sheets from Noel's shed, and slip them into the bag. I met Sheila at the corner of Bridge Street. One last kiss and she was gone. She stepped into her father's car and went off to Loreto. I went in and got my bags and put them into Dermot's car.

Please, said Mother, try not to let us down.

I won't, I said.

Myself and Dermot had 6 bottles of beer and then he dropped me out to St Pat's. I swallowed my mints and a prefect led me to No. 10 dormitory. All the bad boys are in No. 10, he said. There was an open case on every bed. There was this circle with no centre. We sat on the beds talking. Put our razors on the sinks, hung our towels on the rails and stashed away our clothes in the lockers. Some of the lads wore scapulars. Square looked in. The light went off. A voice here, a voice there. Had a hard night of it. Sweating and turning. Sad to leave Sheila.

5 Thur.

Woke up with shoes all round me that had been thrown during the night because I snore. Up every morning at $1/4$ to 7. In bed at 10.

8 Sun. 14th after Pentecost. (The Birthday of B.V.M.)

Have the radio in the room for *Top Twenty*. Wait till everyone is asleep before I go asleep myself.

10 Tues.

Got 4 off Square.

13 Fri.

Have not been beaten in table tennis since came into college.

15 Sun.

Got into town for match and met Sheila for 5 minutes by the gate of Breifne Park.

16 Mon.

Playing football for Class 5. The smell of feet. Snot drying on the radiators. Desperate pong in the clattey jacks. *The 'mell of it. The 'mell of it.* No jacks paper. *Cruiscin Mor.* Long runs. Roars from the showers. My face breaks out into giant pimples that burst and run down my cheek like a nose bleed. Dream of being circumcised all over again. The morning bell. The lights suddenly coming on.

Square glancing into the room.

Stepping along the tiles. The seniors smoking fags in the dark ambulatory at 7 before morning Mass. The football pitches in the early light. The skivvies looking out from the kitchen. A walk around the Half before class begins.

17 Tues. Stigmata of St Francis.

Studying very well.

This big fucker McDonald, who is in first year though he's over 17 and plays on the senior football team, stopped me in the study and said, You're next, Healy. He's the chief bully in the school.

18 Wed. Ember Day. (Fast and Abstinence)

Last night stood by the window looking out at a storm. Everyone else was asleep in the dorm. There was the odd light over the trees from the town, a rosy light, and a light, that I could see through the glass portal over the door, still on in the corridor. It shone onto the black face of the Indian lad sleeping just beside me. The rest were turned this way and that, dreaming and breathing, a hand thrown across the eyes, knees tucked up, one foot out. A small shrill whisper. Then came this distant thunder that was really wind. Rain lashed against the windows and the trees were waving and waving. Then the wind, slapping like sheets, thumped against the black college. Three stories below the shining cars of the priests rocked over and back. The outside world howled. Branches swept across the lawn. The storm felt holy. The sounds pounded by, the next stronger than the last, gaining on something, something that was nearly out of control, and then would come a pause, the trees steadied, the black clouds raced to a stop. A grey space opened in the sky so that you could see the white lip of the moon. A bed creaked in the dorm. Someone called out. The stern breathing from the asthmatic lad from Gowna increased, he held his breath and turned another way. His scapular hung over the edge of the bed. A few moments later the storm came up the avenue and I looked down from another place. I lost my bearings. The window grew huge. I stood there in my pyjamas for maybe half an hour, then got into bed, but every few minutes I was out again to look, and there was the storm still going on, making faces in the trees, and the wind barking. The rain curved against the window panes. The boys asleep.

19 Thur.
Today wrote a letter to Sheila breaking it off for clean soul reasons in terms of marriage, and then made a promise to myself to stop wanking.

23 Mon.
Free day. Spent it in the alley with Brady from Mullahoran. We tossed balls for hours till it got so dark we couldn't see a hate.

24 Tues. Our Lady of Ransom.
The boys made me play football for Class 5. Got the first goal of my life. A cheer went up round the Half.

You jammy fucker, said Big Eye.

28 Sat.
In town today. Supposed to get a tooth filled but don't. Instead tried to move Christine Keeler. No go. Got lift back to college on Ballsy's bike.

Did you get your hole recently, Healy? he asked.

Stop that auld dirty talk, Ballsy, I said.

There was the college again. I sat in the study hall among the other hundred odd. The dean of study was late down so everyone was talking. Then the back door opened. You could not hear a mouse. After a while I tucked my hand round my ear, and with my arm hiding it, began to read *The Vicar of Wakefield* that I placed over my science book.

> *Hot cockles succeeded next, questions and commands followed that, and last of all, they sate down to hunt the slipper. . . . It was in this manner that my eldest daughter*

was hemmed in, and thumped about, all blowzed in
spirits, and bawling for fair play, fair play, with a voice
that might deafen a ballad singer, when confusion on
confusion, who should enter the room but our two great
acquaintances from town, Lady Blarney and Miss
Carolina Wilelmina Amelia Skeggs!

Suddenly Hurley's hand came down onto the open book. I shot into the air with fright.

Aw, I shouted. Aw God, Father!

He started laughing, the lads laughed because I got such a shock. He read the title of the book, shook his head, closed the book and strode on. I started maths but couldn't concentrate. The numbers just went off into infinity, so I tried history. I had to go back and back again over what I'd read and still it was not the same as it had been before. The blur sort of bloomed. I tried to think of something happy, then, I searched for the place, and with the point of a biro I pierced a certain spot in my cheek bone and then my cheek, and as I did so this coldness spread over the side of my face.

29 Sun. 17th after Pentecost. St Michael, Archangel.
Andy and Timmy came out to the college with cakes and lemonade for me. I went to meet them outside the locker rooms. Then this crowd of fourth years gathered.

Fuck off back to the Half Acre, one of them shouted.

They began to mill round.

Stand back, said Andy.

Steady, said Timmy.

Go back to where you came from, another shouted.

We'll see you Dermot, said the lads, mad at me because I could do nothing and they backed off down the avenue while the others hurled abuse. I stood with the gifts they'd brought me and didn't know what to do. Then one fellow poked his finger in my face and said: Don't be bringing the tramps of the town round this college, Healy.

A prefect came and marched me through the crowd and back to the locker room. When I went up to the study there was these remarks passed. Then McDonald decided to strike. He came on up the study to my seat smiling. I could see he was coming for me, all of 6 foot 2, and he was working his hands.

It's time, Healy, he said.

I stood my ground. He put out his arms to grab me and I let him. Then as his full weight came on top of me I fell back and brought my two feet clean up into his stomach and threw him over my head. He sailed through the air and knocked himself out on a desk. He went white and just lay there with a splutter on his lips. I was frightened.

Then his eyes opened.

Are you all right? I asked him.

Yes, he said.

Do you want to go to the surgery?

No, he said. He sat there in a daze. Then got up and walked away without bothering with me.

OCTOBER

2 Wed. The Holy Guardian Angels.
Mutt says that the retreat might do Class 5 some good.

Here we have, he said quietly, a group of assorted dunces. Why do I do it? I ask myself. Oh dear, oh dear. What am I to do? he whinged to himself.

3 Thur. St Theresa of the Child Jesus.
Got six off Hurley for racket in dorm last night. Then as I left his room I passed by Soc's. I'd often heard that he listened to radio stations from abroad. So I put my ear to his door and heard these voices speaking in a foreign language.

Then his door opened and the radio exploded into the corridor.

What are you doing, sir? Socrates asked, with marvelling big-bushed eyes.

I was listening to your radio, Father, I said.

It is a miracle to me, Mr Healy, that you, who can't speak Greek, though we labour to teach you, he said, can understand German which is not on our itinerary.

I could see past his huge rounded figure, with the collar undone, into the scholarly room. The walls were book-lined. Books were stacked on the floor. A little bed sat in a corner like a book itself.

Well sir, explain yourself.

I was passing, I said, and I heard the radio and I was trying to figure out what language it was, Father.

What curiosity, sir. What innate curiosity.

I'm sorry, Father.

If only such curiosity could abound in your normal studies.

Yes, Father.

He folded his hands on his stomach.

Knowledge, sir, is not learnt through a keyhole.

No, Father.

But we must be grateful, mustn't we, for even this meagre effort. Come, sir, be off from my door.

Yes, Father.

The Vicar of Wakefield, Socrates said. He stood looking after me with a pleased grin on his face then the door closed and the German voices dropped to a low hum.

4 Fri. St Francis of Assisi. First Friday.

Square comes in. I have Curry against wall. We're play-acting.

Lie up there till I see if you're any good, I'm saying.

I can see Curry looking over my shoulder.

C'mon, I say, till we see if you're all talk.

Curry bares his teeth.

What's wrong with you? I say. Come here to me till I give you a dose of the clatters.

Curry stares straight past me.

Put them up, I said.

As I turn Square gave me a quick sharp knock with his knuckles on the side of the head. Bed! he said. Later, when the lights went off, Curry said in the dark, Well I tried to tell you. I know, I said. That was a good knock he gave you. 'Twas, I agreed. He's nifty is Square. He is. You want to see the look on your face, said Curry, that was great. I enjoyed that, he added. Fuck off, I say. Oh that was great, chuckled Curry.

5 Sat.

At 8 o'clock this evening we go on retreat.

There is a long spiff in the chapel from a monk.

Then silence. Afterwards, we head off round the Whole and the Half by ourselves, a few single fellows cross the football pitch, some stand alone among the pillars in the ambulatory, others pass in the corridors with averted eyes. Priests suddenly emerge from the woods. Speaking in sign language we climb into bed and hear the squeak of Square's soft shoes as he comes along the corridor and stands a moment by the door of No. 10, then goes on, across through the college to the connors' dorm.

6 Sun. 18th after Pentecost.

In the morning we wash and shave without a word. The monks sing the Mass, answering each other over great distances. In the refectory, the sucks eye the seniors fearfully. In silence we eat dry toast for breakfast while a brown-eyed monk swinging a huge wooden rosary parades by.

When a skivvy shouts in the kitchen he wheels round angrily on his sandals and whisks through the door.

Throughout the day we step into the chapel and sit apart from each other, staring at the altar and praying. When the door closes or opens we all look round. It's only someone else. Some other soul like ourselves. The presence grows. I do 15 minutes at a time, then move on to half-an-hour. And once one whole hour. It left me light in the head. We walked the corridors, making certain journeys that brought you back to where you started from, then you started again.

Then there was a very hairy spiff at 8 o'clock. All about sex. I think I have *vocation*. That night in No. 10 we move about greatly troubled in ourselves, me more than most. And Square didn't even bother to look in.

7 Mon. Feast of the Holy Rosary.

A cheer went up, as if we had won the McRory Cup, just after breakfast.

19 Sat.
Got 60% off Cullen for my comp.

24 Thur. St Raphael, Archangel.
Hurley came up to me in the study and said I was wanted at the
front door. Una is there in a car. She says, Aunty Gerty, Mammy's
sister, is dead.

25 Fri.
Bob came into Benny's class and drove me into town. I sat into the
funeral car in my new suit. We drive to Finea. The hearse stops a
moment outside our old house. Tom Keogh and Mrs Flynn are at
the door of the church. Charlie Clavin puts his hand in mine and
says, Can that be you Dermot?

It is, I said.

Bedad. Dermot Healy?

That's right.

He shakes his head.

I was told it but I didn't believe it. He gripped my hand firmly.
I'm sorry, he says, for your trouble.

I follow the funeral from the church. Mammy, Aunty Maisie,
Aunty Bridgie and Aunty Nancy wearing black veils walk behind their
sister. Behind them come the sons and daughters. Every few yards the
tall O'Neill brothers halt. Uncle Seamus takes a wing.

Let the young fellow in, says Tony.

On the bog road Vincent steps aside to let me carry the coffin of
his mother. Pop O'Neill, her husband, with rheumy eyes and small
feet, perches like a tiny bird by the grave. The grave diggers stand by
with their shovels tucked under their chins.

26 Sat.
Slept in my own bed, listened to Luxembourg and up to the alley first
thing in the morning. Great feed of chicken in the house and Sean
O'Neill gave me 10 shillings. I had a good argument with him. Smoke
30 fags, and although I could have stayed in Cavan town · another
night, I decided, in the middle of the funeral party, to take Flood's taxi
back in the dark to the college after lights out. Went in through the

front door that someone had left open, past the priests' rooms without meeting anyone, up the stairs the same, knowing I shouldn't be doing this I wandered with my bag along the strange celibate world of a corridor that I'd never been through alone at night before: warm lights under doors, coughs, a floorboard giving way, friendly radios on low, the rattle of a coal skuttle, the clink of a glass, a door to a priest's lavatory standing ajar and looking somehow sinful, classical music, dark shoes on a doorstep, a rifle resting against a wall beside a wet pair of wellingtons, intimacies, a loud laugh that for the moment I couldn't recognize, the smell of pipe smoke.

I undressed in number 10 by the light from the corridor, got in and lay there, trying to remember Aunty Gerty's face but all that came back was a fur stole, a trap flying the road from Gorey in Co. Wexford and the sense of a big woman in a wide hat. I try to concentrate on her face. She's wearing lipstick I think. She's laughing at the good of Pop. Then suddenly I lose her face and instead it is the face of my father I see. I try to arrange the features as they once were, but they keep slipping away from each other, but I know it's him from the gaze.

Are you back? whispered Square, suddenly in the darkness, and his torch swept over my face.

Yes, Father.

How did you get in?

The door was open.

And why did you not report to me?

It was too late.

You should have reported to me.

I was too tired.

All right.

He pulled the door quietly to. For the first time in years I travel up towards Finea before sleeping, past the barracks, on by Fitzsimon's, take the bend over the seven-arched bridge, up the village and past Myles the Slasher's Memorial, there's a light in our window, I'm nearly there.

27 Sun. Feast of Christ the King.
Have made some good friends.

28 Mon. SS Simon and Jude, Apostles.

One of the young lads I train for middle-distance running today told me he had the cure for pimples. He got it from his father in Drumshambo. He took me into one of the showers and told me to close my eyes.

You may hear me saying a prayer, he said, but pass no remarks. Just trust me.

I trust you, I said.

So I closed my eyes and his fingers touched my face like the scuff of the wing of a bird. Then it was over. You can open your eyes, now, he said. We stepped out of the shower and Hughie McGovern said, Are yous bum boys or what? I timed the young fellow twice round the Half. He clocked in 30 seconds better than the last time.

29 Tues.

When I woke this morning the dry scabs of the pimples had fallen off my face and were all around me on the pillow.

31 Thur. St Alphonsus Rodriguez.

Tried to get out to town for tonight. Told by Bob that he could make no exceptions. From the window we watched stray fireworks shooting over Cavan town then in the dark we passed round bags of nuts.

NOVEMBER

1 Fri. Feast of All Saints. First Friday.

Got home after High Mass, broke a false tooth with chocolate and went to the Central. The women and Sheila are there. Had dinner. Had a beer and vodka in Stick Donoghue's with Dermot. In Central with Sheila alone at last.

I miss you, I said.

How long are we supposed to stay away from each other?

I don't know.

It's hard.

I know.

Is this what other people do?

I think so.

You're strange, she said.

Yes, I said, I'm a funny wee cunt.

We played records. I wanted to ask her up to the Castle but didn't. Back to college at 7. The connors are running round the Half in masks. Someone let off a banger behind the alley. All night tossed and turned thinking of Sheila.

2 Sat. All Souls' Day.

Went up to Bob straight after breakfast. We had an argument but eventually got into town to have the tooth replaced. Went to Mr Hickey the dentist, had fitting and asked him to time the visit for the late afternoon then lifted the phone and asked Sheila to the matinee.

Are you sure that's what you want?

It is, I said.

First we sat by each other in the dark without touching then her hand found my hand, and we sat like that for a time through the Pathé News, but when the main picture began we were kissing. It was one of the greatest courts ever. Drank a bottle of wine in Finnegan's afterwards. Then onto the Central for chips. Always remember Little Peggy March's song and Billy Fury's Halfway to Paradise. So near yet so far away. Sheila told her parents she was going back to Loreto with the Saundersons and I told the mother I was going out to college with Burke then we hired Jack Flood and drove first to Loreto, and at Loreto I didn't want to let her go, so we went on towards Butlersbridge then back again, then once more out to Farnham past the golf links, and finally back up Loreto Avenue and we said goodbye in a hail of leaves, and then Jack dropped me at St Pat's.

Jack turned around in the car seat.

I wish you the best of luck, he said.

It cost me what was to keep me till the end of November but it was worth it. Nuts were served with tea, had 2 pictures that night – *Olympic Games* and then *The Globetrotters*, and Square left the light on till late in No. 10 so we could talk and talk.

9 Sat. Dedication of the Basilica of the Saviour.

My birthday. The boys gave me *gallery* at teatime. Great cheer. Took my birthday cake to the table and gave a piece to every fellow. Great feed. Lit up another cake in the dorm. 16 candles lit. Heard Square coming. Blew out the candles and shoved the cake under the bed.

He came in and walked up the dorm and back again.

He sniffed the air and shone his torch round the room. I began to imagine that smoke was pouring out from under the quilt. Then down the dorm he came again and stopped at the foot of my bed. He shone the torch directly onto my pillow, then suddenly clicked it off and went away.

10 Sun. 23rd after Pentecost.
I was inside playing table tennis when O'Connor said there were friends of mine outside. Andy and Timmy were there. They came out to give me 20 Kingsway for my birthday. The 5th years gather round and begin shouting. The boys pass no remarks. We stay there talking. Then a window opened overhead and they began throwing water down on us. We didn't budge. The whole college talks about it afterwards.

16 Sat.
Got into town to get my tooth. Take feed in Central, and off to the matinee. Try Adams. No go. Square gives off stink and phones Hickey the dentist 'cause I'm an hour late. Listened with O'Connor to radio till half-12. Then began wondering about the chance of slipping out of the college and back to town.

I decided to give it a trial run.

I got dressed and put my pyjamas on over everything, then stepped out onto the corridor in my sandals. I walked to the toilet and stood there listening. No one. So I headed for the stairs intending to take the same route by the priests' rooms that I'd come the night of Aunty Gerty's funeral. I was down the first flight when I heard these steps coming up so I ran back, along the corridor and into number 10. Just as I jumped into bed the door opened behind me. It was Square and he was breathless. He shone his torch onto every face. I found it light up my eyes. He stood over me. The sweat ran down my back. Then at last came the darkness.

I didn't move because I had not heard the door close, so I lay perfectly still, breathing as regular as I could, over and back, trying to concentrate on making sleep come, but the heat of my clothes under the pyjamas grew stifling, and still he was out there, I could find him standing there in the dark waiting for me to make one false move, and sure enough about 10 minutes later he turned on the torch and the beam struck my eyelids, he was still directly over me.

I knew he was on the point of asking me to step out of bed when suddenly O'Connor began to rave in his sleep. Square turned. The boys began wakening. I opened my eyes and looked at him.

What's wrong, Father? I asked.

Go back to sleep, he said.

He woke O'Connor and left the dorm. I bundled my clothes off under the sheets, and left them beneath the bed. In a dream much later that night I woke and could have sworn I saw the silhouette of Square still standing out there somewhere in the dark, but I could not be sure.

17 Sun. 24th after Pentecost.
Wear my blue and white jumper. All admiration.

22 Fri.
I was walking round the Half with Pete Duffy, and Gallagher, and Mullaly when someone with a radio to their ear shouted out that President Kennedy was dead.

DECEMBER

13 Fri.
The sucks from first year ran errands for the seniors to the shop, the Belturbet dayboys talked soccer outside the locker room, Arva lads talked cars, the Drumshambos played touch-penny, while next to them cards were slapped down onto window sills in the top corridor in six-penny games of poker by seniors from Balieborough; the Cavan towns sang Living Doll, and on the Whole the Killeshandras were making plans, a brace of East Cavan men sat in the woods without speaking, in an empty classroom a pair of brothers from Manorhamilton cut a ham sandwich in two; a lone lad from Ballinagh

sat in the toilet reading a 64-page comic, the Mullahorans stood behind the alley against the back wall like men standing out of the wind by the gable of a house; a Glan man jumped in the air and hung off the crossbar of the goalpost on the lower pitch; fellows from Killinkere taunted fellows from Drung; the Cootehills rattled off a litany of footballers and argued who was in the goal that day of the final in '61; in the ambulatory the Shercocks played pitch-and-toss; this dapper lad from Ballyconnell stopped by a window to study his reflection then took out a comb and gave a sharp, quick stroke to his quiff; in the study hall a couple of seniors from Mullagh sat five or six desks away from each other humming Down by the Riverside; in the piano room a Carrickgallen fellow slept; an old argument erupted on the upper pitch between two tall neighbours from Glenfarne so they folded their coats and dug into each other; *Lavey! Lavey Strand! Behy! Behy Bog! and Currahoe*, shouted a connor from Bunoe; in the showers three men from Varginee shouted profanities; a man from Swad spat blood into a basin in the surgery; the loner from Moynalty dribbled a ball along the basketball court; a holy man from Latt walked the Half quickly and stopped and took out a matchbox that had a butterfly in it and went on again; a gambler from Ballyjamesduff heard yesterday's racing results from a dayboy and stamped the floor; You're looking ojus well, said a connor from Drum to a senior from Latt who replied I'll clatter you round the oxter; a Dowra man stole into the kitchen while a Bawnboy man kept watch; a scholarship boy tore the wing off a chicken his mother from Kilnaleck had sent him; the lad from Gowna sat in the locker room sewing a vest; then when the dayboys went to the bicycle shed they found that someone had let all the tyres down.

19 Thur.
Had great fun. Myself, Mullaly and Duffy walk round the Whole backwards, roaring our heads off.

20 Fri. Ember day. (Fast and abstinence)
Got holidays today. Up at 6, and reach town at a ¼ to 9. The girls let me in. Made the fire in the private dining room and had tea ready for the mother when she came down. We talked till the shop opened

and I took a stroll up the town, had a bath and went with Dermot back out to the college to collect my cases. Went to pics.

21 Sat. St Thomas Apostle. Ember day. (Fast without abstinence)
Kiss Sally after breakfast, then her father fell in drunk. Went with Mary after dinner in the car to the golf links. Meet Paddy Kelly in the Ulster Arms. Then walked Phyllis out the road.

22 Sun. 4th Sunday of Advent.
The fire in the bakehouse went out three times, then the bell rang and Sheila was at the door. The Labour Band went down Farnham Street.

23rd Mon.
Dermot woke me at 1/4 past 8. We headed down to the Central Café for free coffee and buns then Sean McManus sat us into the sports car and we headed for Dublin singing opera all the way. Beyond Virginia we skidded and ended up facing home. Landed anyway and I went down to the Parnell house to see Ollie, and Johnny and all the barmen. Then off round Dublin. Muck everywhere. Awful place. Muck even in O'Connell Street. Where did it come from? Went and bought a new jumper, then waited an hour outside the Metropole for Sean and when he came at last we went in for a drink. We set out only to stop at the first pub out the road. Then we stopped beyond Navan, in Kells, and in the Park in Virginia. A great sing-song all the way home. At 20 mile an hour we cruise into Cavan. Some day.

24 Tues. Christmas Eve.
Walked back round by Town Hall Street where all the kids were gathered in the dusky yard for Bud McNamara dressed as Santa Claus to give out presents. With Frank Brady in the Ulster Arms wearing the new scarf my mother had bought me. Poor Jack, he said. Buy all present – Sheila, Dermot, Paddy Kelly – a drink. Vodkas and beers. Then Sheila gives me a present.

Don't open it till tomorrow.
I won't, I said.
You promise.
I do.

Then she went home and I went down to Donohue's with the boys. Bridge Street was all go. Drinks and fags. Great fun. We came up Main Street, and I said Goodnight, I was going to go home, I'd promised. In the Breifne window our Santa was still nodding. I looked at him a while going over and back. With his wisp of beard and confetti on his red shoulders, he looked a little tatty and alone, and the window seemed very bare without the cakes and the boxes of chocolates. He'd grown older somehow, still that didn't stop him nodding away in the empty window. Nod, *yes, you can have what you like*, Nod, *indeed whatever you like*, Nod, *just ask*, Nod, *anything, anything at all*, bowing his head like the altar boy below the altar, Nod, *why yes, my good man*, like a Chinaman before his master, Nod, *the whole world if you want*, his small polished boots on a doily, the small shoulders; then, as I let myself in the door, Andy called across the street, Healy, you dosser, so we move off down to the bus station but there's no buses so a crowd of us headed out the railway lines, and sat on the platform drinking. The sky was pure and full of stars. A black frost was spreading.

I went home at 1. The window was empty.

Where were you? said Mother.

I was at Midnight Mass.

A regular saint, said Maisie.

Happy Christmas, said my mother and she was smiling. She was filled with rare joy. We sat round talking and opening presents till all hours. Christmas cards were tucked into the gold surround of the mirror, along the mantel and into the picture frames. We said goodnight and the clocks were set for the morning. The fluorescent lights in the dining room flickered. Then in my room I discovered I'd lost the scarf and Sheila's present.

25 Wed. Christmas Day.

Up at 8 for early Mass for Daddy then went out the lines to get my scarf but though I found the scarf no matter where I looked I could not find Sheila's present. I sat on the platform, smoked a fag and looked down the lines. An east wind snapped at the bare trees. It was like I was waiting on a train. I tucked the white scarf into my blue gabardine and headed home by the Barrack Hill. The ball alley was empty. Dust flew round in a circle by the right-hand corner of the back wall. A mound of holly was nailed to Paddy Woods' door. The town was deserted. Then suddenly the wind smacked the lines of overhead bulbs and bunting in Bridge Street, Smack! Smack! Smack! and in Main Street it was worse, they cracked as if we were in a ghost town, Smack! Crack! Click! Clickety Click!, the lines so taut it looked as if the string would snap, it felt dangerous, coloured bulbs burst, the whole street strained, the overhead lines of bulbs shook as the wind gusted, then eased, not a soul to be seen, even Santa was gone from the window, up into the attic until next year; Nod, *just ask*, Nod, *anything, anything at all*; there wasn't a car, not a dog even, till young Brady appeared, dressed as a cowboy, he walked up Main Street with two six shooters at the ready, You're dead, he said, you're dead, he aimed at me and I ducked, the cap banged, I clutched my heart and he blew away an imaginary wisp of smoke, holstered his gun and said, See you partner, and he went back up Main Street clapping his arse at a trot, and he went into his house, and I went into mine, stood a moment in the deserted public dining room where the end tables with their false white marble tops were piled high with cold coats and hats and presents and I listened to the TV and the family inside chatting and laughing, opened the door and there they all were, Una, Maisie, mother – the ladies – once on the chairs round the table in its white linen, and then again repeated the other way round in the mirror. The mother clapped her knees.

There you are, she said happily.

The wanderer, nodded Maisie.

And look at the *corr* on him.

A regular slouch, agreed Maisie.

And where were you? the mother asked.

I took a walk round the town, I said.

We, chirped Maisie as she cocked her glasses, are waiting on the Queen to make her appearance.

Is that so, I said.

Oh yes, she answered, she's due out on the balcony at any minute and she turned aside to the TV.

BOOK V

It's Lilac Time Again

Chapter 29

Mother is sitting in an armchair by her bed in the County Hospital where at eighty-eight she's to have a scab removed from her head. She fell against a radiator two weeks ago in the bungalow in Cootehill where she retired after the Breifne closed. The move was made so that she and Maisie could be near Una, who lives in a farmhouse down the road. Mother burned herself badly. She'd lain unable to get up for maybe an hour with her head resting against the boiling rad. She was found by my brother Tony and his wife Moira in the middle of the night.

Moira went into her bedroom to see if she was all right but there was no one there. So she searched the house but couldn't find her then she went back to the bedroom and heard this small cry. The mother was lying between her bed and the radiator. It would be the first of many falls. They had come home on holidays from Toronto to see her and went back in deep despair.

At first the swelling from the blow disguised the burn, but in the out-patients' today she was admitted for an operation. A wad of flesh will be taken from her thigh to fill the hole the burn made. Over the wound she wears a small white skullcap. They want to build her up for the operation, but she wants to go home. They won't let her out, so now she's refusing to eat.

Get me out of here! she says.

You're getting better, says Mrs English, who is in bed across the ward from her.

Oh yes, says the mother smiling sweetly, that's right.

Don't leave me here, she commands me.

I won't.

But you're going.

I have to go now, I say.

To the play?

Yes.

On Broken Wings, she says to herself. She raises her voice. He's making hundreds of pounds.

Very good, says Mrs English.

She takes my hand. Take me with you, can't you.

I would if I could.

That's right.

Goodbye, I say.

You look lovely, she says.

Listen to that, says Mrs English.

Blushing I get to my feet, and kiss her cheek and walk in the Farnham Road to the Town Hall in Cavan where a play of mine, named after a song she used to sing, is opening. The song is called On Broken Wings. She used sing it in the kitchen in Finea.

She sits opposite me in Cootehill, her eyes stalking the dark corridors of the subconscious.

Bring me, she says, to the bed.

Soon I will.

Why had this to happen to me?

You fell.

That's right. So take me, she says, down to Una's.

Una is away.

Away where?

America.

America, she repeats, unconvinced.

The repetitions are constant, with tears and implorations added. I know what she means and what she wants but I cannot provide the answer.

Bring me to bed will ya?

It's too early.

Bring me out for a meal.

We'll eat soon.

Take me to my house.

You're in it.

No I'm not.

This is it, Errigal.

Where is my house?

Here, Mother.

Well, bring me down for a meal there.

In the other room, Maisie's Japanese transistor is blaring.

I can't stand this, shouts my mother, I'm over eighty years of age, and she raises her eyes to heaven.

I can't stand it, she cries and her lips yammer. She shakes her dark-veined arthritic hands in despair. On the back of her head are two indentations where the blasted radiator burned into her skull.

This morning the plaster is torn off, taking a few grey hairs with it, so that the wound can be dressed. She lifts a hand towards the source of the pain. She kicks out at me. Yammers. Cries as the nurse dabs the scab.

You're hurting me, she cries. Oh God in Heaven. Why are *you* letting this happen to me?

It has to be changed, I say.

Why is she so rough. Hah?

It'll soon be over.

So *you* say.

We sit here in a house she does not believe is home. At times I am no longer her son. We are all a cruel clique intent on denying her sleep, food, outings and peace.

I lead her into the living room.

Quite nice, isn't it? says Maisie as she watches an Irish Country-and-Western song sung on the afternoon TV. These mammies' boys charm her. And she is reassured to see that Derek Davies the presenter is there.

There's Derek now, she says. And he's losing weight, you know.

At ninety-two she knows them all – Miley in *Glenroe*, Gay Byrne of *The Late Late show*, Pat Kenny on *Kenny Live*, all the news announcers. Her glasses swing round surveying everything.

The new county hospital in Cavan is *beautiful*, she asserts, as if she herself had been there.

She talks about the nurses my mother met as if she'd seen them herself. She describes the doctors, the size of the building, the lawns, the flowers on the lawns. The bad-tempered night nurse. Mrs English.

Mrs English was there?

Amn't I telling you, says my mother, reluctantly.

And what was wrong with her?

Her stomach.

There now, says Maisie.

Bit by bit by constant interrogation she has got the mother to describe all that happened her while she was away. Now the story has passed onto Maisie, and she that has rarely stirred outside the door in years tells it unerringly. Being behind closed doors does not stop Maisie's curiosity. Once in the Eighties, blinded by cataracts, she took to the bed for five years, and survived on soup and Valium. Often we'd find her astray on the corridor of the Breifne feeling her way back to her room. We stopped the Valium, she did cold turkey, and we tricked her into hospital. Then, after the operation on her eyes, she came downstairs and took her place as if she'd never been away, *Yous have all aged*, she said, and started in where she'd left off, recounting things she'd never seen, but telling them so well you'd swear that she herself was there. In the same way she describes, with great exactitude, shops in Cootehill that she has never stood in. Marriages between people she never met are remembered. All that she hears from visitors is retold and sketched out and authenticated.

While my mother is shedding reality, Maisie at over ninety is entering a new phase of complex embroidery of the tangible and the mysterious. Her heart in her mouth she hears talk of space, of astronauts. A moon walk makes her giddy and transcendent.

It must be terrible – she shudders at the thought – to be up there.

Poor Winnie, she says, looking across the table at her sister.

Despite the interrogations they rarely speak now. In fact Winnie can't stand being in the same room as Maisie because she feels unable to look after her. After years of being cared for by my mother (because of that promise made to Great-Aunt Jane), Maisie now finds herself removed from the centre of her sister's world. But Maisie is at least still with us, rocking down the corridor on her steed – her walking aid – and kicking a tin can of piss ahead of her.

The first thing she does when she wakes is reach to the radio. She flicks across stations thinking she's moving the volume control. But she doesn't care what the radio plays. It is her comforter. Anything might come out, Russian stations, heavy rock, classical music, ads, anything at all will do. Eating oranges with a distracted air she listens to the local radio station as it announces the selling prices for sheep and cattle and advertisements for mastitis.

I watch her. She looks at me, focusing hard.

You should dye your beard, she said, it's going grey.

I can't dye my beard.

Why not? And when you're at it you get some highlights into that head of hair.

Scour, says the radio. Lugworm. Redblood. Mange.

I've stolen so many of Maisie's phrases over the years and inserted them into the mouths and minds of fictional characters that she herself has become a work of the imagination. She likes painted fingernails. She studies her fingernails. She looks at my mother, who sits before her unfinished dinner, a bib to her neck, and her hands folded on her lap. The dessert sits untouched.

You should eat for Dermot, Maisie says, raising her voice.

Mind your own business, says my mother.

What did she say? asks Maisie.

She has no appetite, I reply.

You shout eat, Maisie says, loud and clear.

Let me out of here, barks my mother, and she flitters at her bib.

Now look, says Maisie. You'll knock something.

Bah! says the mother and she shakes the saltcellar at Maisie.

I lead the two women next door, Winnie to her armchair, Maisie to the sofa and then I put the TV on.

The green dog is in the wrong place on the mantel, complains Maisie. There's people in this house should have better things to do than disturbing arrangements.

I move the china dog.

Is that better? I ask.

More.

Now?

There, she says. That's better.

Soon she's falling asleep, tipping gently to her right-hand side. Nothing Maisie likes better than falling asleep to the comforting sound of the radio or the TV blaring. Soon the two sisters are sleeping. I steal a brandy. My mother's mouth opens like a fledgling's.

Spit slips out the corner of Maisie's lips. *All I can be is a sweet memory that drifts through your mind*, Jimmy Buckley sings, as if on cue, through their subconscious on *Today at 3*.

I change the station. Immediately Maisie wakes, rights her glasses, looks at *The Clash of the Titans* that's on the box, and then turns to me.

What happened?

Nothing.

Something happened.

I changed the station, I say.

I thought so. And without so much as a by-your-leave. She studies the film. Burps quietly. Were you ever in the reptile house in London?

Once I was, I think, I say.

My God, if one of those snakes got a hold of you! She lifts her closed fists. They'd squeeze you. *They'd squeeze you.* It's terrible.

She returns to the box.

Dreadful looking yokes, she says. What's going on?

A war.

The same as usual, she nods. The night the orphans were burnt in the fire in the Poor Clares the windows of the Breifne were red hot. The poor things were trapped. It was terrible. *Terrible!* And she beat her thigh with a fist.

In the commotion Mother wakes. She reaches for her beads, turns and sees me there.

Where were you all day? she asks.

I was here with you.

I don't believe you, she says smiling. And she takes my hand.

Will you be sleeping here? she asks.

I will.

God bless you. She ponders her surroundings, gives Maisie a cursory glance and asks, What day is today?

It's Wednesday.

And what time is it? she asks, scrutinizing her gold watch that doesn't work.

It's seven forty-five.

Look at the face, says Maisie watching the TV. Imagine wakening up and finding *that* beside you in the bed.

What's she talking about?

The film, I shout.

Trash, says my mother. Nothing but *trash*.

In any case, says Maisie, there was this man Kayton, and he'd be out womanizing. Oh a dreadful carry on, she laughed.

Jazzing, says my mother.

And his wife'd be out looking for him. Your uncle Jim used tell us all about it.

More jazzing, adds the mother.

Well, I suppose it takes all sorts.

Give her a drink, says Winnie.

She has one.

What's she saying? asks Maisie.

She wants to know if you have a drink.

I have.

Well, nod your head to her.

Who, asks Maisie, do you think I am, Father Christmas?

Just nod your head, Maisie.

If you must.

She nods. One two three nods. My mother throws her an oblique eye.

What's wrong with her? she asks.

She's saying Yes.

Yes, that's right, agrees Maisie. I'm nodding like the Santa used be in the window.

Mother shakes her head in disbelief.

Wow, she says.

What? asks Maisie.

That's right, says Mother.

What are you trying to tell me?

Mother rattles her heels.

Nothing but whispering, she says. Whispering Rufus! She raises her eyes to heaven and spots me again. When is your next book coming out? she asks.

It's too warm, says Maisie.

First it's too cold, then it's too warm, I say.

That's right, replies Maisie, I'm a nuisance.

No, you're not.

Yes I am.

She turns to the box.

It's bad enough being an astronaut, she says. But then there's these climbers that get caught in the snow. There's avalanches. And down they go, it's terrible.

She lifts a hand and curls it. My mother watches her.

You should be in your bed, mother snarls.

What!

Give her a drink in her room, my mother says.

It's already there.

What's she saying? asks Maisie.

She wants you to have a drink.

Maisie looks at me. She scrutinizes my shoes, my trousers, my face. Shifts her glasses a fraction and continues this unabashed survey. A long time goes by.

Didn't you go to the nuns in the Holy Clares?

I did, I say.

And then the De La Salle Brothers slapped you. You got beaten up. They nearly killed you.

Put a drink in her room, says mother. I'm not able.

The two drinks are in her room.

Are you sure?

Of course I'm sure.

Who put them there?

Me.

Oh. Did he? she asks Maisie.

Nod, I say to Maisie.

Nod to what?

Nod to Mother.

I'm turning into Santa Claus, she says.

She nods dementedly.

My mother points at her and laughs.

That Santa, I say, is above in the loft.

And then, you got thrown out of college, added Maisie, for going out to see the Bachelors. *The Bachelors* no less. And what about that five pounds you got from the man in Dublin. She gives me a scathing look. Did you pass it on?

I did.

Good.

I get up and give Maisie another brandy and ginger ale.

All donations, she says, are gratefully received. We'll be in the boneyard long enough.

Your drinks are in your own room, shouts my mother and she shakes her fist at Maisie.

What?

She should be in bed, Mother says to me.

Here we are back at the hurt centre of some responsibility. When she was fit to get about the house my mother would have had her sister in bed at this juncture. Night fell in the house at a whim.

Are those drinks in the room for her? Winnie asks, and leans over and nips me.

Yes.

See that they are, and she moves the black beads through her crimson-varnished fingers.

I pour myself a brandy.

Give yourself another one, says Maisie, you need it. Again she begins her scrutiny of me. And Frankie Brady died.

He did.

He was a laugh.

He was.

Yes, the poor fellow.

Son, interrupts the mother.

My mother wears black stockings to just below her knee.

Son.

What?

Nothing.

She reminds me of Charlie Chang, says Maisie.

Who was he?

He was before your time. You see Charlie Chang knew all his sons as numbers. There was son number such-and-such. You had son number one, and you had son number six. And so on. Charlie was Chinese, of course. And then there was the time that Val O'Neill, your uncle Val, Valentine, no less, or Pop O'Neill as the lads called him, took us to the Chinese. Val was a scream. *What's under that mound of grease?* he hissed. *Is there a cat missing in the vicinity?* I could have died.

Go to bed, shouts Winnie. The two drinks are outside.

What's she saying now? asks Maisie, laughing.

At my time of life, my mother says, I'm not able, and she reaches a hand to her knee.

When you were shopping in Cootehill, says Maisie, we couldn't restrain her. You'd have to use force. *Dermot has left us*, she started with. *Dermot is in town*, Eileen told her. *He's gone*, she'd shout. *He's not*, said Eileen, *he's in town.* She'd wait, then start again.

Eventually I pour the two offending drinks and bring them out to Maisie's room. When I'm there I hear Winnie screaming Bed! Bed! Bed!

It's too early, I tell you! shouts Maisie.

My mother yammers.

I told you it's too early.

Bed!

God above!

Bed, I said!

Stop it Winnie!

Yayaya!

The stroke my mother had has left her tongue a temper which refuses articulation. Ya-ya-ya-ya-yama! When I return to the sitting room Mother is on her feet in the middle of the floor.

If she falls, screams Maisie, I can't help her up.

Mother goes back to her armchair and glares at Maisie. The sisters are estranged. There they are, the work of who makes us, variables, fraught, laughing, impatient, disturbed.

The sisters' silence is unbecoming as these wild science-fiction beasts go large-pawed and cumbersome into battle with huge, jungle roars.

Release the dragon, says Laurence Olivier, in the film.

Mother turns to me.

I fell on the fender, she says quietly. It was dark. That's what happened. She touches the white cap on her scalp. But now I'm fine.

The time she fell on the fender she was sixteen. But the two blows to her head – the fender and the radiator – have become mixed up. One mind gone off, the other mind in. On the box Pegasus flies over the cliffs to the rescue. There is a happy ending. We sit before these metaphorical beasts like figures in a surreal soap.

But surrealism is a conscious obliteration of unaesthetic effects. Someone is in control.

There is no censor in my mother's mind. No artist refining an illusion. What's happening comes through unabridged. The hard slog is crude. The repetition of commands surfaces out of a prior world of habit. They once had meaning and that's what makes her desperate. The orders from the diseased subconscious veer from the pitiful to the dignified, while she peels frantically at a button on her blouse that she can't undo.

She proffers her wrist. I lead her through the house. We go to the door and stand there a moment looking out on the quiet estate. The bin, she says. Then back through the house. She looks into Maisie's room, peers into my room and then we arrive at last by her bedside.

Glasses, she says.

I take off her glasses and put them on the sideboard.

Earrings, she says, touching an ear.

I slip off her shoes. I take off her jumper and skirt. I pull the nightdress over her head. All the time she looks at me. She feels her cap. I pull the sheet to her chin. She closes her eyes.

It's no good any longer, she says.

Of course it is.

No, she says, the mind is going.

Before sleep that night I remember a moment in time – myself, nineteen, maybe twenty, walking along in a blue trench coat, under trees, in the rain. I'm going somewhere. I try to imagine where I was going to but can't. No matter. I have great expectations. In the dark the leaves are glistening. I'm happy it seems.

I listen intently for any sound from Mother's room. Nothing.

After a while I hear Maisie.

What's to become of me? she says to herself and the wooden top of the po bangs shut.

Near dawn the door to my bedroom opens a fraction. A hand reaches in, the light comes on. My mother is standing there in her Sunday best with the red hat low over her eyes and the handbag on her arm.

Chapter 30

In a terrible sleep filled with slugs which are turning into black cats. I try to wake and go out to see if the mother is all right. I struggle to reach consciousness, but can't. It's maybe that I'm too lazy, maybe too tired. Instead I try to listen in my sleep to whether I can hear her.

I hear nothing but feel something is wrong. So many nights this happens that sometimes I want to get bedrails and cage her in so she can't get out. Now, although her room is only a few feet across the corridor, and both our doors stand ajar so I can hear the least sound, still and all I cannot summon myself from the depths of sleep. I want to wake but can't move. Instead of getting to the surface I'm going deeper. At last I shout, Helen! Helen!

What!

Helen!

Yes.

Go and see is she all right.

Helen goes out and runs back shouting Granny is on the floor! Dermot! *Granny is on the floor!*

Inside her bedroom door my mother is stretched out on her stomach. Her glasses are pressed into the carpet. She's shaking her legs like a stranded fish. Like a fish landed into a boat. We lift her together. She comes up straight as a plank and can't stand. The legs go backward and drag behind her. She tries to smile.

Mother, are you all right?

They moved something on me, she replies.

Yes, I say.

It was not where it should have been.

I know that.

She has done her lips. Has on a blouse. She shakes uncontrollably.

Mother, why do you get out of bed? Why?!

I can't hold her, says Helen.

We find it difficult to bend her legs. We seat her on the bed.

I'm eighty years of age, she cries in despair.

Would she like a cup of tea? asks Helen.

Yes, Mother says smiling.

She sits in the kitchen in her slip and red blouse, green pus on her bandaged head where the wound has become infected, and her chin is shaking like a piston. She drinks the tea gratefully and calls for bread. Then, when we don't bring the bread immediately, she calls for something sweet. So we give her a slice of swiss roll.

The three of us sit at the table. She constantly adjusts her glasses. In the fall one of the arms was bent. It's six in the morning. The central heating is purring in the background. A deep white October frost covers everything.

Is today Sunday?

No.

Are you sure?

Yes.

When it's Sunday you'll have my outfit ready? she asks Helen.

I will.

We lead her about the kitchen, she undoes the back door, peers out, then we stop a moment at the draining board, she stands before all the items she once knew intimately, then on we go to the living room, I lead her to her armchair, then along the corridor, she pauses by Maisie's door and incongruously laughs and puts a finger to her lips.

Shsh! she says. Maisie's sleeping.

We enter her room. She puts her hand on the cursed radiator to check for heat. We undress her.

Glasses, she says.

She touches her glasses. I put them away.

She touches her ears.

I take her earrings. Then cup one hand under her backside and another under her back and lift her into bed while Helen holds her hands.

Don't rough it, she says.

After we put her beneath the sheets, I watch her from the foot of the bed, lean down and kiss her.

There's one thing, she says. I am afraid those are not my glasses.

As I lie in the dark I keep hearing her falling. But each time I look into the room she's sleeping, as Helen says, like a bird.

250

Within a week the hints of Parkinson's disease have crept from her chin, down her hands, along her thighs. Our trips to the bathroom are frenzied affairs.

What was once a tic you pretended not to see has become a spasm, a physical morse code that's tapping out some painful message from a ravaged interior.

But for the rosary beads, her earrings and glasses she would have little. Lipstick and nail varnish are her only decorations. But she has an attachment to certain bright colours on a Sunday. Once she was a very vain lady, now she'll turn aside at dinner and spit out meat she cannot chew onto the carpet.

And she, says Eileen, who does a few hours in the house every day, that was a great woman to look after herself.

What was once impatience is now an obsession. She fills her mouth at table in such a manner that her small gorge cannot accommodate it, then up it comes, and she's on her feet to the door. Except for dessert.

Dessert, she calls. *Dessert!*

Dessert is fruit biscuits crumbled into tinned mandarins. She spoons it into her mouth without stopping, takes off her bib and pushes against the table while Maisie runs through the stations on the radio. The disco has started. After spinning the dial Maisie finds heavy rock, then music from the Sixties, including Clarence Frogman Henry, and finally rap.

If there's one thing I hate, explained Maisie, it's silence.

I open the dining-room door.

Wait for me, says Mother. I'd wait for you.

She's up and on her feet. I lead her to her armchair. She dips into the metal cup at her side and lifts out her rosary. She dips again, lifts out a small prayer sheet to Padre Pio and scrutinizes it. Replaces it in the cup and prays.

The head is tipped back, and the whispers are low to begin with, then after a while the sibilants grow in intensity, she barks out the name of God, and stops suddenly, her rounded back straightens, then drawing the rosary into the air, she finds her place and begins again.

What's coming now? laughs Mother as I advance with the pills across the sitting room.

She picks them out of my hand with her painted fingernails and places them on her palm, then picks them again, one by one, and drops them under her tongue. She sips the milk, and throwing her head back opens her mouth like a minnow in a stream, and shakes her cheeks and gargles.

She gets two down.

I hand her another.

That's enough, she says.

No, two more.

Why do you want to do this to me?! And she nips me.

It's good for you.

With eyes narrowed in frustration she takes the second lot of pills. The red aspro stains her tongue. She swills the milk around. Goes through all the same motions again, closes her eyes and swallows. Then gags on the final pill. Her eyes water.

God in Heaven, she says.

Oh, she was always like that, says Maisie, ever since she was a child.

The mother glares at Maisie.

What would you know? she says.

Ha-ha, says Maisie.

Now, Winnie says.

We head to the toilet. I steady her over the bowl. Afterwards I make her clean herself. Then I turn on the taps for her to wash her hands. Instead she reaches for her false teeth.

No, not the teeth, I say, not yet.

Dear God, she says.

First wash your hands.

The teeth, the teeth, she says.

I take her hands away from her mouth. She fights me. I slap her hands.

I am over eighty years of age, she cries, and you are abusing me.

I stand ashamed beside her as she washes her hands, dries them and then we do the teeth together. She gags again as I replace the plate. The teeth push through her cheek like ribs. She plops them into place. All her former intimacies, the habits she'd learnt when alone, are following a different pattern than before.

Before the teeth, wash the hands, I say.

That's right, she says.

We go back across the carpeted floors, looking into the other rooms as we go, like two people in a fairground. Arriving by her armchair again she reaches for her beads, and with one hand dropped over the other, and the knees delicately crossed, she closes her eyes.

She reaches a hand to correct her glasses. These are not my glasses, she says, then the beads inch through her fingers.

I said to Eileen that at night I'd hear a thud and rush into Winnie's room to find her safely asleep and then realize that the sound I'd heard was Maisie in her room slapping the seat down on the wooden commode. So Eileen took the seat away to stop the sudden commotion at night, but now there was nothing to cover the unseemly contents of the po.

The following morning Maisie entered the dining room like the Maisie of old. As I sat next door with Mother I could hear the tirade begin.

I demand the return, she said, slapping the table when Eileen brought her dinner, of the seat of the commode.

You were waking Dermot with it at night.

Tell him I want to talk to him, she said slapping the table louder. How dare he!

It was not him that took it, said Eileen, it was me.

I want it back where it was.

Yes, Maisie.

We *cannot* live without the seat of the commode. I want it back, no matter who took it.

All right, said Eileen.

We want it back *immediately*.

Yes, Maisie.

It's disgraceful, she said and she switched on the radio, that we have to look at our own piss.

The seat of the commode went back. Down it banged in the middle of the night with, I thought, an added intensity from then on.

My mother snores with her head back and her mouth open. The glasses have slipped. She wakes.

Are the potatoes boiling?

Yes.

Did you feed Maisie?

I did.

What day is it?

To prove that today is not Sunday I show her the date and day on the front of the *Irish Press* that is delivered along with the milk.

Did you pay the man?

I did.

Did the bins go out?

Bennie took them.

And how are things in Sligo?

Fine.

Will you bring me there some day?

I will.

You'll bring me to your place by the sea?

I will.

To see the chainies, you bugger you, she says. Chainies is her pet word for china. She'd once visited me in Sligo and saw us washing the delft under the outside tap and was horrified. She skips through her beads. I fill a glass of wine.

Supping, she says.

That's right, I agree.

Always supping.

A bit.

Your father never drank, she says and nips me.

Yes, he did.

No, he didn't. It's you are the guilty party.

Mother, he did.

Never. Never. *Never.* Nor did he smoke.

He died of smoking.

He did not. And he walked from Finea to Mullingar for court and back again.

It's your own father you're talking of.

What are you saying?

You're talking of Thomas Slacke. Not Jack Healy.

Jack Healy, she repeats, savouring the words.

Yes, Jack Healy. You married him.

I know all that.

Not Thomas Slacke.

Thomas Slacke. Oh, she says, again savouring the words. He was a very religious man. A saint. Praying all the time. We never saw him.

But Jack Healy, I say, do you remember him?

Of course I do.

Well he drank.

No, she says uncertainly. Then she adds: He died young.

He did.

That's right, she says, and she goes back to her prayers.

Will you bring me to the altar, she asks at some moment of every day. Or: Will you bring me to Mass?

Each day of the week tends towards Sunday. She wakes at night and dresses for Mass, steps into her finery and does her lips, then slips into the sitting room and waits, with the red hat on. This can happen any day, Wednesday, Thursday, any time.

Phone Una, and get the car, she'll command.

Once myself and Helen took her to Mass. Usually she would go with Una, but this Sunday Una was away. Mother was wearing her purple suit and incongruous red hat. She entered church like an elf. Nodded and smiled at faces she didn't recognize. The beads ran through her hands. Communion started and we watched the crowds, forgetting all about Mother. For whatever reason we did not get her to the altar rail in time. The priest had finished with the last communicant and was turning aside with his chalice of wafers when my mother's hand came down on Helen's like a claw.

Startled, Helen, who had been away in another world, looked at me. Mother dug her fingers into the back of Helen's wrist. She shook her head and gritted her teeth.

Get me up, she whispered shrilly.

What? said Helen.

Bring me to the altar, Mother cried and stood. Wait! Wait, you! she called to the priest.

Helen dutifully got up, the people in the pew stood aside and my mother, angry and defiant, hauled Helen with her towards the rails.

I pretended I wasn't there. The priest had already turned away and knelt before the sacrament. He was stirring the leavings of wine in the chalice with the Eucharistic cloth when he caught sight of my mother. She was beckoning him with her index finger while Helen, embarrassed, stood behind her in front of the multitude.

The priest returned, fed her her portion, and she bowed. She looked at Helen with disdain as she led her back. She knelt beside me.

What was going on in your head? said my mother. To think you'd let me miss communion.

I'm sorry, said Helen.

Humph! she said, you're not with it.

OK, Mother, I said. Take it easy.

Mass without communion! she spat.

Then she smiled falsely at someone across the aisle and swallowed the host.

And the strength of her hand, Helen said afterwards, I wouldn't have believed it.

In the middle of all of this, Helen and Mother and I went to a wedding – Miriam's daughter was getting married in Athy. We holed up in a castle on the outskirts of town. The journey there took nigh on five hours, with mother despairing and wanting to go home, and wanting to arrive, and asking, *Why are we lost? Ask a guard can't you. A guard will know. Dear God in Heaven when is this journey going to end?* By the time we were in the bedroom Helen was demented, so she went outside, got into the car to take a break, saw the mother's red hat on the back seat, leaned over and drove her fist into it in frustration, only to find later it was her own hat.

I bring Maisie her breakfast on a round imitation silver tray. On one plate are little portions of banana and cheese, on another a slice of toast minus its crust cut into squares, a bowl of Frosties and a mug of tea with two and a half sugars.

I tap on her door.

Good morning, Maisie, I call.

Good morning yourself, she says, with her back to me in the bed. Here we are again.

It's raining.

I wouldn't be surprised.

I have your breakfast.

You must be beginning to wonder, she says, when all of this will end.

Not at all.

She puts one hand to the side of her face.

I couldn't care, she says, if I never ate another thing. She turns. Did you ever feel like that?

Sometimes. Do you know what they call the swan in Rosses Point in Sligo?

No.

The Drumcliffe pilot, I explain.

The Drumcliffe pilot, she says.

For you see when the people see a swan flying over the village the story goes that whatever house he flies over in there someone will die.

Now, says Maisie.

And because in those days the nearest graveyard was over the sea in Drumcliffe, the swans were known as the Drumcliffe pilots.

Swans, says Maisie.

That's right.

We learn something new every day, and she folds her hands on her lap. I leave her sitting on the edge of the bed. She eats and ponders every morsel. Combs her dyed, thinning hair. And sometimes, if I've forgot to empty it, she trundles on her steed to the bathroom across the aisle tapping ahead of her the can of pee from her commode. She's in there for ages. When I go in after her the place is in a shambles.

What's going on, I ask her. I had to clean up after you in the loo.

I have the trots, she says. There was so much talk of shit in this house yesterday that I caught the runs.

I bring her radio from the bedroom to the kitchen table. Soon she appears on her steed, stands in the middle of the room and checks that every one of the figurines on the sideboard is in its correct place. Then she scrutinizes the photos and the statues on the windowsill. If there is any strange object among them she'll ask to have it removed. Everything must be where it was yesterday and the day before.

The same scrutiny takes place in the sitting room.

Leaning on her walking-aid she lifts the Spanish Lady and looks into her face, toys with her dress and replaces her exactly where she should be. She moves the yellow-haired china boy a fraction so that he is closer to the yellow-haired china girl. She touches the big green dogs that sat on the old wireless in the Breifne. Touches the flower lady.

Returns an inch at a time to the sofa. Drops into it.

Aren't they beautiful flowers, she says pointing at a plastic arrangement of faded roses. Have they been watered today?

They're plastic, Maisie.

Oh. She looks at the flowers in disbelief. She focuses on me. Who was that girl you went out with when you were young?

Sheila.

And we had to close our gobs when we walked by her door.

That's right.

And that beard. She shivers. Why don't you take it off?

I've always had it.

That's the problem, she says, nodding.

She fixes her cushions and rests her elbow, leans sideways to watch the TV.

What nonsense is this?

Some old film.

Charles Laughton.

Aye.

And Cagney.

Yes.

Where's Winnie?

Sleeping.

It's lonesome without her, says Maisie. Poor Winnie. She doesn't know the time of day. But you want her there all the same.

She turns to me.

Ring Nancy, Dermot, she says. Ring her and tell her to come round.

Chapter 31

I sit with the mother in the early mornings. She prays, I write. It is a private meditative time, broken by visits to the toilet, exclamations to the Mother of God and to Jesus, and explosions from Maisie's radio in her bedroom.

I look up. The mother is watching me.

Is that you? she asks.

Yes.

Dermot?

Yes.

Hm. Where is Helen?

At work in Sligo, I say.

And how are all her people?

Fine, I say.

She's at her best just after breakfast, the curtains thrown wide, and the late autumn light not quite flooding in. We sit with our backs to the outside world. We are trapped in what apparently is. We cannot take off elsewhere. But though this is not a fiction where everything happens in the so-called world of make-believe, sometimes the mundane everyday feels like an illusion – anything might happen, the authentic is a trick, and the story is not really known till it's told.

Today she is blissfully benign. She looks over at me and laughs while I make up things that never really happened, or if they did, happened to some other, some distant self that's been quietened by time, that never existed till words bring it again into being for further scrutiny. Then the inevitable happens. You come to a stop. The whole philosophizing sours. She even loses her earlier calm.

She flings the rosary into its pot.

Get me up, she says.

No, I say, stay there.

Can I not go to my blessed bed?

No, I say. Not till later.

Why?

If you sleep now, you won't sleep later. If you get up by yourself, you might fall. And Nancy is coming this evening.

Nancy?

Yes, Nancy.

She goes back to her prayers. I feed Maisie, make dinner, Eileen hoovers the house, cartoons explode from the telly. Three times in the afternoon I bring Mother to bed, and three times she gets up again. So that by the time Eileen comes to relieve me at five Mother has not had her usual nap. I slink off in the rain to town and into the supermarket. They ask after Mrs Healy. Then, on to Gene Bannon's bar. When I get back from the pub after six with tomorrow's dinner and wine and brandy, Eileen has mother dressed up in a pink blouse, her fingernails are newly painted and her hair is neatly brushed.

You look lovely, Mother, I say.

You left me, she declares.

He had to go to town, shouts Maisie.

And I had to hold her down, says Eileen, to keep her from going to bed.

Blasted bitch, snaps Mother.

We've been a bad girl, Mrs Healy.

Yayaya, says Mother.

And the strength of her.

I want to go to bed, says Winnie, and this yoke here won't let me.

It's too early, Eileen says. If you go now you'll be there for the night.

That's right, says Maisie.

What's she saying? asks Winnie.

And anyway, Mother, I say, Nancy is coming.

Nancy?

Your sister.

I know she's my sister.

That's right, Winnie, Maisie shouts, Nancy will be here soon.

Who's talking to you? says Winnie.

At seven as she promised, Aunty Nancy, eighty years of age and sister of the two dames, steps out of Dr Magauran's car. She arrives with a bottle of wine, a huge pizza from Quinnsworth, and a large pavlova. My mother explodes into laughter at the sight of her.

There you are, she says.

How are you, Winnie?

My mother smiles.

I said, How are you!

That's right, says Mother, and she turns to me. That one loved riding horses, she says.

So I did.

You faggot, you, get Nancy a drink, Mother says, prodding my shoulder with a bony finger.

And what about me, chirps Maisie, have I not got a mouth on me?

And give her one as well.

Now for you, says Maisie.

I split the pizza in four and the three sisters sit down to the meal with gusto. I cut Maisie's and the mother's share into small pieces. Then all three ladies fire a wad of salt onto their plates.

The wine, Dermie, says Nancy.

What's this? says Maisie, looking at her plate.

A piazza, announces Nancy.

A what?

A piazza.

It's not one of those curries he makes? she asks.

No, it's not a damn curry. Try it and see.

We'll be poisoned.

Maisie tries a piece. The mother watches us. She's on the verge of being bold, of refusing. I tie her bib. Still she makes no move. Then she lifts a slice. Then another. Hilarious chat ensues. They love the pizza and to my amazement not a scrap remains.

Now, didn't I tell you? says Nancy.

Dessert! calls Mother.

Hauld your horses, says Nancy, can't you?

Dessert! calls Mother again.

Jesus, you'd think she had a firecracker up her arse, laughs Nancy.

Stop the dirty talk, says Mother laughing. She lifts a strawberry and dips it in the cream, rolls it around in her mouth and swallows.

Nice, she says.

We'll be on the throne all fucking night, says Maisie.

By the time we've eaten the pavlova myself and Nancy have finished the first bottle of wine. Then we start on a second and move on out to the living room. Maisie is on her third brandy and ginger ale. I stroll, with the mother in tow, to her armchair.

She's like a guinea hen beside him, says Maisie, God help her.

Now what? says Mother.

Nothing, I say.

Mother starts to push herself up out of the chair.

Where are you going? asks Nancy.

The mother sits back and smiles.

Take something, can't ye, says Nancy.

No, my mother says.

Take a port.

No.

It will do you no harm.

I'd be up all night.

Give her a brandy and port, says Maisie.

I won't drink it. She shakes her fists. And that's final.

She was always stubborn, Nancy says. And always fussy.

Oh always, agrees Maisie.

But Bridgie was the favourite.

She was.

Soon Mother is calling out to go to bed, Maisie wants clove balls and Nancy wants brandy.

There's no clove balls in the house.

Well, can I have grapes? asks Maisie.

No, I say.

You see that? says Maisie. He won't give me grapes.

They only give you the runs.

And I love salted peanuts, says Maisie, and I declare he won't allow me any of them either.

They only give you heartburn.

Doctor Healy, she says scornfully.

Oh I suffered from heartburn in my day, says Nancy.

So you did, nods Maisie. I loved onion sandwiches, she adds reflectively and studies me.

So used I, Nancy remembers, and then you wouldn't let me into the bed with you.

Why would I? She slaps the cushion. She'd eat onion sandwiches and get sick. And then she'd come into my room on her tippytoes. She peers at Nancy. *Maisie*, she'd whisper and she only five.

Go away, you'd say.

And then she'd get in behind me.

And what was wrong with that? asks Nancy.

You were like a cold frog after standing in the outdoor closet.

Let me up to your stalk, I'd shout.

No, I'd say.

The clock goes back tonight, I add.

And the country people, says Maisie, will say: *Is that auld time or new time?* You see it used to confuse them.

What are you saying? asks Mother, and she leans over and nips me.

I said the clock goes back tonight.

In more ways than one, shrieks Nancy.

Look at her, adds the mother. Jazzing.

The bottle of brandy is sinking. Finea and its people enter the room as the three women, who between them add up to a total of 262 years on this earth, begin reminiscing about the village around the turn of the century – the Clarkes, the Clavins, the Keoghs, Brian Sheridan, women, dogs, death. They break into gales of laughter.

Mary Jane slept with her two brothers, roared Nancy.

What's that? asked Maisie.

Mary Jane, she slept with her two brothers.

And she used to milk the cow into the fucking pisspot, agrees Maisie, chuckling, with her eyes to heaven. Into the fucking pisspot.

Dear God, says Mother, she did.

And the priest came in with the host for the stations and found the three of them in bed.

Dear God, repeats my mother and she claps her knees.

Then auld Clarke got randy at the end of his days. He leapt on Josie Flynn.

Jazzing, says mother.

And he all of ninety years of age.

263

Well, that had to overtake him sometime, states Maisie.

He was old enough not to know a mickey from a pussy, shrieks Nancy.

And by God, says Maisie, if he didn't come back for more.

What are they saying? asks Mother.

Oh, as if she wouldn't know, Nancy says.

Are they talking dirty?

They are, I say.

I thought so.

And a gypsy woman, continued Nancy, came into the shop to old Clarke and she said: *Could you give me something for the childer? I have seven childer. Out! Out! Out!* he roared – *you had the sport of them, not me.*

There's no doubt about it, says Mother.

I fill more glasses.

Squealer McHugh, sniggered Nancy.

Oh, Squealer McHugh.

He got so drunk one Christmas he couldn't walk.

And they put him into a barrow, says Maisie, with a lantern on it and pushed him up the village.

And someone saw him and thought it was the Holy Family coming.

Dear God, laughs my mother.

Then there was the Marcus Somerville. He wasn't the full shilling. Do you remember Marcus Somerville, Winnie?

What are you saying?

Do you remember Marcus?

Marcus? The Marquis of Somerville, she says, correcting the pronunciation. Of course I do, the poor creature. He was put out of the big house and came to us.

He did, agrees Maisie.

He had a very good speaking voice, Winnie declares.

He was aristocratic, agrees Nancy, and I was intrigued by him.

You were intrigued by anything in trousers, laughs Maisie. She turns to me. Did she ever tell you of Matti Sheridan?

No, I say.

Oh, Matti Sheridan, says Nancy.

He came to Nancy and said: *It's lilac time again.*

That's right, nods Nancy, he did.

He was trying to work up an affair with you. And you a grass widow.

Your uncle Jim at the time, Nancy explains, was in England.

Yes, *It's lilac time again*, Matti Sheridan said to her.

He did, agrees Nancy, and the two laugh outrageously.

My mother blinks, feeds the rosary through her fingers. Maisie studies her, burps suddenly, then exclaims, Dear God.

Winnie, she says.

My mother does not reply.

It's terrible to think she doesn't know what's going on, says Maisie sadly. And she can't hear a word we say.

Winnie, shouts Nancy, have a drink.

My mother throws Nancy a hostile eye.

Take me to my bed, she says, and then leans over and nips me.

In a minute, I say.

Blessed God, she sighs.

She dribbles her beads into the pot, and sits with her hands joined in her lap, and her eyes on the ceiling.

Seamus, says Nancy, in a low voice, was very cut up when Mammy died. *I never told her I loved her*, he said.

That's right, agrees Maisie.

We go quiet for a while, the central heating shudders and figures go by in silence on the TV. Nancy looks into her glass and nods to herself. She weeps a little and shakes her head. Maisie leans on her arm and watches Mother.

Dermot.

Yes.

What time is it in Canada?

I don't know.

Are they before us or behind us?

Behind us, I think.

Well, ring Tony in Canada, said Maisie, and let him speak to your mother. She'd like that.

Do you want to speak to Tony, Mother? I shout.

My eldest is far away, she says.

I can get him on the phone.

Don't be bothering me.

I can phone him, Mother, I shout.

Stop shouting at me.

Tony, says Nancy. Do you want to speak to Tony?

The mother forms the word Tony on her lips a number of times, then closes her eyes, as if she were tempting providence. I reach over and take her hand.

What now? she asks wearily.

C'mon with me, I say.

Are we going for a walk?

We are.

Good.

She tries to rise from the chair and falls back again. I take both her hands and haul her to her feet. She adjusts her glasses and plods fearfully across the room. She heads in the direction of her bedroom so I steer her before me along the hallway to the front door. We open the door and look out at the stars. I close the door and ring Tony. Nancy and Winnie wait behind me. When he answers I say, Hold on there, Tony, the mother is here. I hand the phone to her. She looks at it uncertainly.

Mother, I can hear Tony saying, is that you?

It's Tony, I say. I raise my voice. Mother, it's Tony.

She drops the phone and heads off.

Come back, says Nancy, and speak to your beloved son in Toronto. I bring her back again. She lifts the instrument to her ear.

Mother, says Tony.

Say something, can't you, Nancy orders.

Will you take me to the toilet? Mother asks.

I will, says Tony.

Then she replaces the phone.

Chapter 32

In an ironic piece some time ago in The Irishman's Diary in the *Irish Times*, Kevin Myers wrote that out beyond where I live in north Sligo every few years Hy Brazil, like another Atlantis, rises. This was news to me. I have not seen it yet, but I think of it this morning, rising out of the sea like a whale, or resting gently on the bottom of the ocean, waiting for the next time.

I think of Hy Brazil as I sit in the living room with a terrible hangover, my mother asleep in her armchair, Nancy asleep in my room, Maisie perched by the radio in the dining room, the central heating going up into a whine. Lack of sleep after spending the night on cushions on the floor has made me start to hallucinate.

If I close my eyes I think I can see Hy Brazil, a little beyond Inishmurray Island, not exactly land, not even someplace eternal, but a place imagined by people long before me that I must imagine in my turn. Imagination hands on a duty to those who come after. So it is with Hy Brazil.

So it is with Hy Brazil. Because it doesn't exist we wish it into being because someone else did in another age. Like a star that appears say once every two hundred years, you watch for Hy Brazil every seven years but in truth it has no definite orbit, no mathematics can accurately predict its appearance at a definite hour on a definite day. But you want to be there when it happens. Even if it never happened. Even if it never existed, you wish it into being. You wish for the language to recover it from the void.

I don't have any books to hand here in Cootehill in County Cavan that tell me who the imaginary folk were who inhabited Hy Brazil, how they arrived there, whether it is like Tír na nÓg. Are they ageless folk who live there? Is it an island inhabited by heroes? Shape-changers? Is it where suicides go? Or has it been long deserted, and rises out of the sea as a reminder to us of another civilization that has long disappeared off the face of the earth. Did the inhabitants do wrong that the island sank? Did a catastrophe greet them because of some terrible evil doing?

Is Hy Brazil the place we go to after we die? I don't know, so I make up my own Hy Brazil.

But the minute I start imagining it, my mind refuses Hy Brazil. The language won't budge. Instead I think of trivial things, irritations, domestic affairs; a dream of the previous night where an old lover, with astounding familiarity, visited, and a book that I can't finish writing presented itself. Nursing. Drinking. How the smell of my mother's waste made me retch as I cleaned her this morning.

But I suppose those who dreamed up Hy Brazil must have also known these irritations and mood swings. Mythology is full of sordidness. The fears of the storytellers are exaggerated in the tales. The unbelievable takes on a human presence. What has happened repeatedly turns into a ritual. What has not happened turns into the mystery. The island is peopled with our uncertainties. Peace is only allowed a certain passage of time before terror intrudes again.

So that is how it must be on Hy Brazil for those who live there, and how it must have been for the makers of Hy Brazil, the ones that dreamed it up and make it sink and make it rise.

It's not the island that rises out of the sea but the observer out of the torpor of everyday. And on the Hy Brazil I imagine there is someone looking back at us, wishing that they might begin again, be trapped once more among all that human and domestic trivia. Someone out there would probably like to swap places with me, they'd like to hear human voices again, listen to human despair and laughter, wake to a new day.

By thinking of Hy Brazil I get homesick for my cottage in Sligo. I sit there thinking of the cottage in the same way I used think of Finea before sleep. I go up the road that was taken away in the storm. The asses roar. The sea is thumping the rocks. Beside me my mother sleeps with a cooing sound. She – despite infirmity, spasms and weakness – is on her own Hy Brazil. Next door Maisie calls for green grapes. On the TV, 7000 people gather in the Shankill Road in Belfast to mourn nine out of ten killed in an explosion in a fishmonger's shop.

The tenth they will not mourn.

He planted the bomb.

Nancy staggers out of bed. She looks pale and wasted.

God, she says.

Nancy, I say.

I didn't know where I was.

Can I get you something to eat? I ask.

No, thank you. She pats the air with her hands. I'm off solids and on a herring.

Tea?

A cup I suppose.

Are you all right?

I feel dreadful. How do you feel?

Terrible.

What time did we go to bed?

About two.

God of almighty.

That's the way.

Was I drinking brandy?

You were.

I thought so. She sat and laid her hands on her lap. Her chin shakes. And I'm eighty years of age.

I know.

Why do we do it?

I don't know.

Neither do I. And those cursed radiators. The din they make. It's like a hothouse. She gets up and looks into the mirror. Dear God. I better get home. Will you ring Raymond.

I will.

She looks at my mother.

Are the dolls all right?

Yes.

Poor Winnie, she'd drive you crackers. I did two weeks here by myself and I thought I'd never get home. No one called. I was demented. By the second week I thought of climbing up onto the roof like those prisoners. This place is worse than Strangeways.

You're right, I laughed.

Strangeways, she laughed. God, she grimaces, I shouldn't laugh.

I bring her a cup of tea.

And Maisie?

She's inside at the table.

Did she eat?

A whole breakfast, I say.

How does she do it?

I don't know.

And she's over ninety. My God. Nancy drinks a little tea then lays the cups aside. And they ate the pizza.

They did.

That's something, I suppose.

Maisie appears on her steed at the doorway.

Is that you, Maisie?

It is. I'm still here. You can't get rid of a bad thing.

So I can see.

And how is poor Nanny this morning?

Don't mention it.

Well, you can't be told.

I have a head.

Oh, and last night we were on top of the world.

Don't, says Nancy.

We were drinking brandy to beat the band. We were going to go courting again.

Stop, says Nancy, raising a hand.

It's lilac time again, says Maisie chortling. *It's lilac time again.*

And she went away on her steed.

The minute Nancy returns to Cavan the mood drops in the house. Eileen is away so my niece Grainne stands in for me for an hour while I go to town to shop and have a drink. When I return Mother is ill but asleep and Maisie is vomiting. Maisie's hernia has erupted. I bring her paper towels, a plastic bowl, and talk to her.

I'm destroyed, she says.

You'll be all right.

I'm not well. Oh God in Heaven.

Drink this.

I can't.

She sits with the bowl on her lap, and her hands on her knees. I turn down the TV.

And leave the TV on! she orders.

This goo, not from her stomach, pours out of her mouth. A latticework of blue veins clusters on her cheeks. Her eyes water. She gasps for breath.

Between bouts of this she says: You must be fed up with us.

No, I'm not.

This is terrible.

Never mind.

I hold her forehead. She's sweating badly.

Oh God in Heaven.

Drink some water.

I can't.

Do, please.

Then another fit of retching goes through her.

Get me to the toilet, she says.

I walk alongside her. From the toilet her cries carry out. In one hour everything has gone wrong. No one is right. And I cannot wish everything better. Maisie cries out again. I sit waiting. If she gets trapped in the toilet I'll have to break down the door. With each cough of bile I hope for the sounds of relief. This is the ordinary – nobody caused it! – ordinary shameful everyday. It's what Una and Eileen and the rest go through when I'm not here. I wait on the silence which means she's getting well.

Why, she cries inside, had this to happen to me?

Terrible! Terrible! Terrible!

I hear the basin emptied, the plunge of water into the toilet bowl and relief pours through me as she appears.

Now, now, she says to herself as she goes a step at a time on her walking-aid.

Now, oh. Her voice that of a young girl.

She stops.

Where is it? she says to herself.

Goes on.

Now see, she says.

Stops.

Oh God bless us! she says.

I follow her into her bedroom.

Will I put the radio on? I ask.

Yes, she says, at least let's have music.

Then I go to clean the toilet. You'd be surprised how quick vomit sticks to porcelain. Why am I recording this? Because it's worth while telling that at the end of awfulness there's always a generous spirit who says: At least let's have music. The music would not mean what it does if we had not been in the bad places.

So I scour the bowl with Vim that's handy and think: *Stop panicking. It's not me that's having an awful time here – it's the two girls.* But I feel powerless. I ring Maura, the mother of my daughter, Inor. She lives in Cavan, nursing her mother, who is also ill.

How are things? I ask.

It's hard going, Maura says.

I think I'm losing it.

Hang in there, she says.

A few days before this Maura and Inor had come to call.

Who's this? asked my mother.

Inor.

Who?

Inor, I say. My daughter.

She peered at Inor and lifted her hand and waved as if she were seeing her from a great distance, waved very slowly with her fingertips while Inor smiled, uncertain of what to do; so she waved back – the two waved at each other – then Mother dropped her hand, and, dismissing us all, closed her eyes.

I put down the phone. Peer in at Maisie. She's sitting on the edge of the bed, with her head down.

Maisie.

What?

Get into bed.

I thought I might get sick again.

You won't. It's over.

You think so?

I do.

So can I have a brandy?

Why not.

I step into the mother's room. She's praying. Her eyes without her glasses on are weak and colourless. The room is boiling. Nevertheless, I pull the sheet round her.

Is that you, Dermot?

It is.

Was Maisie sick?

She was.

But you got her to bed.

I did.

Will you call me in the morning?

I will.

Don't forget.

I won't.

Because you see I don't think I'll be much longer here, she says. She turns her face to the wall. And leave the light on, she adds.

I bring Maisie her brandy. The lamp on the side table is dim. The room is dark. She's in her blue nightdress.

Do I only get the one?

I'll bring you another later.

Do, won't you?

I will.

My God, she says.

Try a sip.

She takes a little taste.

And Nancy's gone with Raymond.

Yes.

She's good fun, Nancy is. And how is Winnie?

She's gone asleep.

Poor Winnie.

I stand in the doorway a while longer.

She rests a hand on the side table, lowers her head and puts her two wrists together on her lap. She raises a hand to her thinning scalp, then puts her wrists together again, as if she were handcuffed. I wait a while. She doesn't move.

Maisie?
What! she says startled.
It's Dermot.
Are you still there?
I am.
Well I'm all right.
Are you sure?
Yes. You can go now.

Hy Brazil is a place that is hard to imagine inland. Sitting in the living room drinking Rioja I can barely remember the place I live, never mind imagine the impossible rising out of Sligo Bay, trailing seaweed and gravel. But standing at the headland of Dooneel it's easy to imagine mermen strolling the rocks at night. It's easier there for the weather and the rushing light to make an imaginary island before a storm breaks.

There is magic in the calm as far out black clouds gather. The swell rises into the air and salt lands on Moffit's field. A wave strikes the rocks from some disturbance far out. But there are days you don't even bother to look. You hang around indoors.

There are days Hy Brazil rises when you're not there.

I push Maisie's door ajar. She's lying on her back piping breath into her lungs with her hands folded on her breasts. I put off the light. Then I tiptoe into Winnie's room. Her eyes are open. The Sunday suit is hanging ready from the handle of the wardrobe. The blouse folded on the other bed.

I tuck her in. Her eyes follow me.

That's right, she says.

Chapter 33

What age was Somerset Maugham when he died? asks Maisie.

He was ninety-six, I think, I say.

Mother watches us. She's wearing a blue cardigan buttoned to the neck. She looks away.

Was he indeed? says Maisie.

He was.

He couldn't be got rid of, I suppose.

Mother studies her beads. She kicks. She sighs.

And Vincent Price died today, I add.

God bless us.

And he still, I said trying to make a joke, had all his teeth.

Some do, nodded Maisie.

Let me out of here, cries Mother, as she jumps to her feet. The girl has arranged to collect me in the car.

Stop where you are, I say, pushing her back into the chair.

But the girl is waiting, she complains.

There's no girl.

Dear God is there nothing I can do? She holds the bag dearly in her lap, and kicks at me. They are outside! – she glares wildly – waiting for me!

No, they're not.

Yes they are. The car is outside.

There's no car. Una is in America. Helen is in Sligo. There's no car.

She puts the handbag down, lifts her beads out of it, then lifts the bag again and slowly, bead by bead, trails her rosary back into it.

I have an arrangement, she says rising.

What are you saying, Winnie? asks Maisie.

Look, I shout, opening the curtain behind her, there's no one, but Mother stares straight ahead at the sitting room door, the handbag over her arm.

There is no one, shouts Maisie.

Who is that old woman? asks Mother pointing at Maisie. Who is she?

Sitting down again she throws Maisie a caustic stare. So I lift her up till her feet are off the ground and carry her to the door.

He's abusing me, shrieks Mother.

I put her down. Arm in arm we walk out of the living room, along the corridor, past the mirror from the Breifne that now fills the hallway, and stop at the front door. I open the door and we step out into the cold October evening. Her fingers dig into my wrist. She turns her head scrutinizing what is out there.

You see? I say. *There's no one!*

Flowerpot, she says.

Yes, that's the flowerpot!

Eileen's light is on, she says.

It is.

She studies Eileen's house for a moment, her head cocked as her eyes vainly try to focus on the familiar. Eileen's house floats in the gathering dusk. Winnie turns away abruptly. She's finished with all that. We come back slowly. Tour the rooms. Halt a moment in the kitchen. Return and stand before the mirror. She touches her hair. When we re-enter the sitting room she pauses and studies Maisie, who smiles at her. I leave her back in the armchair. She dips into her bag for her beads. Lifts the Virgin's prayer, puts it away. Rights her glasses and closes her eyes. Who was to collect her has not come. Roddy Doyle wins the Booker Prize on the TV.

Coca-Cola, says Maisie quietly when the ad comes on. She lies sideways on her right arm on the sofa. Another ad.

Persil, says Maisie, for a brighter wash.

And she chuckles when the next programme begins.

Arthur Daley, she says. I like that thing. He's always chancing his arm.

Maisie loved the pictures. Her routine never varied. She went each night, except Saturday, catching every change of programme. It was the Magnet on Sunday night, the Town Hall on Monday, the Magnet on Tuesday, the Town Hall on Wednesday, the Magnet on Thursday, and the Town Hall on Friday. Each of my brothers and sisters, and all my cousins as they visited the Breifne, went with her.

On the wooden chairs in the Town Hall we sat in a pool of

Afton butts tipped with red lipstick and Yorkshire toffee wrappings discarded by Maisie. A latecomer went up the central aisle, and forgetting where she was, genuflected before she entered a row of seats. Aunt Maisie went to pieces. When an actress shrieked in terror Maisie's hand would slap down on your knee. As Peter Lorre, one of her favourite actors, stumbled round a dark mansion her hand stayed put in the sweet bag. When the good guy got hit she'd crack her heel off the floor and shake her fists into her lap.

She loved gangster movies, period pieces, courtroom dramas, but prison films above all. Her favourite films were *Witness for the Prosecution, The Barretts of Wimpole Street, A Tale of Two Cities* and *The Birdman of Alcatraz.* Her favourite stars were Stan Laurel and Oliver Hardy.

Some have it, she'd say, and Stan had everything.

She learnt the patois of the gangsters and used it constantly in the shop. Channel-hoppers were lads who collected butts off the street. Easy Street was where no-gooders lived. Do you want to take a trip up river, she'd say to the house painter Brennan. We'll soon be in Boothill. Doing time, that's what we're at, she'd say to Mrs English, as she handed her her scones.

In the Magnet cinema the tickets were collected by Catho Morgan while Mr Charlie McGriskin the manager and organist hovered about.

Good evening, Miss Slacke, Catho would say.

Good evening, Miss Morgan.

The Magnet was up market. She would be steered through the dark to her seat by the light of a long torch held by one of the O'Rourke twins. We saw *The Robe* there and *Dracula.* Across the road Mr McKiernan ran affairs in the Town Hall. They showed black-and-white thrillers and cowboy films. His man on the tickets was Packie Cullen, who also maintained the Town Hall and kept cattle in the Market yard. He'd lead Maisie to her seat and wait in the aisle till she was seated. We saw *The Five Fingers* there.

Between reels the film would stop and the audience clattered the floor with their feet.

The Gods, Maisie would say, are angry.

The house lights would come on. Packie would patrol the space.

Courting couples on the balcony withdrew their arms from round each other. Elder citizens looked about them with disdain. People raced to the toilet. Mr McKiernan called for order. The lights went down and numbers raced across the screen till we were back where we left off, at some moment of horror. The Half Acre folk in the front went quiet and grew mesmerized. Maisie, cigarette slanted, suddenly gripped my wrist when the Five Fingers were thrown into a roaring fire. Peter Lorre, eyes rolling, backed off. The hand came out to get him. It got him by the throat.

Maisie squeezed me tighter.

When Peter Lorre got free of the hand she relaxed and tapped her Afton politely on the floor. No one moved till the final frame had dissolved. The curtains came across. We left regretfully and walked up Town Hall Street, not in this world at all, through the bristling cold nights of winter. It was like walking home after Benediction on Wednesdays. And the next night there we were again, midway up in the Magnet, her Afton tilted, the Yorkshire toffee bag in her lap.

Nowadays the Magnet cinema is totally forgotten by the ladies. All those nights in the dark might never have happened. And the strange thing is the Magnet was run for a number of years by Eric Kinane, Nancy's son, and later by her other son Ernie. Eric had seen his first picture with Maisie. Films entered his blood, and one of his jobs was as a projectionist in London.

He worked in the Academy in Oxford Street. It was a privately owned cinema that for two years ran *Ulysses*. By the time it finished Eric knew the dialogue by heart. He worked in the Classic in Chelsea where I got in for nothing to see *Repulsion* by Polanski. As the demented hairdresser in the film walked down the King's Road she passed the Classic cinema in which I was sitting. I got an awful land. It was a special effect Polanski would have been proud of. Eric became manager of the Paris Pulman in Drayton Gardens in South Kensington. Here I saw many of the classics – by the Indians, the French, the Russians, the Italians. The three cinemas are now gone, I think.

By the time Eric came home and set up in the Magnet, Maisie's days at the cinema were over. She made, I think, one excursion down to see her nephew at work. But it was not the same. She went blind, the cataracts bloomed, while Eric, her protégé, sat in a spill of phosphorescent light on a tall stool by the spinning reels in the high-up projection room, tapping tobacco into a roll-up while voices boomed round him.

At Midnight Mass at Christmas an epileptic screamed. From the organ loft I saw a man carried out. It terrified me. But the walk home afterwards through the dark expectant town was magical. The happy voices on the street. The cheerful drunks calling out greetings.

Tiredness exalted you.

In the Breifne they were all transformed. There were brandies, ports and a big fire. Two trees in the mirror. Maisie was courteous. All the Christmas cakes and boxes of expensive chocolates had been sold. Uncle Seamus began performing. Mother sang. She waltzed with her brother. My father gave me a taste of his Guinness. We were up till all hours.

Neither Maisie nor Winnie is nostalgic for those times. Cavan is only mentioned in passing. An earlier Milseanacht Breifne, when it was governed by their great-aunt Jane McGloughlin, one of the founders of Fianna Fail, is more often recalled. It was a time when the two girls served tea to groups of Republicans who sat up with Aunt Jane till late in the café – Paddy Smith, who had faced the death penalty after 1916, Countess Markievich, done up in a veil and quite lah-de-dah, and the chief, De Valera, who was like a turkey, Mother said.

But little is recalled about the days when the responsibility for the Breifne became theirs. The Milseanacht might as well have never existed. It is as if Cavan was an aberration that occurred after they left Finea in their youth and before they arrived in old age in Cootehill.

By coincidence, Una married Joe Smith, who was from Cootehill, son of Paddy Smith, a frequent minister in De Valera's government. So after the Breifne finally closed down for good, the pair moved to be beside my sister Una in Cootehill. By then both ladies were approaching eighty. In between, the business had made a cruel bonding between the two.

My mother was servant to Maisie for all that time. Wherever she went she worried about her sister. When the business was left equally between the pair, Aunt Jane said: *Look after Maisie, Winnie, that's all I ask.* And so she did. I cannot remember Maisie ever making dinner for herself. It's maybe twenty years since she made a cup of tea.

Now, because of my mother's state of mind, that bond has been severed, and both parties are unsure what relationship remains. It's Maisie now that worries about mother. She tries to remember for her a past which is quickly escaping. She gives off to me if I'm angry – *That's your mother you're talking to,* she says. *That's your mother!* She slaps the table. The impatience I sometimes feel at Mother's sighs, her stubbornness, her complaints fills me with shame. The faults she has are exaggerated by the disease while her goodness is being daily eroded.

She is no longer the sedate lady people speak of. But it remains somewhat in the delicate way she folds a towel, toys with a bracelet, pulls a comb through her hair or hangs her Sunday suit. They say that if someone you love is mentally available, then your self-image is enhanced. If they are not, then your identity is belittled. You'd be surprised how much you once did was, in fact, a charade to meet with the bestowal of her favours. Now praise is not forthcoming. Looking after Mother is like watching language losing its meaning.

Then sometimes out of the blue she unearths a newspaper clipping from an old *Anglo-Celt*, brings it into the sitting room and deposits it in my lap.

Read that, she says.

And there is Una dancing at various *feiseanna*, or Miriam performing in pantomimes, Tony sitting in the sun in Aden, or myself claiming to have written a play for ITV. Out come photographs of herself and Aunt Bridgie at the Niagara Falls. She points at a photograph and smiles.

Bridgie, she says, fondly.

Then looks at me. *Straighten your back, you bugger you,* she says, and starts laughing.

Once when I lived in Pimlico in London an astrologist on a grant from some esoteric group in America moved into a room on the third floor. He had an aggressive mind. He was seeking the mathematics of mystery. I met him on the stairs at various times and soon we became vaguely acquainted. He was interested, he said, in the Irish psyche because of its waywardness and femininity and confusion.

So I sent him off to a Beckett play in the Royal Court.

He left disturbed at half-time because he kept seeing me on stage. That's why you sent me, he said. No, it wasn't, I told him. How was I to know you'd start seeing things? You knew, he said. Then bit by bit I began meeting him everywhere. I worked as an underwriter at Sun Alliance Insurance in Soho, and when I'd leave the office in my pinstripe suit, he'd step out of a shop doorway on Piccadilly to greet me. I met him outside the police barracks in Rochester Row. He fell out of the crowds in Victoria Station. Then, one evening, I found him waiting for me on the landing outside his door.

He said we should all go round the following evening to see this woman in the House of the Mediums in Eaton Square. She – as a medium for various dead composers, Beethoven among others – was able to play compositions the composers might have written or left unfinished. So we agreed to meet him there some time before seven. The next evening John McCaffrey, Becky and myself found ourselves entering this white Victorian five-storeyed house which was perched among various embassies. We arrived at a minute past seven. We told the receptionist where we wanted to go.

You're late, she said, I'm afraid.

Only a minute or so, I said.

But you see, she explained, Mrs — has already begun.

Oh.

And you can't go in once she's started.

That's a pity.

I'm dreadfully sorry.

We were about to go when she added: But you could see Mrs — at seven-thirty.

We could?

Why, yes.

And who is she?

She's a medium.

Can we walk just right in?

Of course you can. We are delighted to see new people.

We entered a pink room with an ornate ceiling. Incongruous wooden chairs, six each side, formed about nine rows. People arrived singly and sat at respectable distances from each other. Two couples, outsiders like ourselves, quickly sat down and waited. We, of course, took chairs in the back row, in the far corner, at the furthest remove.

There was no whispering. A woman I took to be one of the audience entered. She was wearing a tweed skirt, quite fashionable blouse and pert shoes. She sat down in front of us and began unexpectedly talking in a matter-of-fact way.

I'm just going to say a small prayer, she said, there is nothing to be afraid of. And for those newcomers among us let me explain that when I speak to you, and you realize that I have met someone you've known who has passed over, please say *yes*, say *yes* when they speak to you, for if you say *no* well then I will lose them.

She smiled, said a short prayer, and turned immediately to a woman halfway down the room.

James sends his regards, she said.

The woman nodded. Yes, she said.

He believes you *should* go to Canada.

Oh yes, the woman agreed enthusiastically.

And forget about the piano.

I will.

Then she turned to a man with ginger sideburns wearing an off-white suit, who was seated in the front row.

Madeline is here, she said.

Yes, he said.

She is trying very hard.

Yes.

I see sadness.

Yes.

But she wants you to know that that is all over. You can forget about it now, she desperately wants you to know that.

Yes.

She's happy.

The medium moved so fast at the beginning from one person to another that I did not know the mediumship had begun. I thought these were people she knew. That she was calling out greetings to old companions. But then she began to call out to people, *You* in the red hat, yes you, or, *You* in the raincoat, and suddenly it struck me she was talking to strangers. Her features would twitch. Some spirit would possess her ever so slightly, she'd give a small grimace or smile, and without hesitating pass on to another lost soul. Without stopping, she ran through the available dead, offering advice, encouragement, intimacies, to which the people in the room said *yes*, and nodded, and I was wondering was all this real when suddenly I heard her saying, *You*, you down there at the back.

We held our silence.

She bowed her head a moment then stared at me.

You in the blue shirt.

John and Becky looked at me.

Yes, I said.

I have a man here.

Yes.

He appears to be in a uniform.

Yes.

And he's saying *Straighten your back!*

Yes, I said, for that was something my father always said to me.

Is he a soldier, I wonder?

He's a policeman, I replied.

Ah, she said, for he holds himself very, very correct. Yes. And he's saying not to worry about the writing.

I could feel John look at me in wonder.

Yes, I said.

He's saying that you'll never come in the front door, you'll always come in the back.

Yes.

Are we in a village?

Yes, I said.

And there's water.

Yes.

And you're on a horse.

I was never on a horse.

Yes, it's a big horse. And the policeman, who is your father, is holding the reins.

No, I said.

But I see it, she said crossly.

I'm sorry, I said, I was never on a horse.

But I can see it.

No, I persisted.

This was the first time since the mediumship began that such a negative hiatus had occurred. I was ashamed of myself. Everything had come to a stop. Some of those who had already spoken turned to look at me with curious disdain or to urge me on to say *Yes, yes.* I wanted badly to say *yes,* but knew I had never been on a horse. There was silence a while as she contemplated me. She was not going to give up.

Have you ever had a pet monkey?

No, I said with great certainty.

Then a young lad who had come in last and was sitting next to me slowly put up his hand.

I had a pet monkey, he said.

Strange, she said, I could see it sitting on his shoulder. Oh well.

Then the conversation passed on from me to him, and from him to others, as I sat there light-headed after a visit from my dead father which ended with a question about a horse, Becky was visited by her grandmother in Texas, others spoke to dead husbands and wives, and then, just as she had arrived, the woman got up purposefully and thanked us, strode off and went away into the night and a few moments later we followed her.

The astrologist was peeved that we'd missed Mrs — but delighted to find that I'd been unnerved by contact with my father.

And the monkey, he said excitedly.

What about the monkey? I asked.

Don't you know what having a monkey on your shoulder means?

No.

It means having an addiction, he said with a great deal of satisfaction.

Years later I told the story to Anne-Marie after we got married. One night she came racing into our bedroom in the Breifne with an old

Healy family photograph album she'd been looking at. She placed it in front of me and pointed. There was a photograph of my father standing, with just the side of his head in view, by a horse in great wonderful winkers, Tom Keogh's horse in Finea, while I, about four years of age, sat astride it happily.

Chapter 34

Today Mother is quiet. The nurse came and said Mother looked wonderful so both myself and Eileen were pleased and proud and she ate a brave breakfast.

Today is Thursday, I leave Sunday when Una returns from the States, so we have only a few more days together. The routine we've established will be broken. And of course I'll be glad to shed the responsibility of the twenty-four-hour day, and yet in another way, I don't think I've ever been this close to her, not maybe emotionally, but in some intimate way I can't articulate.

There have been moments I thought I was going off my head, but then the routine would re-establish itself, Maisie would cheerfully reappear on her walking-aid and send us off down some vitriolic *non sequitur*, Eileen would come in. I think of Mother's death, a death to which she constantly refers, and yet I find it hard to imagine her giving up the body which is refusing her peace. She is strong physically and when she is quiet like now, she is endearing, innocent, a porcelain doll again. She was always impatient whether cleaning or polishing, and this impatience now controls her every need. Housework haunts her. The things she would have done slip through her mind with a guilty sense of *déjà vu*. The ghost of her earlier self flies ahead of her through the rooms, dusting and clucking, and she totters along in her own wake. Even an orange, upon which she once used gorge, is a mystery. She hurries towards work to be done only to find that the actual act eludes her. She rushes headlong from bed to table, table to armchair, armchair to toilet, toilet to bed, searching for something, but wherever she ends up that something is missing.

Only prayer and sleep halts this rush to duty. These two poles are her only peaceful states, except perhaps for sitting in a car. Going someplace is a powerful peacemaker, but to arrive is to grow impatient again. I know this feeling in myself. Her genes have put in mine the same need to be away. Like her I speed between moments of rest, impatient to arrive and then impatient to be gone again.

At various times, we have shared intimacy but not for long, we must be always bustling ahead, and then with each departure, we're again embroiled in loss. And this sense of loss makes for telepathy. It's like years ago, the mother was dreaming of me in the Breifne and she suddenly darted awake when she saw something hit my head. At that same moment I was being treated in a London hospital for a wound to the skull. And when we next met she said I saw you bleeding, *bleeding*, she repeated as if she could find the actual word for blood like red fluid gushing onto her tongue, and I woke, she said, and the room was cold.

I felt, she said, the blow.

But telepathy does not bring us any closer. It is the result of the distances between us. Even if we knew the future, we could do nothing about it. It would happen as planned. Our natures are set. The loss is predetermined.

In the same manner as I sit here writing while my mother prays, I used to study in my father's sickroom over the three years he lay dying. I'd have my tea in the room with him, he'd eat off his tray and I'd eat off mine, then I'd go off for a game of handball, return and study beside him till nine. I used love those times with him. The silence I found then, I do now with Mother. When he'd fight for his breath, he'd dab a handkerchief to his purple nose. I'd wait for the outburst to subside and we'd go on as before, in the same way as I wait for my mother's restlessness to pass.

When we are alone together for hours in the morning Winnie and I rarely speak. She looks over her shoulder at me sometimes as if startled at finding a stranger in the room. Yoh! she says. She tries to reassemble my features into somebody familiar. I smile, she touches an earring. I roll a cigarette, she concentrates on this.

Leaves? she asks.

Tobacco, I answer.

God, she says, and goes back to her rosary. Her breathing eases. This little exchange has reassured us both. Then within seconds her mood changes and she tries to get out of the chair.

Where are you going?

To the room.

No.

She clasps her hands on her lap. Her chin stirs. She looks down-cast. She studies the shining aluminium dessert dish that contains her beads, the prayer to Padre Pio and an Address to the Virgin. The earring shakes. She bows her newly dressed head and ponders her fingernails. I hear a noise off. Soon we head on a tour of the house and encounter Maisie illicitly searching drawers in the kitchen.

What are you looking for, Maisie?

Apples, she says, green apples. Will you give me one?

They only give you heartburn, I say.

Never mind that. Everything gives me heartburn – can I just have one?

All right.

Oh you could supervise the devil, snaps my mother and she pulls sharply at my arm.

We go to the front door, visit the toilet and head to the bedroom.

She lifts the pillow to see if the second rosary is beneath it. I put on her hairnet and she dabs her skull. I turn her onto her side.

Are you writing another book?

I'm trying.

You're spending a lot of time with the pen in your hand, she says with extraordinary lucidity and I realize that while I've been watching her, she's been watching me.

Will you call me in the morning?

I'll call you for tea.

God bless you, she murmurs, content at last. I turn her again so that the wounded part of the head is not touching the pillow. I ease the door to. Go back to my armchair. Putting together the banal events of these days seems pointless, yet it gives me relief. It passes the time. It is a record of days I would otherwise not recall.

Soon I'll have to wake her. The earrings, the glasses, will be replaced with shaking hands. Whatever dream she's in will accompany her for hours. Because her sleep is so deep she cannot shake off who she encounters there.

There will be things to be done that cannot be done. Stray figures out of the past will be at the door. The house will be totally new, not like the house she encountered in sleep, or the bend for home she was on before she was rudely awakened. And when she'll encounter Maisie across from her in the dining room some sort of mania and distress will make her flinch. She'll eat with relish the first few spoonfuls then push the plate away. I'll push it back. She'll stuff her mouth one more time. Then push the plate away. I'll put it back.

She'll drink the tea with great gusto. And when the mug is finished she'll shake it as as she used to do in the good old days when there were real tea leaves in it. And before she's quite finished she's struggling to get out of the chair.

Away! Away to where?

At four I enter her room. It's stifling. The bottom false teeth have come loose in her mouth. The edge of the plate is bared like a fang. The set pushes against her lower lip and swells out the cheek she's lying on. The loose teeth give her a demented look. The side of the face has fallen in. It's as if she's had a severe stroke.

The minute I touch her she opens her eyes.

Dermot, she says and smiles.

She struggles to say something else but the sentence will not allow itself to be articulated. She babbles incoherently for a few seconds.

Time to get up, I say.

No-ono, she mutters and begins to weep.

Out with the legs.

I can't.

Yes you can.

I reach an arm under her back, put her chin on my shoulder and lift her. She falls back. I hold her. She grabs me. I get an arm under her knees.

I want – I want, she stammers. I put on her shoes. I put on her earrings. She puts on her glasses. She touches her hair. With her tottering badly behind me, I lead the way through the house. We are walking through a dream of unremembered objects. She follows me, her body hanging to the left and her knees quaking.

I sit her a while in the armchair.

Have you got it fixed? she asks me.

289

I have.

Then sign it, she says, holding out her hand.

I will.

And hurry up!

She prays with shaking chin.

Dermot!

What?

Take me up.

No. You're only out of bed.

Dear God.

She prays, then kicks, glowers over at me. Prays out loud.

Tch. Tch, she says and touches her scalp. You got me out of bed for what? she demands succinctly.

For tea.

There's silence a while, but she is not settling.

She returns to her beads. Like a bold child she stamps her feet. Touches an earring. Commands me again.

Dermot!

Yes.

Get me up.

I do and bring her into tea.

There you are, says Maisie cheerfully.

The two ladies face each other over small plates of tinned salmon and mayonnaise, sliced tomatoes and buttered white bread. Mother lifts her mug of tea and drinks thirstily. Maisie picks and contemplates. Mother shakes the saltcellar repeatedly. She eats everything. Afterwards I wash her false teeth while she hangs onto the sink. The minute we're back in the dining room she starts again.

Bring me up, she says, to where there is peace.

No, I say quietly.

Get me out, she says after a while as she reads Padre Pio's prayer, to where there's peace and quiet.

There's peace and quiet here, I say.

She starts her chant that is much like the lament of the Marsh Arab women, and makes to get out of the chair. I put her back in. She kicks at me and claws at my face. I slap the back of her hand.

My God, she cries, walloping! Walloping! And me eighty years of age. For an hour she stubbornly fights to return to bed. She gets up. She makes fake excursions to the toilet. We go back and forth like sleepwalkers till eventually Maisie enters like a saviour.

Weep, says Maisie, and you weep alone.

Soon Eileen arrives. I'm out the door like a shot. It's my hour in the pub. When I come back the mother greets me like a long-lost stranger.

Did you enjoy yourself?

I did, I say.

I pour Eileen and Maisie a glass of brandy.

When you were out, says Eileen, she asked me to phone Una. So I said Una was in America. Phone, said your mother, for the gig of the thing, and she started laughing. I couldn't believe it – *for the gig of the thing*, she said.

I start the crossword. The mother relaxes. The ladies chat.

How do you spell earring? I ask.

Earring? says Maisie speculatively.

Is there two r's in it?

I don't know, replies Maisie. We're regular dunces. She considers Eileen. Princess Anne got remarried. And I don't blame her.

Did you not like Captain Mark Phillips? asks Eileen.

A regular tramp.

God, but you're severe, Maisie.

Captain Mark Phillips, God bless us.

I cough.

You have a frog in your throat, says Maisie.

I have. A cold one.

The cursed fags, says Maisie. You should give them up. As Monty Montgomery said to Mary Kate – *you'll make a fucking job of yourself yet.*

She turns to my mother. Winnie!

What?

What age would Mary Kate Dowd be now?

Forty, says my mother.

That was then. I mean now. Do you hear me?

I hear you.

See that – she can hear you when she wants to, remarked Maisie. Winnie.

What?

The travellers will be back Sunday.

What travellers?

Una and Joe.

Una, Mother says, testing the word.

Yes, they're coming back from their stint abroad.

Eileen takes Mother to the toilet. When she returns Mother asks me: Were you on holidays?

I never budged.

It's Una is on holidays, confirms Maisie. Your son is here with us pair of dolls.

Una, says Mother ruminatively.

As Shirley Sheriff said, remarks Maisie, we all have to die.

I know what you mean, I say.

I know what you mean, answers Maisie with a smirk, but the grass is wet.

She grins lustily.

And the train is gone and you with your chicken in your hand, she continues with glee. Then there was the time Andy B. was in the church after his wife died. He was kneeling in the pew next the coffin. And the sacristan came up to say the church was closing. *Well you see, child,* said Andy, *she was always difficult.*

She was always difficult, repeats Maisie, and tears of laughter come to her eyes. Oh Andy B. He was standing at the door of the shop looking out and he saw Fegan go by on a bike. *Look at Fegan, Miss Slacke,* he said to me, *and a pair of balls on him like the weights on a grandfather clock.*

Maisie! says Eileen in mock horror.

Then there was that cursed fiend out of hell. A Jesuit. I stepped into the confessional and he asked me: *How many times?* I said, *I can't remember. Well, I have plenty of time,* said he, the cursed fucker.

What did you do that brought him down on you? I asked.

Nothing. It was only trivial. Now that I've become a great sinner I can see that. The cursed fucker. I could wring his neck. Did you ever have that Eileen?

No.

Back then we did.

I give Mother her pills.

God help her, says Maisie, she's taking her pills. If you shook her she'd rattle. And when she was young she couldn't. She'd hold it in her mouth till she soaked the coat off it. And then it would poison her.

My mother spits the red aspro out.

See, says Maisie. What did I tell you? Poor Winnie, she says sadly.

Then Eileen's husband looks in.

There's the binman, says Mother.

On comes a documentary about wildlife in Africa on the TV. Maisie starts laughing.

When the elephants passed by the Breifne in a procession with Duffy's circus, declares Maisie, they appeared to be up to the windows.

Didn't you go off with an acrobat?

I didn't. Babs did.

You were too grand.

Not at all, they were nice people.

Jazzing, says my mother, just jazzing.

He gave Babs the eye in the tent, Maisie continues. And if she didn't give me the elbow. And when we were going home he stepped out from behind one of the caravans and without a by-your-leave took Babs's arm. Then out came the other acrobat in a lovely suit and says to Babs, *Your friend is very nice.*

More jazzing, says the mother.

She wanted to square me off with him but I wouldn't go. *What next?* said Rose Smith, *Duffy's Circus, no less!*

You walked down the town with them, I say.

I did not.

You did.

Were you there by any chance, she asks, with a scolding eye, at the turn of the century?

No.

Well I did not, she nods firmly. I let him go to hell. I was afraid Aunt Jane would hear all about the carry-on.

Look at the giraffe, I say.

I like the frog. They're harmless. Betty Ronaghan put a pair of trousers on one once. Lord above! She sniggers, and turns back to the box. There's the elephant again. And look at the small elephant. He's making his way, the poor thing.

I farted.

Who's blowing? Maisie asks with happy eyes.

We watch zebras drinking from a stream.

And people pay to see them, she says. Isn't it wonderful.

I'm going, says Mammy.

And a whale is so huge. Did you ever see one, Dermot, out there at the sea?

No, there's no whales in that part of the world.

No whales, says Maisie sadly.

Eileen, says my mother, put out another drink, then she leans over and nips me.

I will.

I have a pain in my head, she says, else I'd do it.

I know that, Winnie, says Eileen.

My mother claws the air.

I have a pain in my head! she screams.

God sent a message down to say you have no pain in your head, I say loudly.

What? asks the mother.

I said *God says you have no pain.*

She watches me strangely.

Your son has a line to God no less, says Maisie. You put me in mind of the Bible. What does it say? It says death is like the sea. Make room for me, says the sea, and it comes in and out.

Whispering Rufus, snorts Mother.

Look at all those birds, nods Maisie. When you come to think of it.

There's three thousand barnacle geese fly in over the house in Sligo every day and then in March they go home.

They know, says Maisie nodding.

Wow! shouts Mother.

They know when it's time to go.

Wow! Wow!

Wow! says I clapping a hand to my mouth, we have an apache in the fucking house.

The mother smiles, then she says: It's all right for you.

Eileen brings Mother a cup of tea.

How many children have you? asks Eileen.

Three and one overseas, she answers promptly.

And was Dermot a good boy?

He was. I'm going.

And what does Dermot like?

She studies me a moment. He likes wandering around.

God bless us, says Maisie.

Up! mother screams. *And stop the interrogation!*

Maisie laughs across at Winnie.

The queen is having her problems too, she says. *Weary is the head that wears the crown.* Then she taps her cheek with a finger. *Where's heaven now?* she adds.

Where did that come from? I ask.

Where's heaven now? the astronaut said when he stepped out into space, declares Maisie.

Did he?

He did. Oh yes, nods Maisie, he did indeed, and reclining on her arm she turns towards the TV to catch the news. Two Catholic workers have been triggered into eternity, states a priest. Dick Spring appears with a formula for peace. Just more Irish blarney, announces John Taylor, Unionist MP.

At four in the morning I woke to find her wandering the house nude except for her blue blouse. All the lights are on. The carpet beside the commode is wet and her slip that she'd managed to take off is wet also.

Take it away, she said.

I redressed her and put her to bed. Just as I was lying down I heard a door open. I slipped out and found Maisie about to set off on her travels. Her painted fingernails came round the jamb.

Where are you off to, Maisie?

What is the cause of all the illuminations? she asked out of the darkness of her room.

It's Mother, I said.

She appeared in a wide flowing red nightdress to her ankles and a white cardigan over the top.

And who is going to pay the bills?

It was Mother walking the house, I said louder.

Oh, she said, I see.

Timidly she closed the door.

At six I suddenly woke when the light in the room came on. My mother's hand with its painted fingernails was on the switch while she stood out of sight in the corridor. Then the head appeared.

Will there be food?

There will. Soon.

I lead her back to bed. This time she had the blue cardigan on over the blouse and she had on her slip-on shoes. She'd done well. I tuck her into bed. She watches me strangely.

At seven-thirty I find her seated in her room at the bottom of her bed struggling with a button on her cuff. The teeth are jutting out of the left side of the mouth. One eye is partly closed. When she sees me she proffers her wrist.

Una, she says.

Yes, I reply.

You're a good girl, she says. You're all I have, God bless you.

I button the cuff. We tiptoe to the bathroom. I fix her face. Across the corridor Maisie moans, calling on God. We sit in the half-dark of the dining room like it was an early school morning. As I make tea she calls me.

Dermot!

What?

Bring us dessert.

Yes.

Dermot!

What?

Where is the proper room?

This is it! And Helen will be here this evening. In her car.

Helen?

Yes.

That's good. For dessert, dessert is all I want.

I light a roll-up.

Lovely, she says and smiles. Then she points to the table where the new dressing is laid out for the nurse when she comes.

Get the thing out of the weight, she says.

I nod.

She beckons me.

I hate being with Maisie, she says. She cups her mouth as if she's said something wrong. Whispering Rufus! she says gaily. And so we have only you, you bugger you.

Later, after the paper arrives, I lead her through the headlines. I put my finger under the words and she reads them out:

THE DICK SPRING TRAGEDY.

2 DIE IN NEW SAVAGERY.

LOYALIST DOUBLE KILLING SETBACK TO PEACE HOPES.

DOHERTY CRUSHES KNOWLES.

WITCHES FLYING VISIT!

NURSES RECEIVE THEIR BADGES.

Only the photograph of the witches draws a response. She laughs and points. *Witches*, she says. The rest of the items are only words. More words. What they once represented is of no significance. I open the front door and slowly she moves her head from side to side, like some small seabird. She checks where the milk should be, then she withdraws, staggering.

In Maisie's room the Travelling Wilburys are playing.

At last we hear Helen's car.

The mother stands and takes her hand.

How are all your people? Winnie asks.

They're fine, says Helen.

But they've left the drapers, confirms Maisie.

They have.

And why wouldn't they? You can't be a slave to the public all your life.

So how long are you staying?

Till Sunday, says Helen. We'll go back Sunday.

We, says Maisie, what do you mean *we*? And she throws me a terrible eye.

You're abandoning us, says Maisie when I tell her I have to leave tomorrow.

Una is coming home, I say.

That doesn't matter, she says crossly.

But she'll look after you.

I don't need looking after.

I make you your breakfast. Your dinner. Your tea.

Eileen can do that, thank you. She slaps the table. I don't need you. She slaps the table again. *Your mother needs you.*

But Una will look after her.

You are abandoning your mother.

I need to go home.

This is your home, she says and her voice rises.

I have things to do at home.

There's nothing you do there that you *can't do here.*

Stop fighting, says Helen, the two of you.

This is his home, shouts Maisie, and this is where he should be, and she turns resolutely to the TV.

I feel like I used to when I was young, guilty and terrified of her temper. Mother sits there silently watching these things happen.

Are you going away? she asks.

Yes.

Why?

I have to.

Then I'm going to bed.

Why?

I don't want to watch the sorrow.

You see, says Maisie, bitterly.

On Sunday I sleep till twelve and Helen feeds the dolls. I go to the pub and when I return dinner is over. I've done everything wrong.

I sit with Mother.

I'll be sad when you go, she says.

I'll be back in two weeks.

You promise?

I do.

Stay till tomorrow.

I can't.

What are we going to do?

She takes my hand.

Please.

No.

She goes to get up.

Where are you going?

To the toilet.

I bring her. When we return Maisie is on the sofa.

There yous are, she says quietly.

Yes, I reply.

But you'll be back soon?

I will, I say.

Good.

We watch the snooker. Helen sits down.

Maisie, she says, got three numbers up in the Lotto.

Go on.

And do you know what she wanted to do if she won?

What?

To hire a spacecraft and go to the moon.

But the moon is not the moon anymore, says Maisie, since *those crowd* got there. It used to mean an awful lot more.

That's true, says Helen.

My mother reaches for my hand.

Take me to bed.

So I do. She slips beneath the pink sheets in her purple dress. She watches me. Soon Una arrives with tales of New York and Canada. Mother totters in and smiles.

America, she says to her daughter.

Yes, says Una. How are you, Mother Healy?

I'm fine.

* * *

The bell rings in the dusk. I answer it to find this group of children dressed up as Halloween spectres, in masks and black dustbin bags, jingling boxes of coins.

Come on in, I say.

My mother watches them anxiously.

Witches, she says and she darts a hand to her mouth.

Sing, says Maisie.

We can't, they say.

Wren boys, says Mother pointing.

Whoever heard of wren boys that can't sing, says Maisie, scornfully.

So one of them starts The Town I Loved So Well, but the song breaks down after the first verse. Then eventually a girl plays *Eileen a Run* on the flute and my mother shakes her feet in time. Another calls out Trigger Treat! – an ominous sound since that's what a killer called out the night before in a village in Derry before shooting seven people dead. They all stand around while money is found. The dustbin bags crackle. The kids spill out the door. We sit a while longer talking and going through the routine with Una. Then we put our bags in the Mini Metro. I kiss the mother's cheeks, then Maisie's.

Your beard is going white, says Maisie, you'd want to have something done about that.

Like what?

Put some colouring in.

Goodbye you, says the mother. She pats her hair and passes the mirror from the Breifne without looking into it.

She closes her eyes and kisses me again on the doorstep of the house. Una steers her out into the November night. She watches Helen reverse the car, then suddenly goes in without looking behind her.

Chapter 35

It is the week before Christmas '93 and Mother has not eaten in over two weeks. She rarely recognizes anyone but Una, sometimes Joe, sometimes myself. More often than not I have become Joe. Una becomes Grainne, her daughter. Or Grainne becomes Niamh, her sister. We have all become representations of each other, no one person dominates, and this is perhaps how it should be.

I slept last night holding her hand through the bedrail. She is about to go, like her husband before her, in the festive season.

We feed her 7-Up and Ballygowan water through a syringe. Eileen and Una get her out onto a chair for a few minutes at the beginning of every day. How are your people? she called out to Helen once as they washed the mother down. It was one of her last complete sentences. Her body has shrunk. Her feet are deathly pale. The toenails are like those of a corpse. Yet her face is still pink, but getting smaller everyday.

Her sleep is a series of regretful sighs, and sudden moans. When she wakes she reaches out, pushes the quilt off, then pulls it back again. She is too weak to fight now when the nappy is being changed.

During the night snow fell. Una and myself slept at intervals in the room. All night long the mother kept pushing the quilt back, nearly fanning herself with it, her knees tucked up against the bedrail and her hand cupped in mine. I had terrible dreams. Leapt out of a car before it went down a cliff.

A couple of weeks ago she fell in her room while I slept across the hall. I was struggling to wake up, eventually I did, and listened and heard nothing but knew something had happened still the same. And yet couldn't get out of the bed. Something clicked in my brain. A small sound went off. A sharp bone sound. And still I couldn't get out of the bed. I imagined that I had run across the corridor and found her head bashed in where she'd fallen.

And when I did at last get up and throw open her door I found her on the floor, shivering wildly, her legs shaking and her right eye a mass of painful purple.

She must have struck her temple off the chest of drawers. She looked terrible. I gave her tea and bathed her forehead in the dining room. She sat in her chair looking across at her reflection in the mirror. She rose a hand to her eye.

The hurt is there, she said, in that person.

She pointed over at herself.

There, she said.

If we have changed into other people, even she herself has become someone else. But she knew something bad had happened. Now I knew we could not go on like this. So that day I put the iron bed in her room, clamped a bedrail to it that I got from the hospital. Then too late for the shops remembered nappies. So that evening for the first time I put her into nappies loaned to us by a woman up the street suffering from MS.

She cried bitterly as the nappies were put on. I lay her down and closed the cage around her.

I'm helpless now, she said.

She watched me sadly from her cage and turned away.

At night she'd try to pull the nappies off. Eventually even the false teeth were gagging her. They had to go. Then the earrings. From that day on the mouth and the spirit collapsed inwards.

Journeys get mixed up in my mind. Journeys to Cootehill and journeys back to Sligo. Una's anxious voice over the phone. Guilt and anxiety and helplessness plagued us. I began to hate that road to Blacklion, the turns at Glenfarne, the potholes round Clones. Into the sad bungalow where a grieving Maisie stood on her steed outside Mother's bedroom door peering in at her in the bed. Then back again to the shunting sea at Dooneel, to the asses roaring at dawn for their winter feed. Removed from the company of the two ladies I could barely remember them. I could see them physically but could not hear their voices.

It's as if I had removed myself from some relationship that was so intense my conscious mind would not consider it.

I'm home, and yet I'm not home. My home is in their minds, among their nuances, memories, chatter, repetitions, but now I'm at one remove. I've lost responsibility for them. Then suddenly my mother's face will rear up like a sign. With a shudder of shame I recall holding her down in her chair. We were talking of private nursing homes, or the County Home. Home became the key word. But they are really all places pretending to be home. For Mother home is an illusion.

Joe rang to say things are looking bad. I packed the car for the morning and went down that night to see Jimmy Foley, a man of eighty-two who lives alone down the road in a three-roomed cottage without electricity. Salt was pouring over the banks. The bothered sea was rolling hard against the gravel. I tapped his window and shouted out my name. He was inside playing the box to himself. He put the accordion aside and we sipped a glass of whiskey in the dark.

He dipped a finger in the whiskey and Victor the dog licked it. We lit Woodbines. He stirred the fire.

Do you ever get lonely? I asked.

Lonely, he said, pondering the word. No, he answered eventually, I know that *I* am here.

Next morning at six, hungover, I head off in the car through a sea mist. Clifford the cat is in my lap. It takes for ever to reach Cavan.

Maisie gets onto her steed and visits her sister.

Winnie! Winnie! She touches her cheek. Winnie will you not get up and come out to the sitting room. Winnie! It's not the same without you.

Maisie puts her steed aside and sits in a chair by the bed and holds her sister's hand.

I'm going home, says Winnie in a pleasant way.

What did she say? Maisie asks me. Did she say she was going home?

I think so.

Winnie! Tony is coming to see you. Isn't that good? She presses Mother's hand. And you are all style. You'll be delighted to see Tony.

Mother looks at her and her lips move.

Why won't she speak to me? asks Maisie.

She's talking to you, says Una, but you can't hear her.

Winnie! Now, Winnie.

Maisie looks at us.

No answer, she says.

She's mumbling to you, says Una.

I suppose she is.

She's restless.

She is. What is she saying? Maisie inclines her head. What love? What are you saying pet?

Mother tries to get death over with, through not eating, and now, through not drinking. Una wants to wash out her mouth with glycerine but she fights her off, waving her hands like some ghostly conductor. Only a dab of 7-Up on a cotton stick for cleaning ears is keeping her alive.

Then we lose Eileen because her husband Bennie falls sick and a girl called Anne-Marie arrives to take her place.

Tony comes from Canada and, jet-lagged and disorientated, takes up his position by her bed.

We all want to hear our names on her lips, but the only name she calls is Una, her constant companion to dances in the White Horse, parties, shopping sprees. Tony sits there, his hand in hers, waiting on a flicker of recognition. Then Miriam takes his place.

Mother, she says, it's Miriam.

It's a strange phenomenon, this wish of ours that the dying should know who the living are. Then there is too a type of competition between us for her final favours. Who will be there when she finally lets go? But the truth is, the reason you sit there, that one person replaces another, is that when the moment comes the others will be called.

The past flies by in great whirling, giddy spasms. I make a stew in the kitchen. The young priest visits. Brief moments fix themselves and are gone. And sometimes grief turns to anger. We lose control.

She purses her lips for a kiss. I kiss her. She lifts her head a little, then settles again.

You sit there by waiting for the next person to come and relieve you.

I slept alongside her last night, not all the time holding her hand, or feeding her 7-Up, because it only makes her gag, but sleeping till she woke me with a screech.

I forgot she was dying.

Instead I took her hand in mine through the bedrail and lying in our two beds we commenced whispering like children who, not only have been allowed to sit up late with the grown-ups, but have been given permission to sleep together, that is, if we stay quiet. So here we are with everyone else asleep, in a strange house, and snow falling.

Mother?

She turned her eyes towards me, as if to say, That's right.

That's right.

She was speaking not in words but sighs that were strangely lucid. The sighs were animated, her breaths hurried, the tone everyday. We spoke of mundane stuff, agreeing, it would appear, about many things and not too bothered by what was beyond our ken. It was the sort of casual chat you might have with someone in passing. *Someone in passing.* We'd crossed some threshold, and wondered where the things were, and what was needed. Out of me came these long articulate sentences that you are only permitted every so often, and she'd answer, though none of the words articulate, in an understanding way.

It all made sense. It was comforting.

I tucked her in. She was very cold. I called Una, who was sleeping across the hall.

Is she all right?

She's cold, I said.

I went to have a shower. As I was drying myself in the bathroom I heard a gang of people passing by the door like a herd of cattle.

Who's there? I called.

Miriam, said a voice.

Then I heard more shuffling. I ran through the house and found that Una had called the family, thinking death was imminent. She was so cold. But there was another day to go. I went in and sat by Maisie.

How are you? I asked.

I have my regrets, she said.

Tell us one.

Well, she said, I would have joined the acrobats if I hadn't so much lead in me arse.

I fall apart laughing.

Well, I said, I love you.

She appraised me.

Are you sure? she asked.

I am, I said.

Tony appears and fills himself a brandy, tips it smartly into his gullet with the precision of a soldier saluting on parade and then sits by Maisie, whose face is very drawn. Broken veins cluster on her cheeks like measles.

Will we take a walk to town, young fellow? he says.

Watch the drinking, Una whispers in an aside to me.

First we chanted, my cousin Ernie and I, some mantras.

If you don't cut out the singing, said Joe, we won't know when she's gone.

Then we sent her out on a wave of prayer. All the family were there. The sign was her hand began to sweat in mine as I held her beneath the blanket. For hours I breathed alongside her, up and down the incline, then when Joe heard the sign he called the others.

Una started a makeshift rosary and she and Tony took the mother's hands. We found it hard to finish a decade because we'd all forgotten the Glory Be to the Father. Now it really snowed. Her breath dropped, when we finished the prayers, into a softer key. Her eyes were seeing straight in front of her when the next breath never came.

Anne-Marie was called. She tied up the mother's skull in a head scarf and sat for hours with a finger on each of her eyelids. Get the teeth, she says to me. She closed the mother's lips into a smile. Then she ordered Tony to open the window to let the soul out.

Mother died on 23 December 1993, at twenty to five in the morning. Maisie died a year later on 26 December 1994. She, too, fell against one of the blasted radiators and was found by Grainne, who slept as her companion in the bungalow. She died from that blow a while later. At Mother's wake, prepared by the people of Kill and Cootehill, Maisie stayed up all night and would not sleep. She was indomitable. We carried Mother out of the house on our shoulders; her coffin, for such a nimble gal, was strangely heavy because our heights were all uneven. Both funerals left Cootehill and stopped first, for a moment, outside the Milseanacht Breifne on Main Street in Cavan town. The Breifne is now a building society. Locals wondered who had died. Both funeral parties were held in the same hotel, the Crover House, overlooking Lough Sheelin, the lake where the ladies went boating as girls. Both were buried in the same plot in Castletown graveyard, my mother with my father, and Maisie beside her, with her aunts and parents.

On the far side of the lake from Crover, up the Inny river, is the village of Finea where both hearses stopped a second time for a moment outside the old family home, where my father's funeral had paused for a moment thirty-one years ago before going on. Uncle Seamus carried all three coffins. The day my mother was buried the fields were filled with snow. After we took the bend round Myles the Slasher's monument the house looked cold and damp and unlived in. All the trees had been cut. The ivy that used stir round the windows at night was gone. Aunty Nancy, the last surviving sister, turned away. We stopped, went on. As we climbed the hill over the lakes the Fineas joined the cortège and Brian Sheridan, who had been in Babies' Class with my mother, came out of his one-room mobile home, tipped his cap to the funeral, and took a kick at his dog to keep him away while he fed a heel of bread to a swan he'd recently tamed.